Giftedness

101

Linda Kreger Silverman, PhD

SPRINGER PUBLISHING COMPANY
NEW YORK

Springer Publishing Company, LLC
11 West 42nd Street
New York, NY 10036
www.springerpub.com

Acquisitions Editor: Nancy S. Hale
Composition: Newgen Imaging

ISBN: 978-0-8261-0797-8
E-book ISBN: 978-0-8261-0798-5

13 14 15 / 5 4 3 2

The author and the publisher of this Work have made every effort to use sources believed to be reliable to provide information that is accurate and compatible with the standards generally accepted at the time of publication. The author and publisher shall not be liable for any special, consequential, or exemplary damages resulting, in whole or in part, from the readers' use of, or reliance on, the information contained in this book. The publisher has no responsibility for the persistence or accuracy of URLs for external or third-party Internet websites referred to in this publication and does not guarantee that any content on such websites is, or will remain, accurate or appropriate.

Library of Congress Cataloging-in-Publication Data

Silverman, Linda Kreger.
 Giftedness 101 / Linda Kreger Silverman.
   p. cm.
 Includes bibliographical references and index.
 ISBN 978-0-8261-0797-8 (alk. paper)
 1. Gifted children. 2. Gifted children—Education. I. Title.
 BF723.G5S55 2013
 155.45'5—dc23   2012040247

Printed in the United States of America by Gasch Printing.

Giftedness 101 is dedicated to Dr. Annemarie Roeper—my friend, my colleague—whose inspirational work changed the lives of multitudes of gifted children. She *saw* who they are, and her brave insights allowed others to see them as well. May the Annemarie Roeper Method of Qualitative Assessment be appreciated as a legitimate means of assessing giftedness. May the *Roeper Review* and The Roeper School continue to reflect her passionate regard for the emotional lives of the gifted. I dedicate my life to carrying on her work. May our hearts, souls, and voices intertwine.

Contents

CONTENTS

Preface

What is giftedness all about? This topic is mired in controversy.

- Is there such a thing?
- Aren't all people gifted in some way?
- Doesn't this type of labeling give a child a swelled head?
- Is giftedness just the result of "hothousing" by helicopter parents?
- Are programs for gifted children elitist and undemocratic?
- Can't smart kids make it on their own?
- Won't the other kids catch up eventually?
- Does giftedness disappear or cause untimely death ("Early ripe, early rot")?
- Are people with unusual gifts born with some sort of compensating handicap?
- Is there a link between giftedness and insanity?
- Is the notion of giftedness obsolete?
- Shouldn't we be talking instead about talents in different domains or multiple intelligences or expertise developed through years of effort and practice?

These are some of the perennial misconceptions with which the gifted and their parents must contend. Few topics engender such strong reactions. While it is comfortable to acknowledge that some individuals are less intelligent than we are, the idea that some individuals are smarter than us poses an emotional threat to the insecure (Persson, 2009). Tannenbaum (1983) discloses the history of "persistent undercurrents of suspicion and negativism"—widespread resentment—toward those who are highly intelligent (p. 3). The gifted are lonely in a world of misunderstanding.

It is not uncommon to hear an educator say to a parent in a patronizing tone, "We believe *all* our children are gifted." While all children are a gift to the world, saying "all children are gifted," robs the term of any meaning. It would be equally absurd to say, "We believe *all* our children are developmentally disabled." In Lake Wobegon, all the children are "above average"; in the rest of the world, there exists a vast range of individual differences in ability. These differences do not disappear by the time a person reaches adulthood. Individuals with impaired intellectual development, whose intelligence measures 2, 3, or 4 standard deviations below the norm, deal with specific psychological issues. The same is true for those who are developmentally advanced, with IQ scores 2, 3, 4, or more standard deviations above the norm. Those whose abstract reasoning is significantly keener than the majority have qualitatively different life experiences and qualitatively different psychological needs.

The purpose of *Giftedness 101* is to dispel many of the myths about the gifted, define the term in a nonelitist manner, explore how it manifests in individuals, describe why it is important, consider its origins, examine its psychological implications, and provide guidelines for its recognition, assessment, and development. An important topic that will be visited several times is the individual assessment of twice exceptional children (gifted children with learning disabilities). Expertise is required in several areas in order to detect high intelligence, ferret out specific learning disabilities, and recognize their interaction effects. Psychologists also need to understand the interplay of giftedness with gender, gender preference, socioeconomic status, cultural diversity, linguistic background, location (rural vs. urban), creativity, birth order, personality type, and learning style, as well as the factors that contribute to underachievement.

In this book, giftedness is viewed as a psychological reality. Within psychology, there has always been an interest in outliers; they show us the range of human abilities and illuminate the possibilities of human development. The study of giftedness originated in psychology, central to the analysis of individual differences. The first course on this topic was created at Columbia University, Teachers College, by Leta Stetter Hollingworth, in 1922: "Education 254" (Borland, 1990, p. 163). As the first clinical psychologist in New York State, Hollingworth was completely fascinated by the minds and development of profoundly gifted children. Her textbook, *Gifted Children: Their Nature and Nurture* (1926)—the first in this field—described the psychology of the gifted; only two chapters were devoted to their education. Another psychologist, Lewis Terman (1916b), developed the first popular IQ test with the specific intention of identifying the gifted, as well as other groups.

Over the years, this discipline lost its psychological focus and became imbedded in the field of education as a curricular and instructional issue. The role of school psychologists in identifying and serving the gifted is rapidly dwindling. Returning to the origin of the concept, *Giftedness 101* endeavors to re-establish the study of giftedness as a legitimate segment of psychology. Talented individuals need coaches to spur them on to greater achievement. Gifted individuals need psychologists who understand the depth and complexity of their interior worlds, and their struggles adjusting to the exterior world.

Education has not always welcomed its brightest students. Outliers upset the apple cart. They don't conform to the lesson plans. They force us to think outside the box. Mirroring society's ambivalence and anti-intellectualism (Tannenbaum, 1983), the education of gifted children has been on a perpetual roller coaster. The gifted have been applauded, attacked, mined as a national resource during the Space Race (after the Russians launched Sputnik), neglected, resurrected, and, during the school reform movement, scapegoated. Subject to the whims of educational fads, political agendas, and budget cuts, the field of gifted education has been swept in many competing directions. It has never been on secure ground. Throughout the world, there is no agreement as to whether or not gifted children should be recognized or served in school (Geake & Gross, 2008). There is no agreement regarding the definition of giftedness, its incidence in the population, methods of identification, assessment procedures, or appropriate provisions for its development (Martin, Burns, & Schonlau, 2010; Pfeiffer, 2003). Even the term "gifted" is not unanimously accepted; often it is replaced with more politically correct words, such as "talented" or "able and ambitious."

Giftedness 101 provides a cohesive conception of the psychology and development of a group with special needs. This perspective was shaped through 50 years of concentrated study and is informed by my experience as a teacher of gifted elementary students, a counselor of gifted adolescents, a teacher educator of graduate students in gifted education, a psychologist specializing in the assessment of giftedness, a clinician with gifted clients, the creator of a refereed psychological journal on adult giftedness, and a researcher. Scattered throughout the book are *italicized* quotations drawn from the files of over 6,000 children assessed at the Gifted Development Center (GDC) since 1979.

While there may always be controversy around the idea of giftedness, the inspiring words of Hollingworth (1939) offer hope that eventually this group will be embraced by society as a genuine special needs group, worthy of our attention and our support:

> We know that we can select in childhood those endowed with...extraordinary intelligence.... We know that the endowment of intellect is a permanent one.... We know that the range of intellect among school children is simply enormous, and that this will still be the case when these children become adults.
>
> .... These facts would be epoch-making, if applied to the limit of their power to apply. For a long time, people will not believe them, will be afraid of them, will not know what to do about them, but in the end the truth will be admitted and utilized, as everything is finally utilized that has power to bring order to human life. (p. 579)

Acknowledgments

I am deeply indebted to all the gifted children and their families who have shared their journeys with me. They have taught me all that I know about the gifted.

Giftedness 101 was inspired by Leta Stetter Hollingworth, the foremother of the psychology of giftedness; she found the minds of gifted children endlessly fascinating. I consider Leta my mentor, even though the two of us did not walk the earth at the same time. I am profoundly grateful that I had the opportunity to work closely for three decades with Annemarie Roeper, who understood the hearts of the gifted. This book represents a continuation of the work of these two child-centered giants.

Thanks to Nancy S. Hale, my editor from Springer Publishing Company, who was enormously patient with a book that was nearly a year overdue, got me unstuck, kept me on task, and put my feet to the fire to support my assertions. Donna Stumpp came to my aid by garnering evidence from refereed journals. I particularly wish to thank James Kaufman for inviting me to contribute this volume, for his excellent suggestions of additional resources, for his appreciation of my clinical perspective, and for holding my hand during the final revisions. I also appreciate Alan Kaufman's confidence in me, and his delightful defense of ipsative analysis.

John Wasserman, who has served as a continuous fountain of wisdom about assessment, offered feedback on the first draft of my chapter on Comprehensive Assessment of the Gifted.

Kathi Kearney, known to her friends as "Nancy Drew," provided historical research on the origins of the term, "gifted," as well as 19th-century citations.

During the course of writing this book, we had a flood leaving us without a kitchen for 6 months, we survived a major remodel of our house, we moved the Gifted Development Center after 18 years, we organized an international Dabrowski Congress, we conducted a national study to create extended norms for the *Wechsler Preschool and Primary Scale of Intelligence, Fourth Edition* (WPPSI-IV), and I lost my dear friend, Annemarie Roeper. Talk about stress... I am forever grateful to the staff of the Gifted Development Center, particularly Lee Ann Powell, for handling our move single-handedly, and Bobbie Gilman and Ann DeMers, for filling in for me, while I worked on the book. Thank you to everyone connected with the Gifted Development Center for all the support you have offered to me and to families of the gifted throughout the last 33 years.

The source of my strength has always been my family. This book could not have been written without the constant support of my husband, Hilton Silverman, who took care of me throughout the entire process, as he has for the last 52 years. He fed me, soothed me, read drafts of several sections, and cheered me on. When I pushed myself too hard or became frustrated, I was not fun to live with, and he was the one who suffered most. Yet, his love and compassion never wavered. Our daughter, Miriam Darnell, introduced me to invisible dragons. From our son, Brian, I learned about twice exceptionality and forgiveness. Our son, Damion, helped me stay in the vortex. And, our grandsons, Connor, Caelan, and Adam, endless sources of delight, remind me every day why this work is important.

I am exceedingly grateful to all those who care about the gifted and who take their needs seriously. Their future is in your hands.

Creativity 101
James C. Kaufman, PhD

Genius 101
Dean Keith Simonton, PhD

IQ Testing 101
Alan S. Kaufman, PhD

Leadership 101
Michael D. Mumford, PhD

Anxiety 101
Moshe Zeidner, PhD
Gerald Matthews, PhD

Psycholinguistics 101
Wind H. Cowles, PhD

Humor 101
Mitch Earleywine, PhD

Obesity 101
Lauren Rossen, PhD
Eric Rossen, PhD

Emotional Intelligence 101
Gerald Matthews, PhD
Moshe Zeidner, PhD
Richard D. Roberts, PhD

Personality 101
Gorkan Ahmetoglu, PhD
Tomas Chamorro-Premuzic, PhD

Giftedness 101
Linda Kreger Silverman, PhD

Intelligence 101
Jonathan Plucker, PhD
Amber Esping, PhD

Invisible Gifts

Individuals whose gifts have been discovered and cultivated have been as chance outcroppings of precious rock, while the great reserves of human talent lay undiscovered below.
John W. Gardner

"Am I gifted if no one can see it?" Some would say no, you are only gifted when you do something others deem remarkable. But the fox would disagree. *"And now here is my secret, a very simple secret: It is only with the heart that one can see rightly; what is essential is invisible to the eye"* (Saint-Exupery, 1943, p. 87).

Invisible gifts do exist. When they are deeply buried, the individual, and everyone in the person's world, may be completely unaware of them. If they do not receive nourishment from the environment, they may never flower into achievement. Do they wither and die or do they lie dormant waiting to be discovered?

Potential does not reach fruition without recognition and support. The potential concert pianist can never reach the

1

concert stage without a piano. Talent development requires expert tutelage and dedicated practice. We cannot know how much talent has been lost for lack of discovery and development, nor can we assess the magnitude of that loss to our society—the music that was never composed, the medical cure that was never discovered, the political strategy that might have averted a war. Undetected ability is an immense loss to society; the pain borne by the individual is beyond measure.

> Full many a gem of purest ray serene
> The dark unfathomed caves of ocean bear:
> Full many a flower is born to blush unseen,
> And waste its sweetness in the desert air.
> Thomas Gray (1751/1949)

There is inestimable waste of extraordinary endowment. What happens to those whose gifts remain invisible? Yearnings, shame, doubt, estrangement—feelings with no explanation.

THE SLEEPING DRAGON

There is more to some people than meets the eye. When one knows what to look for, giftedness appears in unanticipated places, expressed in unexpected ways: plaintive graffiti, a very clever reason for not having one's homework, a really good joke, a fascinating question, a turn of phrase (such as the use of "marinate" in the movie, "Kissing Jessica Stein"), painstaking absorption in an activity, a drawing of the inside of the pumpkin instead of the outside, an abiding passion, the courage to defend the underdog, stillness in the midst of chaos. Qualitative indicators of giftedness. If one notices that there is something special about a child and conveys a glint of recognition, the sleeping dragon within may awaken and begin to breathe fire into this little person's soul.

Giftedness is not addressed in the training programs of counselors, psychologists, and psychiatrists (Amend & Beljan, 2009) and is rarely covered in the field of education (Kane & Fiedler, 2011). Why? For the same reason school districts frequently cut gifted programs when budgets are tight and proclaim that there aren't enough funds to test gifted children. Few people "get it"! Few grasp the fundamental experience of giftedness—the outsider status in a society suspicious of outsiders (Geake & Gross, 2008). And many educators and academics mistake the tracks—visible achievements—for the beast itself. Achievement is easy to see. Giftedness is a dragon that can only be seen by those who can conceive of dragons. There are a lot of nonbelievers in this world. I remember being enchanted by the title of Deirdre Lovecky's (1986) article, "Can you hear the flowers singing?" I knew she "got it." Believers spot giftedness in grocery stores and airports. They see that certain spark that nonbelievers miss. Sometimes that moment is captured in films like "Hugo," when the toymaker recognizes Hugo's unusual ability to put a toy back together.

If most of the population does not acknowledge giftedness, or resents those of high intelligence, then multitudes of gifted individuals must camouflage who they really are in order to survive (Colangelo, 2002). Coleman (2012) found that of several coping mechanisms gifted youth use to deal with the stigma of giftedness, "invisibility is the most often used strategy" (p. 378). Pretending to be someone you are not is emotionally costly. It can lead to self-alienation. Most gifted children and adults are hidden from view because it is risky to reveal the depth of their awareness. They only trust those who believe in their existence, who "get" who they are, who appreciate their kookiness, who embrace their individuality. That is why professionals who "get" this population are so desperately needed. They provide a secure haven for dragons to feel comfortable enough to reveal themselves.

School is based on group norms. A gifted mind may not be well received in the classroom. Questioning that is irrelevant to

3

the lesson plan can throw the entire schedule off course. Some teachers find it exasperating when students ask complex questions they cannot answer or when gifted students know more than they do (Kane & Fiedler, 2011). The playground is even more perilous. Gifted children often question the rules of the game. Their sophisticated variations may make games more interesting to them, but too complicated for their classmates. Rejection is common. It is painful to be left out of games, to eat alone, to be excluded from birthday parties. There are emotional consequences of being different.

Giftedness is rarely expressed in groups; outliers conceal their differences. Shape-shifting dragons are easier to recognize away from the crowd. This is where psychologists have a distinct advantage. Psychologists work with individuals. Like grandparents, they have the freedom to give what Carl Rogers (1961, 1969) called *unconditional positive regard*. Their agenda is to see and understand, rather than to mold. They have the capacity to appreciate differences. In a psychologist's office, free from the imposition of group norms, it is safe to reveal secrets that remain veiled in group settings.

Does a gift imply an obligation? Many of the arguments in favor of educational provisions for the gifted are based on the value of this group to society. Gifted education is marketed as an investment in future leaders. "In current thinking in giftedness and education, the utility value reigns and the intrinsic value of the gift is virtually nonexistent" (Besjes-de Bock & de Ruyter, 2011, p. 205). Prized as a utility, the gifted are expected to yield a return on society's investment that is advantageous to the social order. Little attention is paid to their inner lives; "emotions are of minor importance" (p. 199). While some gifted children covet the goal of achieving high grades and crave the accolades of success in school and adult life, others march to their own drummers. One mother wrote: "*We say that A doesn't march to the beat of a different drummer—she has her own band.*"

Driven by their passions and curiosity, they may resent expectations that they maintain high grades in subjects that hold no interest for them. These children do not become stars in school. Instead, they may be labeled "underachievers" or simply fail to be noticed.

How might we find this buried treasure? In *The Republic*, Plato (n.d./1944) recommended testing the metal of youth to find the veins of gold. Testing—an uncomfortable subject. From a utilitarian perspective, IQ scores are considered insufficient evidence of giftedness. Demonstrated performance is what counts. Despite widespread aversion to placing a numerical value and rank on intelligence, IQ tests can expose a precious asset: an extraordinary mind. Children with extraordinary minds frequently do not divulge their true capabilities in unstimulating environments. Like caged cheetahs, their full capacities never have the opportunity to be displayed (Tolan, 1996). Instead of being valued only for what they can produce, which frequently happens in school, the gifted need to be cherished for who they are and the unusual ways they think and feel.

HIDDEN GIFTED POPULATIONS

When schools only recognize high achievement as indicative of giftedness, untold numbers of gifted children from diverse backgrounds are missed.

The Exceptionally Gifted

Strangely enough, the most intelligent are among those missing in action. In 1942, Hollingworth wrote:

> In the ordinary elementary school situation children of 140 IQ waste half their time in school. Those above 170 IQ waste almost all their time. With little to do, how can these children develop power of sustained effort, respect for the task, or habits of steady work? (p. 299)

In the last 70 years, not much has changed in the education of highly, exceptionally, and profoundly gifted children. "Consistently robbed of opportunities to learn through real struggle," highly gifted students "are among those who are least likely to receive an appropriate education" (Kane & Fiedler, 2011, p. 73). The most able are rarely recognized or served. These children often find it impossible to cope with drill, repetition, Mad Minutes, endless waiting, mindless homework forcing them to prove what they mastered years ago, unchallenging material presented at an agonizingly slow pace, and the lack of connection with other children in their class. Without being given the opportunity to soar, they disappear into daydreams. Thousands of extremely gifted children become so disillusioned that they drop out of school and insist on being homeschooled (Goodwin & Gustavson, 2011; Gross, 2009; Lovecky, 2011; Rivero, 2002). Missing from the roll calls and from the minds of school personnel, their disappearance is barely perceptible. Their absence confirms the entrenched belief that there are too few of them to worry about anyway.

Homeschoolers

Among the gifted that no one can see are the myriad who decide to stay home. Homeschooling is claiming a steadily increasing share of the gifted population (Goodwin & Gustavson, 2012). The most decorated Olympic champion of all times, Michael Phelps, was homeschooled. Christopher Paolini, author of *Eragon* (2003) and other books in his *Inheritance Cycle*, was homeschooled for the duration of his education, and graduated high school at the age of 15. *Eragon* was published before his 20th birthday. The number of homeschoolers is mushrooming (Livingston & Nachazal, 2009). Partial homeschooling and early college entrance are gaining in popularity in the gifted community (Goodwin & Gustavson, 2011). While no census of gifted homeschoolers exists, one indication of their rising number is the growth of organizations such as the Gifted Homeschoolers

Forum (GHF; www.giftedhomeschoolers.org), which provides support to more than 8,000 members nationally.

> The increase in positive popular media coverage and the relative ease of access to free or low-cost resources and homeschool communities via the Internet have increased the viability of this option for many families regardless of their cultural background or economic status. (Goodwin & Gustavson, 2010, p. 22)

Cultural, Ethnic, Linguistic, and Socioeconomic Diversity

A great deal has been written about the underrepresentation in gifted education programs of children of color (e.g., Bonner, Lewis, Bowman-Perrott, Hill-Jackson, & James, 2009; Ford, Moore, & Scott, 2011; Grantham, 2011; Kitano, 2012; McBee, 2010), those for whom English is a second language (e.g., Esquierdo & Arreguín-Anderson, 2012; Harris, Plucker, Rapp, & Martinez, 2009), and those in lower socioeconomic circumstances (e.g., Latz & Adams, 2011; Stambaugh, 2009). Some of the factors contributing to this inequity are lack of teacher referrals, stereotype threat, deficit thinking and deficit-based educational models, negative peer pressure, and, of course, test bias (Silverman & N. Miller, 2009).

While IQ testing has been cast as the Big Bad Wolf, the selection criteria for most programs for the gifted include measures of achievement, and achievement has always favored the advantaged (Hollingworth, 1926). Studies employing intelligence tests have repeatedly documented that giftedness is plentiful in all these groups (e.g., Ehrlich, 1986; Kearney & LeBlanc, 1993). Exceptional abstract reasoning (high intelligence) is found in all cultures and in all socioeconomic levels (Dickinson, 1956). There are many more gifted children in the world living in poverty than those who are wealthy (Zigler & Farber, 1985). Poverty conceals giftedness. Early identification and support of high ability holds the greatest promise of reversing the inequity.

The Highly Creative

Children who think outside-the-box may be perceived as "weird," rather than gifted. Predictability is valued in some classrooms, and these children challenge the monotony by doing the unexpected. This may enhance their popularity with the other students (J. Kaufman, 2009), but probably not their appeal to their teachers. Undesirable creativity can cost a teacher recommendation or a referral to the gifted program. Divergent thinkers "prefer unusual, uncommon, original and creative responses…though they might not produce concrete products" (Lovecky, 1991, p. 7). If products are the entry to gifted programs, the most creative often lose out. Many gifted children are creative and imaginative (Albert, 1980; Louis & M. Lewis, 1992). IQ tests can miss the most highly creative (J. Kaufman, 2009), whose ingenious responses confound test constructors. Even creativity testing does not always reveal creativity. The *Torrance Tests of Creative Thinking* (TTCT) (Torrance, 1974) was once integral to the admissions criteria of many gifted programs, but they have declined in popularity. For a dozen years, the Gifted Development Center (GDC) routinely administered the divergent production sections of the *Structure of Intellect Learning Abilities Test* (SOI-LA) (M. Meeker, R. Meeker, & Roid, 1985), and then abandoned the practice. We found little correlation between the creativity measures of the SOI-LA and observed creative behavior. Unquestionably, highly creative children are at-risk for being weeded out in the selection process for gifted education.

Gender and Gender Preference

There are as many girls as boys in the highest IQ ranges (Silverman, 1986c), but girls are chameleons; early identification is critical, before they vanish in middle school (Silverman & N. Miller, 2009). Gender bias has been demonstrated in referrals to gifted programs by teachers (Bianco, Harris, Garrison-Wade,

& Leech, 2011) and in referrals for assessment by parents (Silverman & N. Miller, 2009). This contributes to declining self-concepts of gifted girls over time (Rudasill, Capper, Foust, Callahan, & Albaugh, 2009). Gay, lesbian, bisexual, and transgender (GLBT) gifted youth are often disregarded (Friedrichs, 2012). They face insufferable prejudice in the schools and need advocates, both in and out of school (Hubbard & Whitley, 2012). Psychologists who appreciate and support them may save lives.

Personality Type and Birth Order

Introverts are also at a distinct disadvantage in extraverted school systems (Cain, 2012; Olsen Laney, 2002); they are more likely to observe than participate. The gifted population is composed of more introverts than extraverts (Silverman, 1998b). A considerable number of introverted gifted children are hidden at school, particularly in the elementary grades. They come to life in one-on-one assessment. Second-born children may be overlooked as well; they often live in the shadow of their older brother or sister. Cornell (1984) found that when schools labeled only one sibling as gifted, invariably it was the first-born. Individual assessment reveals that siblings are usually close in intelligence (Silverman, 1988), even if they differ markedly in achievement.

Rural Gifted Children

Highly intelligent children who live in rural areas are often unseen (Lawrence, 2009). Fitting into the community is strongly valued. Rural gifted students may be conflicted about disclosing high abilities and standing out. Yet, when these children are assessed, they actually may stand a better chance of being served. Karen Rogers (2004) found that smaller, rural schools were more likely than affluent suburban schools to implement recommendations derived from psychological testing. Rural educators may take pride in their identified gifted students and appear to be more flexible in serving their needs. There are advantages to being small. "Small rural schools can, in fact, easily accommodate acceleration through a variety of means—in particular, early entrance to school, grade-skipping, cross-grade grouping by subject, multiage grouping, and dual high school and college enrollment" (A. Howley & C. Howley, 2012, p. 128).

Underachievers

Gifted programs are usually reserved for the able and ambitious. Those students who lack the second ingredient may not even be defined as gifted. The new National Association for Gifted Children (NAGC, 2011a) definition indicates that in adolescence, "achievement and high levels of motivation in the domain become the primary characteristics of their giftedness." "Task commitment" is an essential element of Renzulli's (1978) three-ring conception of giftedness. Motivation takes center stage. Students admitted to gifted programs based on test scores, but who fail to produce, often are invited to leave.

Children underachieve for a wide variety of reasons, including fear of failure, fear of success, fear of lack of acceptance by peers, too low or too high parental expectations, and so on (Silverman, 1993a). Regardless of the reason, the deficits are cumulative. It could be argued that nearly all gifted children underachieve, since few are challenged sufficiently to demonstrate and develop the full extent of their abilities (Silverman, 2011). Those who can attain high grades without exerting any effort fail to learn study habits that they will need in higher grades. They may come to believe that all learning should be effortless (Rimm, 2009). Dweck (2006) contends that telling children they are smart can undermine effort; however, earlier, she put more responsibility on the school. She maintained that the curriculum needs to be more challenging for bright students (Dweck, 1986). "Continued success on personally easy tasks" has been found to "produce lower confidence in ability"

(p. 1046). Effort must come from the school as well as from the individual.

From a school perspective, underachievers are those who refuse to do the assigned work. Teachers and parents often become very upset with a child's nonperformance, and everyone can get into a blaming stance. The child is accused of being "lazy," the parents of being "dysfunctional," and the teacher and curriculum "boring." Psychological services may be needed for crisis intervention and mediation, to investigate the causes, and recommend solutions. Hidden learning disabilities routinely should be ruled out in all students who underachieve, as these two populations overlap considerably (Silverman, 1989). Underachievement patterns need to be attended to as early as possible. With every year, they become more difficult to reverse. However, they can be reversed (Rimm, 2009). Emerick (1992) found that a key element is the good fortune of having a teacher who sincerely cares for the students, communicates with them as peers, engages them in learning, and helps them to see the relevance of education to the pursuit of their interests.

Learning Style

Learning style can pose a barrier to the recognition of high abilities. School is an auditory-sequential playground. Auditory-sequential learners are good listeners, learn in a step-by-step fashion, are timely, and well organized (Silverman, 2009d); they learn the way teachers teach, and they are more likely to be counted among high achievers (Silverman, 2002). Visual-spatial learners do not display these prized school skills. Instead, they are "big picture" thinkers, who need to see the whole to understand the parts. Higher-level visual-spatial thinking is essential to geography, architecture, medicine, design, computer science, and many other fields (Shah & Miyake, 2005). Eide and Eide (2011) dub these children "young engineers," who "typically show their keenest interest in spatial or mechanical activities like building, designing, art, inventing, electronics, computing, and science" (p. 10).

> To identify our next generation of talented engineers, inventors, and physicists, we shouldn't be using pencil-and-paper "talent searches" or seeing who's fastest at the "mad math minutes." We should be searching for spatial prodigies in LEGO Stores and hobby shops—just like athletic scouts hang around ball fields. (Eide & Eide, 2011, p. 73)

Many visual-spatial learners find school painful. In the classroom, they are frequently reminded of their weaknesses, rather than celebrated for their strengths. These children are more likely to exhibit the bright array of right-hemispheric abilities, such as imagination, insight, intuition, emotional responsiveness, three-dimensional perception, artistic expression, inventiveness, and spirituality (Silverman, 2002; Taylor, 2006). These gifts are not necessarily valued in school. Our right hemispheres are nonsequential and mysterious, giving birth to "Aha!" moments (Lehrer, 2012).

> When a solution does appear, it doesn't come in dribs and drabs; the puzzle isn't solved one piece at a time. Rather, the solution is shocking in its completeness. All of a sudden, the answer to the problem that seemed so daunting becomes incredibly obvious. We curse ourselves for not seeing it sooner. (p. 7)

Auditory-sequential teaching appears to be a good match for only one-fourth of the students (Haas, 2011). Haas has found that at least two-thirds of public school students prefer visual-spatial teaching methods; the percentage is even higher among Navajo. Alan Kaufman (1994b) reported that the perceptual reasoning abilities of Navajo children typically were 2 standard deviations (30 points) higher than their verbal abilities, supporting their need for visual-spatial instructional strategies.

Leviton (2011, in press) describes a third learning style— tactile–kinesthetic learners. These children learn by moving and doing. She finds that the current emphases on test scores and academic achievement render most learning environments unfriendly to children with this learning style. Students who have a high need for physical activity may be unable to sit still and work for the better part of 6 hours a day. Gifted visual-spatial learners and tactile–kinesthetic learners tend to be late bloomers, unlikely to be recognized as having high abilities in school.

The Twice Exceptional

Related to learning style, but more extreme, is the condition of twice exceptionality—giftedness combined with learning disability. Baum (2009) notes that students with specific learning disabilities and students with attention-deficit/hyperactivity disorder (AD/HD) both "may prefer spatial tasks" (p. 528). Several researchers have suggested that certain disabilities and gifts seem to go together, such as reading disorders and unusual spatial abilities (Davis, 2010; Eide & Eide, 2011; Gilger & Hynd, 2008; West, 2009).

When IQ testing is abandoned, when children are only deemed gifted on the basis of demonstrated performance, when they are not qualified as disabled unless they are performing significantly below grade level, and when psychologists are left out of the process, most twice exceptional children are imperceptible. Coexisting gifts and disabilities mask each other, making the child appear less able and less disabled. The superb reasoning ability that surfaces in class discussions cannot be demonstrated in written work, which leads to the stinging "smart, but lazy" label.

A remarkable number of gifted individuals suffer from disabilities, and both their gifts and disabilities may be hidden (Kennedy & Banks, 2011). The estimated number of twice exceptional children in the schools ranges from 300,000 to several million (Barber & Mueller, 2011; Baum & Owen, 2004; Foley Nicpon, Allman, Siek, & Stinson, 2011; Gilger & Hynd,

2008; Neumann, 2009). Disabilities come in a variety of shapes and sizes: dyslexia, dysgraphia, dyscalculia, central auditory processing disorder, AD/HD, Asperger syndrome, disorder of written expression, and more. More often than not, the child is graced with a combination of these labels.

> *We're not making up this stuff.* We really do have gifted kids who have various issues that hold them back. Yes, it exists. You can have a highly gifted kid with processing speeds slower than molasses/Sensory Processing Disorder/ADHD/anxiety/school underachievement. Highly gifted is not the same as high achieving. Highly gifted is how a person is wired, not what a person produces. Please remember this. (J. Merrill, 2012, p. 8)

Mood disorders (e.g., depression, anxiety, bipolar disorder) may also be present; they represent another form of twice exceptionality. There are also homebound gifted children who have physical conditions that prevent school attendance.

In most cases, their high abstract reasoning enables twice exceptional children to compensate sufficiently to get by with at least low average grades during their first years of school (Silverman, 2009c), but with each grade level their struggles intensify. They must work harder and longer to maintain passing grades; nearly all of their free time may be consumed by homework. Their gargantuan efforts are often rewarded by their being considered "not good enough" for gifted programs and "too good" to qualify for accommodations. Catch 22! Their underrepresentation in gifted programs is well documented (Assouline, Foley Nicpon, & Huber, 2006; Morrison & Rizza, 2007; Silverman, 2009b).

> My son wasn't accepted to the district's Gifted and Talented (GT) program.... Never mind that I have a full workup from the Gifted Development Center which states very clearly that my son would best be served in a full-time gifted classroom. Unfortunately, I unexpectedly learned this from the principal as my son was standing there, so not only did I not have the opportunity to argue

effectively, but I also had the added pleasure of talking my hysterical son off the ledge once we got into the car. Oh yes, that was a joyful afternoon. (J. Merrill, 2012, p. 22)

Is average good enough? Average work amounts to underachievement for a gifted child; however, grade-level achievement renders the child ineligible for individual assessment and accommodations in today's schools (Postma, Peters, Gilman, & Kearney, 2011). Psychological assessment is essential to documenting both giftedness and disabilities. Instead of asking the typical question, "How does this child's performance compare with the norms?" it is necessary for the examiner to ask an entirely different diagnostic question: "To what extent do the *discrepancies* between the child's strengths and weaknesses *cause frustration and interfere with the full development of the child's abilities?*" (Silverman, 2009c).

The following example is illustrative. An 8-year-old profoundly gifted boy was asked to write a paper. After several failed attempts, he changed his topic to, "The Writing Dilemma." He wanted his teachers to know how he struggled with writing.

> *10-17-11 One of the largest worries about homework is writing. Not just writing, but writing slowly. If I write a paragraph it takes 20 minutes. My mom says to hurry up, but I say, "I can't write quickly." Because of my slow writing it takes me longer to get my homework done and to be able to play. Writing slowly is a homework dilemma.*
>
> *10-18-11 As I write I get **very** apprehensive, for I feel like my writing has to be perfect. My hands shake with worry, as I continue to write; writing stories the very first time is hard.*

The discrepancy between this boy's reasoning and handwriting speed exceeded 5 standard deviations (equivalent to the difference between an IQ of 130 and an IQ of 55). His sympathetic teachers could see that he is highly intelligent, works very hard, and gets frustrated by writing. A Section 504 Plan could assure that he would be allowed more time for standardized tests. However, getting him qualified for a Section 504 Plan was daunting. He was not below grade level, and the decision-makers considered his giftedness irrelevant. Without advocacy from a psychologist, no accommodations would have been forthcoming. Accommodations are not expensive. The majority of twice exceptional children need extra time due to processing speed deficits, which costs nothing (VanTassel-Baska, 2012b).

Twice exceptional children need early intervention and effective support systems to turn their vulnerabilities into benefits. They should not be treated as if they are broken and are in need of fixing (Eide & Eide, 2011; Kennedy & Banks, 2011; Mooney, 2007). "Often these students are so starved for praise that even the slightest bit of encouragement can do wonders" (Eide & Eide, 2011, p. 212). The most effective interventions take both exceptionalities into account (Yssel, 2012). The key is to find the child's strengths first and focus on those strengths, before dealing with the weaknesses (Gilman, 2008a). Too many times, the disability takes center stage, and the child's gifts are ignored (S. Schultz, 2012). Twice exceptional children blossom when their assets are recognized and valued by others.

Vast Numbers of Invisibly Gifted

When all of these factors are taken into account, it becomes clear that giftedness is largely invisible. The visibly gifted are high achievers, and they represent only the tip of the iceberg. The vast majority of the world's millions of gifted children are hidden from view. Less likely to be recognized at home or at school, most of these children do not think of themselves as having special ability. Some may demonstrate unusual facility outside the school walls, while masquerading as "normals" in school, working overtime to disguise themselves. Strength-based approaches, in teaching and in counseling, are most effective with diverse populations (Kitano, 2012). Psychologists entering this field need to be talent scouts, actively seeking giftedness in all groups.

CHANGING LIVES

It is extremely gratifying to work with the gifted of all ages. One well-timed clinical insight can be instantly life-changing. Psychological examiners open doors to special programs and scholarship opportunities; they enable the twice exceptional to gain access to accommodations that allow them to succeed. Counselors ignite passions and reverse patterns of underachievement. Therapists gain as much from their gifted clients as they give. Advocates who understand giftedness transform life scripts.

Professionals who specialize in the gifted are quick to recognize glimpses of gold beneath the surface. They relish these children: they take great delight in their vocabulary, kooky sense of humor, intriguing questions, and remarkable insights—the qualitative markers of giftedness. Their enjoyment becomes a positive mirror of the gifted person's assets. They can hear the flowers singing. They can awaken sleeping dragons. Even a brief encounter with someone who delights in you opens caverns of your inner world that were blocked with "No Trespassing" signs. The following allegory is illustrative.

Max, the Jumping Flea

Once upon a time, there was a little flea whose name was Max. He had many older and younger brethren, but none of them could jump close to the height he could. Every few days, he would jump out into the world; out of the shoebox where he and his relatives lived. When he came back, usually with numerous injuries, he was scolded and laughed at.

His worried mother put a cover on the shoebox. Max tried to jump high, but he hurt himself over and over. He found out that he could not get to the outside world anymore and he was very sad. Soon he learned not to jump high, so that he wouldn't hit his head and hurt himself. Finally, his mother removed the cover, but Max had forgotten the outside world and would not jump high.

17

One day, there was a Jumping Olympics for all fleas. Some remembered Max's jumping abilities and tried to get him to jump, but his abilities were just not there. He tried very hard to get out of the shoebox, but he just couldn't. Those who used to snicker at the injured Max now were disappointed very much. "Oh well. He couldn't jump that high anyway."

Finally, an invisible stranger came. He put invisible stools and books and chairs under Max. Max was still jumping low, but with all the boosts, it was comparatively high. He could see the world again! With a turbulent, bright flash Max remembered the world. His spirit soared and he jumped five times higher than he had ever jumped and won the Jumping Olympics with a titanic effort.

This story was written by a 9-year-old profoundly gifted boy. May you become the "invisible stranger" who makes a difference.

What Is Giftedness?

How glorious it is—and also how painful—to be an exception.
Alfred de Musset

tudents and professionals in the field of psychology are encouraged to understand diverse populations. Most are aware of the psychological impact of ethnicity, gender, sexual preference, socioeconomic status, and disability, but there has been little guidance offered with regard to one minority group: the gifted. Being "too smart" is emotionally unsafe; some (especially boys) have found it physically unsafe as well. Anti-intellectualism is alive and well in our society and takes its toll on our brightest members (J. Jung, McCormick, & Gross, 2012). To be gifted and Black or dyslexic or gay or poor or any combination compounds the risk of being marginalized.

"Geek!" "Nerd!" "Freak!" "Brainiac!" Stereotyping. Ostracizing. Distancing. "I'm not like everyone else. I'm not acceptable. There's something wrong with me." From preschool on, gifted children often feel flawed. How do they cope? The fortunate find others like themselves early in life, feel accepted, and adapt well. Others pretend to be like their peers, carefully monitoring their language, lopping off parts of themselves that don't fit in. Camouflage is a short-sighted solution: it impedes development and undermines aspirations. There are gifted children who withdraw into books, fantasy, video games—solitary pursuits to avoid the slings and arrows of their tormentors. Some fight back and develop behavior problems. A few appear to adapt, but suffer depression, school phobia, suicidal ideation, psychosomatic ailments, or chronic anxiety. Life scripts are formed in childhood, and feelings of alienation seeded in their early years can haunt the gifted throughout their lifespan. Gifted individuals need professionals who understand their striving, their search for meaning, their yearning for connection, and their complexity, sensitivity, and intensity. They need professionals alert to the issues of giftedness—who use this template to help their clients develop greater self-awareness. They need to be recognized.

Giftedness is a political football. Caught in the pendulum between zealous egalitarianism and our country's striving for excellence (J. Gardner, 1961), now you see the gifted, now you don't. Shifting national values concerning assessment place all gifted children at risk for underachievement and disenfranchisement. In lean years, state and district provisions for the gifted are often the first to be cut, reflecting their low priority as a special needs group. "We can't afford to test gifted children" veils the conflicting, ambivalent attitudes with which this population contends. Without recognition, their gifts are unlikely to be developed and their differences can become a source of shame.

In the field of psychology, there is a conspicuous absence of concern for the gifted. Currently, there are at least 54 divisions of the American Psychological Association (APA), none of which focuses on the gifted. Surveys of specialty areas distributed by state psychological associations list nearly all exceptionalities, with the exception of giftedness. There are no courses in psychology programs on the psychology of giftedness. Psychologists frequently report that the gifted were not mentioned at all in their graduate programs (Amend & Beljan, 2009).

School psychologists bear the responsibility of identifying, assessing, and advocating for the gifted during their formative years. Yet, even this branch of psychology does not offer specific training with this population, nor is this training required for certification. "Standards of accreditation of school psychology make no mention of the curricular requirements regarding the unique needs of the gifted" (Robertson, Pfeiffer, & Taylor, 2011, p. 787). A recent survey of school psychologists revealed that "94% of the participants received either little or no training in gifted screening and assessment" in their graduate programs (Robertson et al., 2011, p. 790). Although twice exceptional students (gifted children with learning disabilities) are invisible without assessment, more than 60% of the 298 school psychologists polled in this study reported little or no knowledge of twice exceptionality. This inequity could be rectified if all psychology programs were to include the study of the gifted and twice exceptional, along with the needs of other diverse groups.

IS GIFTEDNESS BORN OR MADE?

The nature–nurture controversy is particularly spirited and divisive among proponents of the gifted. This may seem perplexing. Wasn't this question settled decades ago? Hadn't science conceded that these two factors are so intertwined that their impact is inseparable? So what's the fuss? The problem stems from conflicting ideologies, disagreement about the value of IQ tests, and different populations studied, leading to opposing definitions of giftedness. "Nature" implies inherent differences that create a complex inner world, unusual awareness, and the pain of being an "outsider." "Nurture" focuses on performance and the role of the environment in fostering recognized achievement. "An achievement-based conception of giftedness differs from an ability- or intelligence-based conception of giftedness in its focus on the external manifestations of giftedness and/or talent" (Bland, 2012, p. 21).

The "nature" supporters tend to believe that there are vast differences in native abilities (Gottfredson, 2011) and that heritability accounts for as much as 80% of intelligence. "Heritability does not imply immutability" (Plomin & Price, 2003, p. 114). Giftedness is *not* set in stone and impervious to experience; however, genetics does play an important role (see also Johnson, Nijenhuis, & Bouchard, 2008; Plomin & Asbury, 2005). The "nurture" fans remain unconvinced; they tell us that "many well-known geniuses—Edison, Darwin, and even Einstein—were ordinary bright children who became obsessed with something..." (Dweck, 2011, p. 1).

Those who are interested in success equate giftedness with eminence. They wonder, "What enabled these individuals to have noteworthy accomplishments?" They usually conclude that effort (deliberate practice) is the key to success, and that the motivation to put forth sufficient effort can be influenced by the individual's beliefs about intelligence, as well as his or her support systems (see Dweck, 2006; Ericsson, Nandagopal, & Roring, 2009; Gladwell, 2008). Some of these adherents deny the role of heredity altogether (e.g., Dweck, 2011; Ericsson, 2006), claiming that there really are no differences in ability; success is simply a function of hard work. This viewpoint has captured the attention of the press, reflects the prevailing cultural attitudes ("Everyone should have an equal opportunity to be successful"), and undergirds the current Zeitgeist in gifted education—influencing teacher training programs, legislation, legal decisions, and funding initiatives. The National Association for Gifted Children (NAGC) has proposed a new definition of giftedness that fits within this framework:

> *Gifted individuals are those who demonstrate outstanding levels of apti-*
> *tude (defined as an exceptional ability to reason and learn) or compe-*
> *tence (documented performance or achievement in top 10% or rarer) in*
> *one or more domains....*
>
> .... As individuals mature through childhood to adolescence,
> however, achievement and high levels of motivation in the domain
> become the primary characteristics of their giftedness....
>
> A person's giftedness should not be confused with the means
> by which giftedness is observed or assessed.... a high IQ score [is]
> not giftedness; [it] may be a signal that giftedness exists. (NAGC,
> 2011a)

This "paradigm shift" was heralded two decades ago
by David Feldman (1992), John Feldhusen (1992), The U.S.
Department of Education's *National Excellence* report (OERI,
1993), Donald Treffinger and John Feldhusen (1996), and others. In this paradigm, giftedness or talent:

a. encompasses the top 10% of the population;
b. is domain-specific;
c. involves achievement or the potential for recognized
    achievement;
d. requires motivation;
e. is focused on external manifestations; and
f. is more observable in adolescents or adults.
g. In addition, IQ scores are insufficient evidence of its
    existence.

The term "gifted," which implies inherent differences, is
eschewed in favor of "talent development" (OERI, 1993;
Subotnik, Olszewski-Kubilius, & Worrell, 2011). "Outstanding
achievement or eminence should be the chief goal of gifted
education" (Subotnik et al., 2011, p. 3).

It follows that there are no gifted children; there can only
be promising children with the potential for greatness in a specific domain. In short, you are not born gifted; giftedness is
accomplished through effort. Nurture rules.

The other side of the nature/nurture debate stems from observations of exceptionally and profoundly gifted young children, who demonstrate extraordinary abstract reasoning, overexcitabilities (intensities), and accelerated development (see Columbus Group, 2013; Daniels & Piechowski, 2009; Hafenstein & Honeck, 2011; Kay, Robson, & Brenneman, 2007; Lovecky, 2004). These young children appear to develop differently from birth. They are unusually alert, crave novelty and attention in the crib, sleep less, smile and recognize caretakers early, and have intense reactions (Gaunt, 1989; Henderson & Ebner, 1997; Maxwell, 1995; M. Rogers, 1986). Some parents note signs of giftedness in the first 48 hours of life (Louis & M. Lewis, 1992). Gifted development becomes increasingly more evident as these children race through the developmental milestones, leaving their age peers behind. Verbal abilities, such as early talking and reading, are the most prevalent signs of giftedness, but a substantial number are more advanced than age peers with puzzles, LEGO™ constructions, and understanding how things work (Silverman, 2002).

From this perspective, motivation, achievement, and external manifestations of success are not the defining variables. Instead, giftedness is internal; it:

a. involves developmental differences in abstract reasoning, emotional sensitivity, and intensity;
b. can be observed in very young children;
c. can be documented on measures of general intelligence (g);
d. is lifelong;
e. encompasses the top 2% to 3%, who have significantly different needs from the norm;
f. creates qualitatively different life experiences;
g. leads to a set of issues unique to this group, making them vulnerable; and
h. requires early intervention and accommodations.

James Gallagher (2000) suggests that there are children "who, at birth, have a neurological constitution that allows them to learn faster, remember more, process information more effectively, and generate more new and unusual ideas than their age peers" (p. 6). He cites the undeniable existence of prodigies as support for inherent differences. "It is impossible to assign such remarkable gifts solely to environmental factors" (p. 6). No one can predict which children will become renowned in adulthood; however, for the last century, psychologists have been able to identify children whose development is significantly different from the norm, and who require accommodations to allow them to develop optimally.

The equation of giftedness with achievement seems to resonate with educators more than with parents. One parent writes:

1. Gifted kids are not like other kids. They are more intense, more curious, more everything. When we didn't know what was going on with our son, lo those many years ago, the only word I could choke out was "more." He was just *more*.
2. Gifted does not mean high-achieving. I'd like to make that sentence into t-shirts, sky-writing, tattoos, bumper stickers, jewelry, pasta shapes, and novelty doorbells.... (J. Merrill, 2012, p. 27)

More and more parents of gifted children, like Jen Merrill, are choosing to homeschool their children, partly in response to the growing focus on talent development—"pushing educational institutions in a direction that parents are not happy with, and those parents are voting with their feet" (Goodwin & Gustavson, 2012, p. 8). Annemarie Roeper, who worked with gifted children and their families for nearly 70 years, wrote, "Rarely did parents relate their child's giftedness with achievement." She went on to say:

Linking giftedness and achievement is comparing apples and oranges, with results that may run the whole gamut from huge success to equally huge failure. Giftedness is a personal

25

characteristic, inborn—possibly enhanced by environmental factors. Achievement is often based on outside expectations. (A. Roeper, personal communication, January 27, 2012)

Academic psychologists favor the emphasis on motivation and achievement, while practitioners who evaluate gifted children are often struck by their developmental differences. Their view is similar to the parents'.

The talent development perspective fits a broad spectrum (the top 10%) rather than the top 3% or less of the populace. Broadening the definition of giftedness is more egalitarian, extending membership into what has been viewed as an "elite" group. An inclusive approach acknowledges a wide range of talents and intelligences, and insists on the imprecision of tests in determining a child's true potential. It has the advantages of being more palatable to the public and considered responsive to the needs of children with diverse abilities and backgrounds.

Disadvantages of such an approach include funding issues and the selection process. The cost of providing services increases with the number of children served; selection of children with potential in numerous domains makes the selection process unwieldy and expensive. The broader view often rests on the hypothesis of multiple intelligences, but there is little empirical support for this conception (Simonton, 2009). Pyryt (2000) reanalyzed data derived from a large study of kindergarten students (Plucker, Callahan, & Tomchin, 1996), which used a measurement tool based on Gardner's (1983) multiple intelligences. By means of a higher order approach similar to the procedure employed by Carroll (1993), Pyryt (2000) found that a single factor (g) accounted for 55.9% of the variance in scores.

Consistent with Carroll's findings, the present results suggest that a general intelligence factor underlies the correlations between first-order factors derived from the intercorrelations of performance-based measures of hypothetical multiple intelligences. The current analysis suggests that researchers and practitioners should be cautious when dismissing general intelligence in favor of multiple intelligences. (p. 192)

Plucker (2000), who responded to Pyryt's (2000) reanalysis, indicated that results of the original study were "admittedly disappointing" (p. 193). Only three factors were found—linguistic, mathematical, and spatial—which corresponds to more traditional views of intelligence.

Another serious concern is defensibility (Ronvik, 1993). McCoach and Siegle (2007) raise the question, "Is it possible that by broadening the notion of giftedness, we are less able to make a compelling argument for the necessity of specialized service for gifted students?" (p. 253). Do children in the top 10% of the school population warrant special provisions? They are close enough to the norm to be socially accepted, and their learning and emotional needs do not appear to differ significantly from the norm (J. Gallagher, 2000; Gross, 2009). Does a program that includes 10% (some recommend as many as the top 33%) serve the needs of the children with more extreme differences (e.g., the top 1%)? Gallagher (2000) is skeptical.

> There is good reason to believe that the far high end of the distribution of intelligence requires something different than what is provided for the gifted students who are merely somewhat superior in learning ability to the average student. If we can speak of the "highly gifted," then I believe these rare students (perhaps less than 1% of the total) should be the instructional responsibility of the specialist in gifted education.... (p. 8)

Focusing on motivation, hard work, and adult success may be exactly what is needed for this broader group. But have the needs of the most gifted been sacrificed in the bargain? Each standard deviation of difference from the norm presents its own unique challenges. The rarer the individual's level of ability, the greater the need for psychological assessment and support services. The child who teaches herself to read at age 3 is on a unique developmental trajectory. Her

goal is not recognized achievement; it is self-actualization—
and finding a friend.

THE GREAT DIVIDE: THE ROLE OF IQ TESTING

The Great Divide in the field of gifted education and psychology stems, in part, from polarized perceptions of IQ testing (Simonton, 2009). If our starting point is the study of recognized achievement in adults, then a strong argument can be made against intelligence tests, since many assert that they do not predict who will attain lasting recognition (e.g., Feldman, 1984; H. Gardner, 1983; Simonton, 2009; Witty, 1940). Some suggest that IQ testing can indicate who has the potential to become gifted, but that giftedness must be demonstrated through achievement. Preschool and primary school children are thought to be too young to ascertain talent. From an achievement orientation, it is better to identify the talented when they are older, since the accomplishments of students closer to adulthood are more predictive of success in adult life. There is also the pervasive belief that intelligence tests are biased against diverse populations, excluding them from opportunities for success.

If we focus our attention on infants, toddlers, and preschoolers, measures of development are important to locate children at the extremes. Early identification and intervention are essential to the optimal development of children who develop in an atypical manner. The ability camp relies on IQ tests to indicate special needs in children. As a significant number of gifted children also have learning disabilities, assessment is vital to uncovering disabilities that are often masked by the child's high intelligence. The profile of strengths and weaknesses revealed in assessment becomes a template for intervention and instruction.

It is always surprising to read a scathing condemnation of IQ testing. For example, the opinion that IQ scores offer an elitist way to rank individuals in our society according to some misguided scale of personal worth seems shocking to me. I view IQ tests as a means to clarify the educational needs of children who are discrepant from the average and to provide information needed to create an appropriate educational program for them...because typical educational programs are not working well for these children. (Gilman, 2008a, pp. 59–60)

Early leaders in the field defined the gifted as those children who rank in the top 1% in general intelligence, as indicated by significantly advanced performance on an individual intelligence scale (Hollingworth, 1931; Terman, 1925). This definition had the advantages of being simple, unambiguous, and pragmatic. It was based upon a conception of general intelligence as an interrelated set of mental abilities which provides the individual with greater or lesser power to deal with abstract concepts and symbols. This conception still undergirds research on intelligence (Gottfredson, 2005; Snyderman & Rothman, 1990).

It was not that intelligence tests were considered infallible—quite the contrary. They were simply a great deal more accurate in locating high-ability children than any other means available (Terman, 1925). As both Binet and Terman were aware, the major drawback of IQ tests was that they did not measure the full universe of abilities. In selecting his gifted subjects, Terman originally tried several other means of locating children with special talents in music, art, mechanical ingenuity, and inventiveness. He eventually abandoned this effort, since there were no valid measures of these abilities and "almost without exception, children who showed unquestionable talent also qualified for the study on the basis of general intelligence" (Zigler & Farber, 1985, p. 395). Despite its inherent limitations, the intelligence scale provides a more objective picture of a child's intellectual abilities than teacher judgment, parent recommendations, grades, achievement tests, and other measures.

Hollingworth (1932) wrote, "The only way to identify these gifted children with certainty is to apply reliable and valid intelligence tests. Nothing can take the place of such tests in making a census of the gifted" (p. 241).

We are currently in an anti-testing era. Few school psychologists are involved in the assessment of giftedness. Of the 286 respondents in a national survey of school psychologists, only 6.2% indicated that they conduct gifted evaluations more than once a month (Robertson et al., 2011). In previous eras, only qualified professionals (examiners) could determine if a child was gifted. In 1970, Public Law 91–230 stated that "gifted and talented children are those identified by professionally qualified persons...." Since that time, there has been a steady erosion of the role of psychological examiners in the identification of gifted children. In the Gifted and Talented Children's Education Act (1978), in P. L. 95–561, Sec. 902, the clause, "professionally qualified persons," was removed from the law. The government document, *National Excellence*, issued in 1993 by the Office of Educational Research and Improvement (OERI), was overtly against IQ testing and educators were warned against early identification of the gifted:

> These suggestions are not intended to imply that schools should label preschool and primary students as gifted and talented. They should not. Instead, preschools and primary schools should develop a curriculum for *all* that nurtures the strengths of children and encourages its staff to do the same. (OERI, 1993, p. 28)

The Individuals with Disabilities Education Improvement Act of 2004 (IDEA, 2004), rapidly being codified in state special education regulations, has circumscribed the assessment role of school psychologists even further. Formerly, students with specific learning disabilities were identified through comprehensive assessment of ability and achievement by qualified professionals. Now, under the new legislation, a child must be functioning *below grade level* before any assessment is possible. Many school districts have drastically reduced or eliminated individual assessment. Among the greatest casualties of the new legislation are the twice exceptional (McKenzie, 2010). These children have been rendered invisible under Response to Intervention (RTI) legislation (Reynolds & S. Shaywitz, 2009).

Without access to objective measures, the detection of giftedness is based upon performance in the classroom. Many gifted children underperform. It is difficult to become excited about learning when one has already mastered the skills. But the winds of change appear to be in the wings, as court cases contesting negligence toward learning-disabled children surface (e.g., Dixon, Eusebio, Turton, Wright, & Hale, 2011), and the Office of Civil Rights becomes involved (Ali, 2012; Shah, 2012). Doors appear to be reopening for students who have been denied comprehensive assessment.

The IQ controversy has raged for the last century. While IQ scores do not predict who will be famous, they do provide a pretty good estimate of the advanced reasoning abilities of children who need something more than is provided in the regular classroom. It is true that IQ tests miss some gifted children. But individual standardized measures find more of them than has ever been found by any other means—including children from low socioeconomic and ethnically diverse groups (Ehrlich, 1986; Kearney & LeBlanc, 1993; H. Robinson, 1981). IQ testing was the objective means by which children of immigrants were accepted to schools that formerly had quotas on students from different ethnic backgrounds (Snyderman & Rothman, 1990). And testing locates more gifted girls than other methods (Silverman & N. Miller, 2009). Females have never had equal opportunity to attain eminence, but they have always performed as well as or better than boys on IQ tests (Hollingworth, 1926; Peter & Stern, 1922; Silverman, 2009a; Silverman & Kearney, 1989). Ironically, gifted girls fared better before the testing industry tried to make testing gender-fair!

Talent development models and ability/IQ-based models serve very different populations. The nurture community casts a wide net (10–33%) in order to give all children with potential for success an opportunity to have their talents developed, whereas the nature community feels that a select group at the extreme of the curve has significantly different needs. Paradoxically, those who view gifted IQ scores as "elitist" do not realize that eminence as the measure of giftedness is far more elitist, since so few individuals will ever reach that elite rank of society. It is also adult-oriented, rather than child-friendly.

Some attempts have been made to marry the two views of giftedness. In 1950, the Educational Policies Commission constructed a definition geared to please both camps:

> ... the term "highly gifted" is used to designate those who are in the top 1 per cent of the total population with respect to intellectual capacity (that is, roughly, individuals with an IQ above 137). Similarly, the term "moderately gifted" will apply to individuals who fall within the top 10 per cent below the top 1 per cent (that is, between 120 and 137 IQ). (p. 43)

Apparently, the marriage didn't last. The two perspectives are still in divorce court.

WILL THE REALLY GIFTED PLEASE STAND UP?

There are so many competing definitions of giftedness that even those rare individuals who have achieved eminence within their lifetime do not believe they are "really gifted." When giftedness is defined as recognized achievement, the label must be bestowed upon the individual from the field judging the quality of the person's contributions. "He is gifted" is acceptable; "I am gifted" is not. "Success" is a popularity contest and the public is fickle. They may think you're the greatest today and not so great tomorrow. Are you only gifted when you are in the limelight? What about the artists who did not achieve eminence until after they died? Perhaps the most reliable determination of the influence of one's accomplishments in adult life is the number of biographies written about the person after death (Goertzel & Hansen, 2004; Piirto, 2009). But this posthumous view of giftedness is not useful for establishing which children need educational or psychological support. Moreover, the winner of the biography contest just might be Seabiscuit!

The most agreed-upon definition of giftedness appeared in the famed Marland Report. A page in the history of gifted education was turned in 1970 with the addition of "Provisions Related to Gifted and Talented Children" (Sec. 806) to the Elementary and Secondary Educational Amendments of 1969 (P. L. 91–230). This was the first time that the gifted were recognized in a federal law as a minority group with specific needs. P.L. 91–230 also mandated that the U. S. Commissioner of Education conduct a study to ascertain the need for gifted programs. The report submitted in 1971 and approved in 1972 was a landmark. After 2 years of study and public hearings, Commissioner Sidney Marland, Jr. (1971/1972) declared:

> Gifted and Talented children are, in fact, deprived and can suffer *psychological damage and permanent impairment of their abilities* to function well which is equal to or greater than the similar deprivation suffered by any other population with special needs served by the Office of Education. (p. VIII-3, italics added)

Over 90% of the respondents to Marland's poll indicated that psychological services and guidance counseling were important needs of the gifted. Yet, Marland found rampant hostility toward gifted students from psychologists, guidance counselors, teachers, and administrators.

Before the Marland Report was issued, school districts providing programs often defined gifted children as those who scored at the 98th or 99th percentile on individual intelligence scales. Considered too narrow to include children from low socioeconomic and culturally diverse backgrounds, this criterion also seemed to discriminate against those who are talented in the fine arts or who demonstrate creativity. The Marland Report broadened the definition to include students who scored at the 95th or 97th percentile on IQ tests or who demonstrated achievement or potential in one or more of six areas.

> Gifted and talented children are *those identified by professionally qualified persons* who, by virtue of outstanding abilities, are capable of high performance. These are children who require differential educational programs and/or services beyond those provided by the regular school program in order to realize their contribution to self and the society.
>
> Children capable of high performance include those with demonstrated achievement and/or potential ability in any of the following areas, singly or in combination:
>
> 1. general intellectual ability
> 2. specific academic aptitude
> 3. creative or productive thinking
> 4. leadership ability
> 5. visual and performing arts
> 6. psychomotor ability.
>
> It can be assumed that utilization of these criteria for identification of the gifted and talented will encompass a minimum of 3 to 5 percent of the school population.
>
> Evidence of gifted and talented abilities may be determined by a multiplicity of ways. These procedures should include *objective measures and professional evaluation measures which are essential components of identification.* (pp. ix–x, italics added)

Objective measures administered by professionally qualified persons were considered "essential components of identification." The Marland Report's definition of giftedness was widely accepted and became embedded in many state laws. It is the closest to consensus that has ever been achieved in gifted education. But agreement was not to last.

Six years later, in 1978, Joseph Renzulli challenged this prevailing definition, introducing the concept of gifted behavior. Gifted behavior occurs when there is an interaction among three basic clusters of human traits: above-average general and/or specific abilities, high levels of task commitment (motivation), and high levels of creativity. Applicable to as many as one-third of the school population, Renzulli's Enrichment Triad Model (1977) and Schoolwide Enrichment Model (Renzulli & Reis, 2003) could be implemented in the regular classroom or a pull-out program. Special, full-day classes for that many gifted students would not be economically feasible or ideologically appropriate. Renzulli and his colleagues suggested a "revolving door" model (Renzulli, Reis, & Smith, 1981), in which students are only gifted when they demonstrate gifted behavior. Renzulli's approach became extremely popular (Assouline, Foley Nicpon, & Huber, 2006), not only in the United States, but also abroad, because it is egalitarian; giftedness was no longer reserved for an exclusive group in the top 1%, 2%, 3%, or 5% of the populace.

This departure from the federal definition opened the door for other academics to define giftedness and intelligence in their own manner and make their mark. Howard Gardner's book, *Frames of Mind* (1983), launched a strong anti-IQ movement. Although he conceded that the IQ test does predict school success, "it foretells little of success in later life" (p. 3). A single score could not adequately represent intelligence. Gardner proposed that there were multiple intelligences and the world applauded. Originally, he included linguistic, musical, logical–mathematical, spatial, bodily–kinesthetic, interpersonal, and intrapersonal. New intelligences have been added, such as The Naturalist. Each intelligence is another avenue for giftedness to be displayed. Gardner's mission was successful. It is now common in the literature, on websites, and in education, to hear that there are multiple ways to be gifted, and that IQ scores are passé. Although not his intention, Gardner's theory of multiple intelligences has become a rationale for those educators who claim, "*All* our children are gifted."

A flurry of competing definitions fought for dominance in the 1980s. Abraham Tannenbaum (1983) defined giftedness as potential for becoming critically acclaimed performers or producers of ideas in adulthood. Francoys Gagné (1985), in Quebec, differentiated between giftedness and talent. Giftedness is the possession of natural abilities in at least one domain that places the child at the top 10% of his or her age peers. Talent is superior mastery in at least one field of human activity that places the child's achievement within the upper 10% of age peers who are active in that field. "*Talent development* corresponds to the progressive transformation of gifts into talents" (Gagné, 2012, p. 5). The growing international popularity of Gagné's Differentiated Model of Giftedness and Talent probably stems from the fact that he synthesizes both camps. While he believes that giftedness is natural ability, and he administers IQ tests, Gagné argues that giftedness must eventuate in distinction in a specific field.

In the same year, Robert Sternberg (1985) at Yale proposed yet another definition of giftedness. Sternberg's Triarchic Theory postulates five criteria that need to be met for a person to be judged gifted: (1) excellence relative to peers, (2) rarity of a high-level skill, (3) the area in which the person excels must lead to productivity or potential for productivity, (4) it is demonstrable through valid assessments, and (5) it is valuable—the excellence the person possesses must be valued by his or her society.

Put forth between 1978 and 1985, the definitions of Renzulli, Gardner, Tannenbaum, Gagné, and Sternberg are still prevalent. Until very recently, these were the five conceptions of giftedness recognized by the National Association for Gifted Children Britain (2007) and four of the five are the most well known by school psychologists in the United States. Over half of the participants in a recent national survey of school psychologists considered themselves moderately to considerably familiar with Gardner, nearly 28% with Sternberg, 25% with Renzulli, and approximately 11% with Gagné (Robertson et al.,

2011). Success or potential for fame is the true measure of gift-edness. Or is it?

Researchers who study gifted children instead of adult accomplishments take issue with the achievement-oriented definitions. They claim that the missing element is the gifted child.

> For some theorists and researchers, explaining giftedness means describing the conditions that produce gifted achievements. Trapped by the metaphor of "gifts," they believe that the most important aspect of being gifted is the ability to turn gifts into recognizable and valued accomplishments....
>
> The models and theories set to maximize giftedness regard gifted children much as farmers regard cows and pigs, with an eye to getting them to produce more. They do not describe how gift-edness works—how the gifted think, feel, and experience. (Grant & Piechowski, 1999, p. 8)

"How the gifted think, feel, and experience" is the heart of Annemarie Roeper's (1982) definition: "Giftedness is a greater awareness, a greater sensitivity, and a greater ability to understand and transform perceptions into intellectual and emotional experiences" (p. 21). Roeper was the first to infuse emotional sensitivity into a definition of giftedness. Credited with seeding the concept of "emotional giftedness" (Piechowski, 1991a), Roeper was influential to practitioners in the field. Other feminine voices were also heard in the 1980s. Joanne Whitmore (1980) defined intellectual giftedness as "exceptional potential for learning and a superior capacity to assimilate, manipulate, and utilize abstract concepts and fac-tual information" (p. 61). In her 1983 textbook, Barbara Clark portrayed giftedness as total and integrated brain functioning, including cognition, emotion, intuition, and physical sensing. Abstract reasoning or cognitive functioning is central to sev-eral definitions proposed by women in the field today (e.g., Gilman, 2008a; Lovecky, 2004; N. Robinson, 2005).

DO MEN AND WOMEN TEND TO VIEW GIFTEDNESS DIFFERENTLY?

In the fertile period of the 1980s, it seemed curious to me that the split in the conceptualization of giftedness mirrored the division between masculine and feminine roles in society (Silverman, 1986c). At the Gifted Development Center (GDC) and other assessment centers, worried mothers were much more likely to arrange to have their children assessed for giftedness than fathers. Mothers noted developmental differences in their children, and were concerned that the children would be misfits; fathers rarely believed the label, and feared that it connoted societal expectations that would rob their children of their childhood. "Mothers are more likely to take seriously their children's advanced development, while fathers, who more often think of giftedness as very unusual, may describe even very bright and talented children as 'not really gifted'" (N. Robinson & Olszewski-Kubilius, 1996, p. 428). Skeptical dads would say things like, "He's only five; what could he have **done** to be gifted?" or "He's no Einstein!" Mothers defined giftedness developmentally, whereas fathers thought it meant fame.

Echoes of these moms and dads appeared in the literature. Male writers, dating back to Sir Francis Galton (1869), often equated giftedness with eminence or the potential for eminence (e.g., Feldman, 1984; Gagné, 1985; Renzulli, 1978; Simonton, 2009; Sternberg, 1985; Witty, 1940). Female writers, beginning with Hollingworth (1926), usually defined giftedness in terms of abstract reasoning and developmental differences in childhood (e.g., Clark, 1983; Hildreth, 1966; Maker, 1986; Roedell, 1989; Roeper, 1982; Whitmore, 1980). Galton studied prominent men and Hollingworth was the champion of gifted girls and women.

Hollingworth challenged Galton's assumption that giftedness leads to eminence. He had only studied men, not the sisters of those men. Most of these illustrious men came from wealthy families. Hollingworth (1926) contended that women, the poor, and those of lower social standing had no opportunity to gain eminence; therefore, it is an unfair criterion upon which to judge giftedness. She embraced IQ testing as an objective method of locating gifted girls. "Mental tests proved the existence of gifted girls" (Hollingworth, 1926, p. 347). Nearly a century ago, Peter and Stern (1922) in Germany, and Hollingworth in the United States, found that not only did girls equal their male counterparts on IQ tests, they often surpassed the boys and attained the highest scores—findings replicated today (Silverman & Kearney, 1989; Silverman & N. Miller, 2009).

The call to abandon IQ tests came from eminent men. While Gardner's concept of multiple intelligences has been touted as egalitarian, little notice has been taken that the exemplars of Gardner's seven intelligences were all male (with the exception of dancers). Convinced that IQ tests are biased, educators insist on culturally responsive definitions of giftedness that increase access for diverse ethnic and socioeconomic groups, but females rarely enter the discussion. The relationship between viewpoint and gender has become blurred in recent years. Women, even those who studied gender differences (e.g., Dweck, 1986), have become proponents of the eminence paradigm (Dweck, 2011).

Women do not fare well in the race for eminence, and neither do minorities. Of the 549 Nobel prizes awarded between 1901 and 2011, 44 were awarded to women—8% of the total—with two of them won by Marie Sklodowska Curie (Silverman, 2012b). Only 2% were in the sciences (Charyton, Elliott, Aahman, Woodard, & DeDios, 2011). There is no listing of Nobel Laureates by ethnicity.

> Few women relative to men have managed to achieve positions of eminence.... Men received almost 98% of the Nobel prizes in science areas and 99% of the prestigious awards in mathematics during the 20th century....
>
> Women of color, often the targets of double discrimination, have even less representation in the ranks of the eminent than do their ethnic majority counterparts....

Only 2% of the directors of the top 100 companies in Britain are women.

....Females and males are socialized differently with respect to achievement,...males are often automatically accorded more status than females, and...women and men frequently differ in their access to the resources.... (Lips, 2005, pp. 461–463)

It is puzzling that in recent years the elusive golden ring of eminence has assumed such prominence in gifted education. Very few gifted individuals become eminent. Most who covet lasting fame are doomed to fail. Nonetheless, over 2 million (2–3%) of the 76 million students in the United States alone are significantly different from their peers and require special provisions and psychological services.

There is another type of success in adult life that has received little attention in the achievement paradigm: the capacity to care about others. Sensitivity, compassion, empathy, responsibility, and ethical concern for the welfare of others are important values in our society (Roeper & Silverman, 2009). Pramathevan and Garces-Bascal (2012) recommend that "youths who have gifts such as profound empathy and sensitivity to human concerns must also be recognized and nurtured" (p. 153). People tend to think of success in terms of fame, creative contribution, and monetary gain. All of these evidences of success can occur within a framework of self-aggrandizement and the lack of concern for others, or they can occur within the context of ethical responsiveness and compassion.

In the "masculine" perspective, the true test of ability is the quantity, quality, and influence of one's accomplishments in adult life; the "feminine" view is primarily concerned with the impact of developmental differences on the child's immediate needs (Silverman, 1986c; Silverman & N. Miller, 2009). The feminine perspective of giftedness is child-centered (Grant & Piechowski, 1999) and holistic. It involves emotions as well as intellect. As children move into adult roles, they become focused on small fragments of intellectual ability. The fluid abilities of childhood are channeled by experience into specific domains, and we see the great diversity of talents in adult life as a function of experience. It is difficult to grasp a unitary conception of intelligence when studying adults, since adults show thousands of different abilities. Before experience has written heavily on the human being, the cohesive nature of intelligence—the interplay of creativity, intellect, and emotion—is much more apparent.

A DEVELOPMENTAL DEFINITION OF GIFTEDNESS

Developmental advancement is comparable to developmental delay. We appreciate the plight of a 15-year-old with the mentality of a 9-year-old. We understand the need for psychological assessment to identify such a child, as well as the family's need for guidance. No one questions the essential role of psychologists in dealing with the other end of the spectrum. Correspondingly, a child of 9 with the mental ability of a 15-year-old is faced with extraordinary challenges that begin prior to school and continue into adulthood.

As developmental advancement appeared to me to be the essence of giftedness, I proposed the following straightforward definition for educators: "The gifted child is defined as one who is developmentally advanced in one or more areas, and is therefore in need of differentiated programming in order to develop at his or her own accelerated pace" (Silverman, 1986c, p. 58). This perspective is strongly aligned with Hollingworth's philosophy.

A developmental definition of giftedness has the advantage of being consistent with accepted definitions of other areas of exceptionality. Additional advantages are that it is nonsexist, appropriate for children from different cultural and

41

socioeconomic backgrounds, and applicable to gifted children with learning disabilities. The definition applies to underachieving gifted children and other bright children who may be disadvantaged in the educational system.

In early childhood, giftedness can be observed as progression through certain developmental milestones at a more rapid rate than other children. Intelligence tests capture the degree of developmental advancement. The child who performs mental operations at the same level as a child several years older is unquestionably developmentally advanced: Mental age surpasses chronological age by a large margin. IQ scores tend to be stable. Children who score in the gifted range on IQ tests in early childhood—as early as 18 months of age—demonstrate advanced achievement and mastery of skills in later years (A. W. Gottfried, A. E. Gottfried, Bathurst, & Guerin, 1994).

The terms "developmental advancement" or "accelerated development" are not meant to imply that giftedness is defined solely in terms of learning rate. Some researchers have defined precocity as the ability to learn more rapidly than one's peers, such as twice the average rate (e.g., H. Robinson, 1981). Conceptualizing giftedness in terms of learning rate presumes that everyone is on the same learning path, and that the gifted child just gets "there" faster. Developmentally, in addition to learning rate, gifted children are qualitatively different in characteristics, emotions, and experiences.

The emphasis on performance inherent in the achievement-based definitions equates competence with performance, and in so doing excludes the underachieving gifted child. From a behavioral perspective, there is no appreciable difference between these two ideas. However, in developmental theory, the distinction between competence and performance is critical. Competence encompasses the whole range of a person's abilities, whereas performance is a small slice of those abilities—the only part perceived by onlookers. Performance is only a partial reflection of competence; it is as much a function of opportunity as ability. Highly capable children do not always perform at their level of competence. Such is the case with twice exceptional learners and gifted underachievers. Often they cannot be found without the aid of an intelligence test or some other measure of ability. The discrepancy between ability and achievement, which may not distinguish children in the average range, is fundamental to the recognition of twice exceptional learners.

Using a developmental lens, the social usefulness of the child's talents does not merit consideration. Childhood is important in its own right. Significant differences in ability signal unique educational and psychological needs. Disabled children are defined in terms of their needs in childhood, not their potential value in adulthood, or the lack of such potential. Moreover, funding for children with special needs appears to be inversely related to their potential to contribute to society.

Developmental differences are the province of psychology. Psychologists were the first to study individual differences. They will always have a role in identifying children who develop atypically and designing ways to meet their social, emotional, and educational needs.

GIFTEDNESS AS ASYNCHRONOUS DEVELOPMENT

A newer conception of giftedness emerged in 1991 in response to the increasing national focus on products and performance. The construct of giftedness as asynchronous development (Columbus Group, 1991, 2013) is phenomenological, rather than utilitarian. Focused on the psychological milieu of the individual, it highlights the complexity of the individual's thought process; the intensity of sensation, emotion, and imagination; and the extraordinary awareness that results from this fusion. Asynchrony also involves uneven development, which has gained the lion's share of attention, as well as feeling out-of-step with societal norms. All of these factors contribute to the vulnerability of the gifted.

> Giftedness is **asynchronous development** in which advanced cognitive abilities and heightened intensity combine to create inner experiences and awareness that are qualitatively different from the norm. This asynchrony increases with higher intellectual capacity. The uniqueness of the gifted renders them particularly vulnerable and requires modifications in parenting, teaching and counseling in order for them to develop optimally. (Columbus Group, 1991)

This is the first definition to specify the importance of counseling in the development of giftedness. It is deeply rooted in the field of psychology, having been influenced by the work of Dabrowski (1964), Vygotsky (1962), Binet (1909/1975), Hollingworth (1931), Terrassier (1985), and Roeper (1982). Child-centered, it illuminates the vulnerability of the gifted child and the need for accommodations. Hollingworth (1931) noted the challenges faced by gifted children due to the developmental differences between their intelligence, emotions, and chronological age.

> To have the intelligence of an adult and the emotions of a child combined in a childish body is to encounter certain difficulties. It follows that (after babyhood) the younger the child, the greater the difficulties, and that adjustment becomes easier with every additional year of age. The years between four and nine are probably the most likely to be beset with the problems mentioned. (Hollingworth, 1931, p. 13)

The greater the degree to which cognitive development outstrips physical development, the more "out-of-sync" the child feels internally, in social relations, and in relation to the school curriculum. The impact of asynchrony increases dramatically as the child moves up the IQ continuum from moderately to highly to exceptionally to profoundly gifted. "The very nature and direction of the behavioral qualities suggest consideration of the highly gifted as a vulnerable group" (S. Shaywitz, Holahan, Freudenheim, Fletcher, Makuch, & B. Shaywitz, 2001, p. 20). Wasserman (2007) asserts that "asynchrony is so prevalent among the higher levels of giftedness that within this population it can be considered 'normal'" (p. 61). He has found that extremely gifted children demonstrate unusually wide scatter of abilities in cognitive functioning, emotional development, functional living skills, physical maturation, and social competencies.

Asynchronous development is meaningful to the gifted themselves. After being introduced to the concept during comprehensive testing, a highly gifted teen wrote:

> By the end of the final subtest, I felt as though my attention had been sifted like flour through a series of increasingly fine screens and that every subsequent weave had required more attention, had demanded more powerfully that I be aware of the mesh.
>
> .... The phrase that most caught my attention, however, was offered as an explanation: *Asynchronous Development. I was different in more than attitude; I was singular in awareness.*
>
> Those two words, their pairing making them almost incantatory, struck to the core of my worry, slightly soothed years of self-doubt and guilt, started to abolish the idea that my always-apparent if somewhat unsuccessful intellect was nothing more than pedantry paired with laziness and angst. Relief flooded my head like liquor and, on my way out the door, I grinned into the sun with the expression of a joyful madman, reveling in a sense of well-being I hadn't felt for years. (Gilman, 2008a, p. 90, italics added)

In the two decades since the Columbus Group's definition was published, the term *asynchrony* has found its way into common vernacular in gifted education and psychology. Over 10% of the school psychologists polled in a national survey considered themselves moderately to considerably familiar with the concept (Robertson et al., 2011). This definition has been recognized in the *Encyclopaedia Brittanica* (Asynchrony, 2011), *The*

Encyclopedia of Giftedness, Creativity and Talent (Kerr, 2010), and can be found on the website of the National Association for Gifted Children (*What is giftedness?* 2011b). Counselors and psychologists of the gifted frequently discuss its utility (e.g., Alsop, 2003; Barber & Mueller, 2011; Beljan, 2005; Gilman, 2008a; Jackson & Moyle, 2009; Lovecky, 2004, 2009; Neihart, Reis, N. Robinson, & Moon, 2002; N. Robinson, 2008a; N. Robinson & Olszewski-Kubilius, 1996; Sheely, 2007; Wasserman, 2007; Webb, Gore, Amend, & DeVries, 2007). This psychological perspective can serve as a basis for understanding the unique makeup and needs of the gifted population. It also resonates strongly with parents of twice exceptional children.

> For me, the hardest thing about parenting a twice-exceptional child is the asynchrony. I never know exactly which age I am dealing with at any given moment. Imagine being a young child, feeling intense despair over the state of the world, and not understanding why other kids...don't feel the same. Or having the reading comprehension of a much older child, but lacking the maturity to deal with the topics at that level. Or...knowledge logjams as you try to write about it, because your writing skills lag far behind your racing intellect. In the span of a few minutes, I could have a child who looks his age, discusses cosmology and theoretical physics in great detail, whips out a few bars of his current favorite rock song, feels great existential despair over the unanswered questions of life, then behaves with the emotional maturity of a child half his age. It's parental whiplash. I've toyed with the idea of returning the favor. Look like a mom, talk like an infant, dress like a teen, and act like a toddler. (J. Merrill, 2012, p. 63)

HOW DEFINITIONS DELINEATE PSYCHOLOGICAL SERVICES

What functions do psychologists serve in talent development? When the emphasis shifts from inspiration to perspiration, mental health workers resemble coaches. In her study, Wood (2010) found that school counselors focus on leadership, sustaining motivation and issues related to academic performance. Doesn't this sound a lot like coaching? NASA (2012) defines coaching as "a developmental strategy that enables people to meet their goals for improved performance, growth or career enhancement" (p 1) Another business model applied to education, the purpose of coaching is to transport people from where they are now to where they want to be in the future. This endeavor is becoming quite popular, providing a sort of accountability for those who have difficulty setting and meeting goals. Coaches do not require the extensive education and certification of mental health practitioners.

Potentially, school counselors could foster talent in other ways. They could assure that children from diverse backgrounds gain equal access to talent development opportunities. They could assist with social skill development to improve a student's emotional intelligence (Goleman, 1995), since that is essential to success. And they could serve as academic advisors, guiding talented students in course selection, college selection, career development, and application for scholarships (Silverman, 2012a).

When giftedness is defined as asynchronous development, the spotlight shifts from exterior to interior—to the complex inner world of the gifted—their overexcitabilities, their feeling out-of-sync within themselves as well as with others, their acute awareness, and their need for meaning. The focus is existential rather than behavioral. Psychologists, counselors, and therapists accompany the gifted on their winding journey to understanding who they are and their place in the universe.

School counselors, as well as school psychologists, receive no more than superficial exposure to the needs of the gifted in their training programs (Assouline et al., 2006; Wood, Portman, Cigrand, & Colangelo, 2010). Wood (2010) conducted a study of 153 gifted adolescents to investigate the degree to which best practices in counseling the gifted were being implemented. From the responses of the students surveyed, she concluded that few of these best practices were being implemented in schools. Half of the participants indicated that they felt misunderstood by school counselors and that their concerns were dismissed. The area least understood by counselors was "asynchrony" (p. 52).

> Of note were topics cited by participants as more frequently experienced by them in counseling, including the participant's ability to produce high levels of work, their contribution to society, expectations they had of themselves, and expectations others had of them. (Wood, 2010, p. 53)

Wood's study suggests that school counselors see their major role as increasing school performance, rather than as promoting emotional health of the gifted.

When IQ tests are perceived as valuable, psychologists are integral to the process of identification. Psychological examiners offer objective methods of documenting the degree of advancement of young children. Standardized intelligence tests measure abstract reasoning rather than the domain-specific talent that emerges with maturity and practice. A 5-year-old who reasons like a 9-year-old is considered profoundly gifted, and is likely to have difficulty fitting into a typical 5-year-old peer group. This documentation provides a solid basis for early intervention to allow the child to develop friendships and learn at his or her own pace.

Although the study of giftedness emerged from the field of psychology, over the last 50 years, it drifted away and became embedded in education. Gifted education became the province of curriculum and instruction, which has offered the most graduate training programs related to giftedness. This habitat led to decades of searching for a truly differentiated curriculum for gifted students. Excellent curricular models have been designed, but the longed-for curricular answer was never found (Ronvik, 1993). The question is perennially raised, "Isn't this good for all children?" If we look at most of the fare in one-hour-per-week gifted programs, the answer, unfortunately, is yes. This sad state of affairs has led many educators to conclude that gifted children do not have unique needs. The differences are not to be found within the curriculum, but within the gifted individual. When we recognize the psychological differences of the gifted, we understand their need for differentiated education, counseling, and parenting.

Talent development is educational, whereas giftedness is psychological. When we look for talents instead of giftedness, the lens is focused on what individuals can *do* rather than on who they *are* in their totality. This perspective diminishes our capacity to grasp their dynamic inner experience. Early psychologists (e.g., Cattell, Hollingworth) embraced the notion that one's intelligence determines one's capabilities, while the environment influences what one does with those abilities: one's achievement. The same argument can be made about the distinction between ability and effort. Recent research with 302 gifted adults in Sweden suggests that this distinction fits the lived experience of many gifted adults. "Most participants encompassed an entity self-theory of intelligence, while also recognizing that it takes effort to develop one's ability" (Stalnacke & Smedler, 2011, p. 900).

As this book is written for those in the helping professions, it is designed from the ability rather than the achievement perspective. Giftedness in children and adults needs to be identified by licensed or certified examiners. Only psychological assessment can ascertain the degree of difference, which is essential information to the individuals' mental health and well-being. Assessment is also imperative to examine discrepancies between strengths and weaknesses in order to uncover masked learning disabilities. The gifted need mental health professionals to serve as their advocates, as well as to teach them self-advocacy (Neumann, 2009). They cope with a set of issues that is often misunderstood and mislabeled (Eide & Eide, 2006; Webb et al., 2007). They need therapists and counselors who understand their inner worlds and the role that giftedness plays in their identity development (Mahoney, 1998). Their differences need to be taken seriously.

The Crusade to Vanquish Prejudice Against the Gifted

The public is wonderfully tolerant. It forgives everything except genius.
Oscar Wilde

HISTORICAL PERSPECTIVES

The infinite variability of human beings is so remarkable that one would assume it had been one of the earliest topics of scientific interest. Yet, the exploration of individual differences began less than 150 years ago, in the latter part of the 19th century. This does not mean that there were no gifted children until then, or that no one acknowledged their existence. On the contrary, the gifted have always been with us; it's just science that entered late in the game. If members of the human race hadn't been smart enough to discover how to create fire or weapons, we probably would still be living in caves.

Nature's Ideal or Nature's Mistake?

Ancient Chinese, Turkish, Roman, and Greek civilizations attempted to locate the brightest members of their societies and groom them for leadership. Dubois (1970) attributes the high degree of stability attained by the Chinese Empire to their emphasis on classical scholarship in the selection of public officials. Candidates aspiring for government offices were required to take proficiency examinations in "music, art, horsemanship, writing, arithmetic, and the rites and ceremonies of public and private life" (Dubois, 1970, p. 3). The Chinese Government sought scholars to serve as political leaders for 2,000 years.

In *The Republic*, Plato (n.d./1944) advocated seeking at an early age the most able children from all levels of society, rich and poor, to determine which had the right kind of "metal" to become leaders. He recommended testing children to see which ones could detect deceit, recognize superstition, and profit from trial-and-error learning. The "golden" ones who passed the tests were to receive specially tailored educational experiences in science, philosophy, and metaphysics (Sumption & Luecking, 1960). Through these means, Plato sought to develop "philosopher kings" who could rule with wisdom. Plato set the stage for the identification and grooming of future leaders. Around 800 AD, Emperor Charlemagne is said to have urged the state to provide free education to able children of common birth (Hildreth, 1966). The grandest experiment occurred in the 16th century: Suleiman the Magnificent established a palace school for the education and upbringing of gifted youth. He regularly sent talent scouts to the conquered territories throughout the Turkish Empire in search of the strongest, most intelligent, and fairest youth, without regard to social class. Within one generation, the Ottoman Empire developed into a great power in art, science, culture, and war (Hildreth, 1966; Sumption & Luecking, 1960).

Some of the earliest accounts of the gifted appear in The Bible, including chronicles of Joseph, Daniel, and Jesus. Society's love–hate relationship with the gifted dates back at least to Biblical times. Think of the story of Joseph and The Coat of Many Colors. Joseph was the gifted son in Jacob's family—a quick learner in every respect. His stepbrothers resented him for being their father's favorite and plotted to kill him, but, instead, they sold him into slavery. Joseph's ability to interpret dreams and foretell the future came to the attention of the Pharaoh, who had a dream that troubled him. Joseph predicted that seven fat years would be followed by seven lean years, and warned the Pharaoh to set aside provisions for the famine to come. Joseph's prediction came to pass and he was able to save his family from starvation. Like Joseph, the gifted have been resented and revered—often by the same individuals.

Not surprisingly, the gifted often were thought to have supernatural powers. Although the origin of the term *gifted* has been obscured, surely it must relate to the belief that some individuals are endowed with gifts from the gods (e.g., the gift of prophecy). Even in modern times, giftedness in reference books is frequently defined as an "endowment" (e.g., American Heritage Dictionary, 2000; Kipfer, 2010).

Harking back to Plato, Thomas Jefferson proposed a bill early in the 1800s to identify and educate gifted students at the public expense. Jefferson asserted that giftedness would perish if not recognized and cultivated, and that the talented poor were the most vulnerable (Hildreth, 1966). In the 18th and 19th centuries, interest in child prodigies flourished in Europe, but these children were perceived as freaks of nature—a different species (Hirsch, 1931). This viewpoint was sustained by the Belgian statistician, Adolph Quetelet. In the 19th century, Quetelet set forth his "doctrine of l'homme moyen," declaring that the average man is nature's ideal and that deviations toward the good as well as toward the bad are nature's mistakes

(Boring, 1950). Exceptional talent was ascribed to unnatural forces, and children with special abilities came to be viewed as abnormal. A source of shame to their families, some were even hidden from view.

Until recently, this grim picture was thought to be universal. It may actually be the underbelly of a fascination with the gifted that grew throughout the 19th century. Kearney (2009) conducted a search through Google Books and unearthed 19th century writings in education, medicine, religion, and public policy on "gifted," "highly gifted," and "precocious" children, as well as gifted girls, dating back to 1825.

Still, the vast majority of the population assumed that everyone, with rare exceptions, was endowed with equal intelligence. To claim that some had more of it and some had less was sheer heresy, and that battle continues to rage. Who made this outrageous proclamation? Sir Francis Galton. Most people think of Lewis Terman as the "father" of gifted education and psychology, but Baska (2009, p. 477) insists that this "ancestral laurel" rightfully belongs to Galton, whose work has been largely disregarded. Our story begins with this intellectual giant.

Sir Francis Galton (1822–1911)

The psychology of individual differences is one of many legacies of Galton, along with the nature/nurture controversy, the science of biometrics, inferential statistics (correlation, significant difference, analysis of variance, null hypothesis, regression toward the mean, etc.), mental measurements, the first mental test, the first psychological questionnaire, the word association test, fingerprinting, the discovery of synesthesia, the study of visual imagery, the first weather maps, instruments to chart weather patterns, the first description of the anticyclone as a weather system, a teletype printer, a stopwatch, a photometer, composite portraiture, the "Galton whistle" to measure the highest audible pitch, and much more. Galton was a genius in every sense of the term: intellectually curious, ingenious, inventive, inspired, versatile, prodigiously productive, and precocious (Boring, 1950). His unusual abilities were noted early in life. In a search through Galton's archives in London, in 2008, Ariel Baska (2009) found the letter Francis Galton wrote to his older sister (and tutor) before his fifth birthday:

My dear Adele,
I am four years old and I can read any English book. I can say all the Latin Substantives and Adjectives and active verbs besides 52 lines of Latin poetry. I can cast up any sum in addition and can multiply by 2, 3, 4, 5, 6, 7, 8, 9, 10, 11. I can also say the pence table, I read French a little and I know the clock. (p. 471)

By the age of 6, the siblings had mastered Homer's *Iliad* and *Odyssey*, and begun composing in Latin and Greek. Based on Galton's precocity, Terman (1917) estimated his IQ at close to 200, in the realm of John Stuart Mill, Goethe, and Leibnitz (Boring, 1950). Like many precocious children, Galton liked to count things, a habit he continued throughout his life. He counted anything and everything imaginable—from yawns and fidgets of an audience at a concert as a measure of boredom to the 20,000 brush strokes used by the artist who painted his portrait (D. Schultz, 1981). He believed everything could be measured—even intelligence.

The dictum, "Early ripe, early rot," should have been put to rest with Galton. He continued to demonstrate remarkable creativity and productivity throughout his lifespan. His most famous book was written when he was 47, one that rivaled it when he was 63, and he continued to produce notable works until he was 87. Galton's *Hereditary Genius* (1869) was the first quantitative analysis of human intelligence. Galton arduously differed with the prevailing beliefs in his era:

I have no patience with the hypothesis...that babies are born pretty much alike, and that the sole agencies in creating differences...are steady application and moral effort. It is in the most unqualified manner that I object to the pretensions of natural equality. (p. 12)

To support his contention that intelligence is wholly inherited, Galton traced the genealogy of many prominent British men, noting the high incidence of eminence in their families. He devised the use of percentiles for ranking individuals within a population and demonstrated that there was enormous variability in the population. The Gaussian curve served as Galton's model for the distribution of intelligence, which has become the bedrock of psychological testing.

Galton, himself, came from a prestigious family. His grandfather was Erasmus Darwin, and Charles Darwin was his half-cousin. Cousin Darwin exerted quite an impact on Galton's thinking. Baska (2009) found a letter in Galton's archives that he wrote after reading *Origin of the Species* (Darwin, 1859): "I devoured its contents and assimilated them as fast as they were devoured—a fact to which I am inclined to ascribe to a natural bent of mind that both its illustrious author and myself have inherited from our common grandfather Erasmus Darwin" (Baska, 2009, p. 472). Darwin was also impressed by Galton's work. After he read *Hereditary Genius*, Darwin announced that Galton had "made a convert of an opponent" since Darwin "always maintained that, excepting for fools, men did not differ much in intellect, only in zeal and hard work" (Pearson, 1914, Vol. 1, p. 7).

In 1883, Galton wrote *Inquiries into Human Faculty and its Development*, which is regarded as the inception of mental testing (Boring, 1950). In this book, Galton delved into the feasibility of measuring intelligence with various discrimination tasks (e.g., reaction times and the ability to discern the sequence of a set of weights). A year later, he created the first mental tests, which were measures of sensory capacity. Cleverly, Galton funded his endeavors by creating the first mental test laboratory in conjunction with the International Health Exhibition in London. He charged his examinees 3 pence for measuring sensory capacities, such as auditory and visual acuity, breathing capacity, strength of grip, reaction time, memory of form, and color sense (DuBois, 1970). In the 6 years of operating his Anthropometric Laboratory, Galton collected data on 9,337 men, women, and children, ranging in age from 5 to 80.

Evaluating Galton's findings, Boring (1950) commented, "No important generalizations as regards to human individual differences appeared, however, unless we should note Galton's erroneous conclusion that women tend in all their capacities to be inferior to men" (p. 487). Women were omitted from consideration in Galton's studies of eminence. There was also a conspicuous lack of regard for women in Galton's writing. Even his sister, Adele, who taught herself Greek and Latin so that she could tutor her younger brother, and his mother, who was his close confidant, were not credited for either their intelligence or personal contributions to his life (Baska, 2009). "Women furnish few persons of great eminence, yet sisters of great men are of exactly the same ancestry as their brothers" (Hollingworth, 1926, p. 13).

Not only did Galton fail to consider gender, he made no mention of socioeconomic status. Most of the eminent families he studied were independently wealthy, but Galton insisted that social advantages could not create eminence; otherwise, adopted children would attain distinction as easily as natural children. Neither did the vicissitudes of life inequitably affect achievement: the cream naturally rises to the top, regardless of misfortune. Hollingworth (1926) passionately believed that eminence is a function of opportunity rather than heredity.

> An overwhelming majority of illustrious persons have had fathers who were far above the average in social-economic conditions—nobles, professional men, or men successfully engaged in commerce. Very few children of manual workers become eminent in high degree.... Very few women can be included among those who in the world's history have achieved first rank for mental work.

One possible interpretation is that education and opportunity are the prime determinants of achievement, since nearly all of the great men have been born in comfortable homes, of parents in superior circumstances. If opportunity were indeed the prime determinant of eminence, then we should expect those who belong to socially inferior categories to be virtually excluded from it. This is just what we do find, since the uncultured, the poor, servants, and women are very seldom found to have achieved eminence. (p. 11)

Galton's gender bias did not cause him to lose favor in psychology. However, his belief in the natural superiority of Caucasians was not acceptable to modern science. In *Hereditary Genius*, Galton rank-ordered races as well as men. He concluded that ancient Athenians were genetically superior to Europeans, and that Anglo-Saxons were superior to those of African heritage. Galton zealously applied Erasmus and Charles Darwin's theory of evolution to the improvement of the human race. He founded the field of eugenics and endowed the Galton Professorship of Eugenics at University College, London. The word "heredity" still invokes a chilling knee-jerk connection to eugenics.

Both sides of the nature/nurture tempest in gifted psychology originate with Galton. The nature faction adopted his variability of intelligence, inherent qualities that differentiate the gifted, heritability of characteristics, and the use of intelligence tests to measure significant differences. The nurture faction raised Galton's banner of eminence as the basis for designating a person as gifted.

Giftedness is the manifestation of performance or production that is clearly at the upper end of the distribution in a talent domain even relative to that of other high-functioning individuals in that domain. . . . eminence is the basis on which this label is granted. (Subotnik, Olszewski-Kubilius, & Worrell, 2011, p. 7)

Both factions reject the notion that giftedness is totally hereditary. They both hold that opportunity in society is essential for abilities to come to fruition, and that equal opportunities need to be created for culturally diverse groups, individuals of lower socioeconomic status, and females. If intelligence were entirely a matter of heredity, there would be no possibility of improvement in one's status; history, of course, has proven otherwise. Although Galton's views have not withstood the test of time and his early measures of mental ability proved to be completely invalid (Carroll, 1993), a new field was born.

Before Galton, individual differences were perceived only as nuisances to experimentation—to be eliminated rather than studied in their own right. Scientist/philosophers, the early forerunners of psychologists, attempted to establish general principles of how the mind operates, and differences among their subjects inhibited their progress. It was Galton who had the insight to see that individual differences provided a fascinating area of investigation. As the study of giftedness was the offspring of the study of individual differences, we are much in debt to Galton.

Alfred Binet (1857–1911)

Galton introduced the concept of mental testing, but it took Alfred Binet to perfect the idea. Binet was not aligned with Galton philosophically. To Binet, intelligence was not a fixed entity; it was a continuously evolving process that could be influenced by the environment and improved through appropriate education (Binet, 1909/1975). He viewed intelligence as a rich, complex, multifaceted gestalt—a myriad of dynamically interrelated abilities.

In 1887, Binet began experimenting with mental tests using Parisian schoolchildren. In 1896, with his collaborator, Victor Henri, Binet published a crucial paper on mental testing, criticizing the use of tests of limited, specialized abilities for the measurement of complex mental faculties. Binet and Henri (1896) urged that tests of "higher mental processes" be constructed, such as various types of memory, imagery, imagination, comprehension, aesthetic appreciation, and motor skill. With the assistance of Theophile Simon, a physician, Binet developed the first intelligence scale for children in 1905. The Binet–Simon scale was a composite of 30 of the tests he and his collaborators had developed in the previous 10 years. This was the first time items in a scale were combined to yield a composite measure of a complex function (DuBois, 1970). Binet and Simon revised the scale in 1908, utilizing a new invention: mental age. Mental age was defined as the number of test items passed by an average child of a particular age. They developed age norms based on a sample of 200 children.

Binet had a pure fascination with the developing mind. He observed how thought processes changed at different stages of children's development. A developmental framework proved to be an effective means of measuring accelerated development in gifted children. A strong advocate for the gifted, Binet (1909/1975) wrote that "classes for the gifted should be created" since their contribution "determines the progress of humanity. ...A child of superior intelligence is an asset not to be wasted" (pp. 85–86). Binet was particularly interested in children with extraordinary abilities in calculation, mathematics, chess, and writing (Hildreth, 1966).

Just before his untimely death in 1911, Binet extended the Binet–Simon scale through adulthood, which provided the first opportunity to measure the degree of difference between the development of gifted and average children. Binet (1911) wrote about the potential use of the extended scale to recruit gifted children for special classes. In 2011, the Texas Association for Gifted and Talented commemorated the 100th anniversary of the measurement of giftedness with a special conference for psychologists.

Lewis Madison Terman (1877–1956)

Lewis Terman had profound respect for Binet; he dedicated his book, *The Measurement of Intelligence* (1916a), "to the memory of

Alfred Binet, patient researcher, creative thinker, unpretentious scholar, inspiring and fruitful devotee of inductive and dynamic psychology." It appears that Binet and Terman never actually met, but Binet approved of Terman's adaptation of his intelligence scale and sold Terman the rights to create an American version "for a token of one dollar" (Wasserman, 2003, p. 425). Terman and his colleagues at Stanford University began working on the *Stanford-Binet Intelligence Scale* in 1910 and finished in 1916. In addition, they devised nine other tests, including the *Army Alpha Test, Army Beta Test, National Intelligence Tests, Terman Group Test of Mental Ability, Stanford Achievement Test,* and *The Concept Mastery Test.*

Terman is often considered the "father" of gifted education (Gowan, 1977) because he devoted his career to understanding the gifted and measuring their abilities. This passion surfaced in graduate school at Clark University. He studied with the eminent psychologist, G. Stanley Hall, who did not support his interests. Hall was vehemently opposed to both mental testing and the study of giftedness (Seagoe, 1975). In spite of Hall's disapproval, Terman chose as his dissertation topic, *Genius and stupidity: A study of some of the intellectual processes of seven "bright" and seven "stupid" boys.* Working completely on his own, he devised 40 tests of inventiveness and creative imagination, logical processes, mathematical ability, mastery of language, insight into the interpretation of fables, ease of learning to play chess, memory, and motor ability. The "bright" students were superior on all mental tasks, and inferior on the motor items (Terman, 1906). Over 100 years later, items measuring eye–hand coordination still do not discriminate well between gifted and average children (Silverman, 2009a). Terman's graduate project initiated his lifelong career in measuring intelligence and differentiating the abilities of "bright" children.

In 1921, Terman received a sizable grant from The Commonwealth Fund to conduct an extensive study of the gifted. One component of the research was the investigation of the childhood and development of 300 eminent individuals. This part was completed by Catherine Cox (1926) for her doctoral dissertation, and became the second volume of the *Genetic Studies of Genius* (Terman et al., 1925–1959). The second part was the celebrated study of 1,528 individuals—the first longitudinal study and longest ever conducted. Five volumes devoted to the findings were published during Terman's lifetime. The study will continue until the death of every "Termite" selected. This database has been enormously valuable and is now providing information about the elderly.

Through this investigation, Terman sought to dispel the prevailing myths about the gifted. He stated in the Preface of the first volume of the *Genetic Studies of Genius* that his research was inaugurated to combat widespread "superstitions" regarding the gifted—that they are "the product of supernatural causes, and moved by forces which are not to be explained by the natural laws of human behavior; and ... that intellectual precocity is pathological" (Terman, 1925, p. vii). In later volumes, Terman took on another cause: the notion that gifted children could be created through programs of early training. Terman and Oden (1959) found no substantiation for the view that intensive early training can produce giftedness. They considered attempts to create prodigies through force-fed instruction of young children almost criminal. Instead, they recommended a more responsive approach, following the child's lead.

Terman offered considerable advice to parents and teachers of the gifted. He advocated early identification of gifted children, before the second or third grade, and systematic differentiated instruction throughout their schooling. His studies indicated that gifted children tend to learn inductively rather than deductively; they are more self-directed and independent; they respond best to approaches that require logic and reason; they need a maximum of new ideas and a minimum of drill and review; and they need emphasis on concepts and principles rather than concrete facts. For their social development, Terman contended that gifted children need association with others of similar ability and with older children and adults. A strong advocate of acceleration, Terman suggested that a gifted child who is socially well adjusted could skip up to 3 years before completing high school and another 2 years before completing a doctorate. He recommended college entrance by 16 or 17.

The *Stanford-Binet Intelligence Scale* (Terman, 1916b) may have been Terman's greatest legacy. For 50 years, it was the gold standard in assessment until the 1960s, when the Wechsler scales gained prominence (Lubin, Wallis, & Paine, 1971). Robert Thorndike (1975) called it the "workhorse of psychometric appraisal of cognitive development, the standard against which other tests of cognitive abilities have been evaluated" (pp. 3–4). When the *Stanford–Binet* was first introduced, it caught the attention of Leta Stetter Hollingworth at Columbia University in New York and changed the direction of her career. Hollingworth is the undisputed foremother of gifted education and gifted psychology.

Leta Stetter Hollingworth (1886–1939)

At the same time that Lewis Terman was "turning the first furrows in the field" on the West Coast, Leta Hollingworth "was preparing to cultivate the field from the other direction" on the East coast. "It was in these simple agrarian terms that Professor Hollingworth thought and often spoke of her task as similar to that of her colleague across the country" (Pritchard, 1951, p. 47). The two never met in person, but held an abiding respect for each other's work. While Terman described and measured the gifted, Hollingworth probed their inner worlds and planned educational opportunities to further their development. They philosophically disagreed about the role of heredity. Terman was strongly hereditarian. Hollingworth acknowledged that heredity determined one's ability, but she passionately maintained that the fruition of natural ability is dependent upon opportunity in society. All of her work was focused on the psychological, sociological, and educational conditions that support the development of giftedness.

Before she embraced the study of giftedness, Hollingworth founded another field of psychology: the psychology of women. While in graduate school, she mounted a campaign to prove empirically that females were the intellectual equals of males. The scientific community, including Hollingworth's advisor, E. L. Thorndike (1910), had wholeheartedly embraced Darwin's variability hypothesis. In 1897, Darwin had concluded that male members of all species were more advanced on the evolutionary scale than the female members because of greater variability of secondary sex characteristics. The reason so few women had attained eminence was clear to Darwin—they were less variable than males, therefore far fewer were extremely bright or extremely dull.

Hollingworth dismantled Darwin's variability hypothesis piece by piece. Her first published study in 1913 of 1,000 individuals refuted one aspect of Darwin's variability hypothesis—that there are more extremely dull males than females. The following year, she undertook an even more ambitious study of 2,000 neonates and demonstrated that the variability of infants was no greater in male infants than in female infants. Where variability existed, it favored the girls (Montague & Hollingworth, 1914). By the time she earned her doctorate in 1916, Hollingworth had published nine scientific articles and one book, successfully challenging the natural superiority of males. Heralded as the scientific bulwark of the women's movement, Hollingworth's career path seemed well established. However, in that same year, an event occurred that ignited a new passion, one that was to fascinate her for the rest of her life.

A position in educational psychology opened at Columbia University, Teachers College, and Hollingworth accepted it. The *Stanford-Binet Intelligence Scale* had just been published. She demonstrated the new test with a child of "subnormal" intelligence and thought it would be a good idea to test a "bright" child to allow her students to see the contrast. "Child E" scored 187 IQ, one of the highest recorded IQ scores at that time (Garrison, Burke, & Hollingworth, 1917). From this moment on, Hollingworth's future was sealed. Although she contributed classic textbooks in several areas, her greatest contributions were to the study of giftedness. The first volume of Terman's *Genetic Studies of Genius* was released in 1925, and Hollingworth published the first textbook on the psychology of giftedness in 1926—*Gifted Children: Their Nature and Nurture.*

Hollingworth created and taught the first course on the psychology of giftedness in 1922, officially inaugurating this field of study. She developed programs for gifted children of diverse ethnic and socioeconomic status, and collected data on their social and emotional development, as well as on their academic progress. Her methodology and educational principles are still in use today. She conducted 30 original studies of the gifted, which helped refute the popular myths that gifted children were physically weak, odd in appearance, and eccentric. No research funds were granted for any of these projects. Reviewing the quality of Hollingworth's contributions, Benbow (1990) found them "a model to be aspired to even today" (p. 214). Hollingworth conceived of the concept of "above-level testing" and inspired Julian Stanley (1990) to initiate today's nationwide talent searches. Her book, *Special Talents and Defects* (Hollingworth, 1923), was the first recognition of gifted children with learning disabilities. She was the first to study the emotional and social development of the gifted. She conducted intensive studies of the adjustment of children of different levels of ability and found that the farther the child is from average in intelligence, the more adjustment problems occur. She developed "child-centered therapy" and trained Carl Rogers, whose "client-centered therapy" was a derivative (Kerr, 1990).

Ironically, Hollingworth is best remembered for a book she never finished: *Children above 180 IQ: Origin and Development* (1942). The book was completed from her notes by her husband, Harry Hollingworth. It stands today as the most comprehensive longitudinal study ever conducted of children in this range of abilities. By studying the profoundly gifted, Hollingworth understood giftedness in a profoundly different manner. She documented their difficulties negotiating the social and educational world, their early philosophical interest in origins and destinies, their uneven development, their imaginary worlds, their need for meaning, and their loneliness. It did not matter to her whether they grew up to become famous or not. She just prayed that they all survived to adulthood, and one did not. She recognized the barriers faced by gifted girls, children of low socioeconomic circumstances and children of color.

> The work of Leta Hollingworth...on gender differences and environmental influences in the study of ability, altered the thinking of Terman and Thorndike on the question of gender and race differences in mental testing (Rosenberg, 1982). Thus, her research helped to encourage environmental understandings of human behavior. (Fagan, 1990, p. 160)

The connection between Hollingworth's two unpopular passions could be found in what she termed, "the woman question."

> Stated briefly, "the woman question" is how to reproduce the species and at the same time to work, and realize work's full reward, in accordance with individual ability. This is a question primarily of the gifted, for the discontent with and resentment against women's work have originated chiefly among women exceptionally well endowed with intellect. (Hollingworth, 1926, pp. 348–349)

Terman (1944) noted that had Hollingworth been a man, she would have been elected president of the American Psychological Association and gained membership in the National Academy of Sciences. It is unfortunate that her contributions and her philosophy have been overlooked in modern times as well.

DEBUNKING MYTHS AND STEREOTYPES

No great genius has ever existed without some touch of madness.
                                                            Seneca

A great deal has been written about the deleterious effects of stereotyping. All those who work in the helping professions are required to take coursework to become aware of the false beliefs and generalizations they hold consciously or subconsciously about diverse groups in society. The gifted fall under the radar and are excluded from these discussions. Stereotyping the gifted is commonly accepted and, in the past, has mushroomed into scapegoating (Silverman, 1992) and persecution (Hollingworth, 1926). "Giftedness is stigmatizing" (Coleman, 2012, p. 376). Stigma occurs when a person or group is perceived as tainted; it interferes with social relationships. Parents of gifted children are also "vulnerable to the stigma that differentness holds" (Alsop, 1997, p. 28).

What sayings have you heard about the gifted? What stereotypic messages were conveyed by these aphorisms? Did you believe them? The gifted have been plagued for centuries by superstitions, misinformation, and hostility. The American psychologists who championed giftedness nearly a century ago battled 19th and early 20th century clichés, many of which had been imported from Europe. They conducted empirical studies to dispel these misconceptions. But deep-seated prejudices endure, despite research evidence contradicting the underlying assumptions. And, sometimes, inaccurate interpretation of early studies of the highly intelligent led to new myths and distortions.

What are gifted children really like? Are they puny weaklings with two left feet? Are they prone to physical and mental illness? Are they all social misfits? Will they be likely to burn out early or die young? Are people with exceptional gifts born with some handicapping condition? No, none of the above is true. Yet, these enduring old wives' tales linger on, and before the old ones crumble, a whole new crop blooms, injuring gifted children and adults beyond measure. One of the first tasks mental health workers are called to do with the gifted is clarify the misperceptions and help them shed the burden of erroneous beliefs. This section would be helpful to share with gifted adults and parents of gifted children.

Early Myths

Myths about the gifted appear to have arisen in two stages. The older maxims attacked their character and foretold doom and gloom for those who have the audacity to develop quicker than the norm.

- "Early ripe, early rot."
- "A man at 5; a fool at 15."
- "Genius is akin to madness."
- "The law of compensation: Any special ability is compensated for by a deficit."

"Early Ripe, Early Rot." "Early ripe, early rot" comes in many flavors. It may have originated as a Chinese or Swahili proverb. Its most literal meaning is that children who develop too quickly die very young. Support came from the early demise of celebrated precocious children, who were often mercilessly displayed as curiosities and required to perform feats beyond their endurance. It is little wonder that only the strongest of them survived (Hildreth, 1966). One of the earliest published accounts of these "Wunderkinder" was Christian Heinrich Heineken, born in Lubeck in 1721. His tutor wrote that Christian learned all the stories in the *New Testament* by the age of 14 months (Hollingworth, 1942). When he died, at the age of 4 years, 4 months, it is reported that he was fluent in German, French, and Latin; knew 1,500 Latin proverbs, the fundamentals of arithmetic, and the skeletal system; could answer all questions about history; and so on (Whipple, 1924). Doctors and educators in the 19th century warned that overtaxing the brains of precocious children would surely bring about early decrepitude and decay (Kearney, 2009). Babcock (1895) declared that the most frequent outcome of genius was early death.

"Early ripe, early rot" also bore a meaning similar to "A man at 5, a fool at 15"; it was the slogan of those who favored slow maturation (Terman & Oden, 1947). Terman assailed the prevalent belief that great geniuses were often dunces in childhood and the corollary that those who demonstrate precocity in childhood will "burn out" before adulthood. "Burn out" frequently appears in modern times in the literature on child prodigies, since they rarely attain eminence in adulthood (Winner, 2000). The conviction that slow maturation is superior to fast maturation dates back to Aristotle. He and others proposed that the early maturation of females signaled their inferiority.

> In human beings, the female foetus is not perfected equally with the male...after birth it quickly arrives at maturity and old age on account of its weakness, for all inferior things come sooner to their perfection or end.... (Aristotle, 4th Century BCE/1962 translation, Chapter 6 of Book IV)
>
> Girls begin to talk and to stand on their feet sooner than boys because weeds always grow up more quickly than good crops. (Luther, 1533/1967, p. 187)
>
> The nobler and more perfect a thing is, the later and slower it is in arriving at maturity....That is why women remain children their whole life long.... (Schopenhauer, 1851/1914, p. xxvii)

"Giftedness Is Akin to Madness." Before the turn of the 20th century, the connection between genius and insanity was established scientific fact. It was cemented by Lombroso (1888/1905) in Italy, Nisbet (1893) in England, and Babcock (1895) in the United States. Nisbet credited Aristotle with this observation. Others cite Plato and Seneca. However, Schlesinger (2009) suggests that "madness" for the early Greeks, "meant inspiration and illumination, and was a desirable, rather than dreaded state" (p. 63). Lombroso (1888/1905) concluded that the gifted are often undersized, emaciated, dysfluent, lame, and strange in appearance—even hunchbacked. Nisbet

(1893) provided physiological evidence and case studies to demonstrate that genius disturbs the healthy equilibrium of the brain and nervous system.

"Aberrant brain development" of the eminent is still discussed in the literature today (e.g., Mrazik & Dombrowski, 2010), with prenatal exposure to increased levels of testosterone posited as the likely culprit. Babcock (1895) considered genius a sign of inferior genetic endowment, along with early death, criminality, and insanity. Nisbet (1893) cautioned parents that discussing their children's gifts with them could lead to the transmission of insanity. A contemporary admonition is that such discussions will lead to "swelled heads" (perceiving oneself as better than everyone else), lack of effort, and perfectionism. The "mad genius" notion continues to be quite chic, as shown by the popularity of the "Creativity and Madness" conferences, sponsored by the American Institute of Medical Education (AIMED), aimed at physicians, social workers, psychologists, and marriage and family therapists. Since 1982, AIMED has held 120 conferences throughout the world on this topic. Schlesinger (2009) sees it as an enduring legacy of the law of compensation.

> The "mad genius" has been a cherished cultural icon for centuries, a romantic and compelling concept that helps demystify our geniuses and make them more accessible....The mad genius idea also neutralizes any envy of their abilities, for if we cannot share their talent, at least we don't have their problems. (p. 62)

"The Law of Compensation." "The law of compensation" and "genius is akin to madness" are close relatives. "The doctrine that great talent exacts a great price is so popular that few people think to question its validity" (Schlesinger, 2009, p. 62). The assumption is that all gifts come with deficits. Strength in one area necessitates weakness in another to balance it out. At the turn of the 20th century, this "law of compensation" was believed as firmly as the law of gravity:

> Just as giants pay a heavy ransom for their stature in sterility and relative muscular and mental weakness, so the giants of thought expiate their intellectual force in degeneration and psychoses. It is thus that the signs of degeneration are found more frequently in men of genius than even in the insane. (Lombroso, 1888/1905, p. 42)

Lombroso still serves as a credible reference for those who maintain that there is an indelible connection between creativity and mood disorders (e.g., Andreasen, 1987). These myths probably developed from our inability to reconcile our belief in equality with our observations that some individuals are vastly more capable than the rest of us. By giving the gifted person some form of handicap in our minds, we make it less desirable to be gifted, and we can dismiss the inequality.

What Does the Research Say? Terman (Terman & Oden, 1947) was disturbed by the increasing number of treatises he found in which gifted children were depicted as abnormal, neurotic, likely to die in childhood, or headed for stupidity or insanity in adult life. Parents were being warned to protect these children from intellectual stimulation and to discourage signs of cleverness. It was within this milieu that he launched his study of 1,528 gifted children, hoping to rid the world permanently of these disparaging beliefs.

As a group, Terman's subjects were found to be above average in all categories studied: height, weight, early physical development, physique, general health, emotional stability, social adjustment, moral character, and school achievement. There was greater variability within the group, however, and these composite results did not reflect individual performances

(Terman, 1925). Later reports of these individuals at mid-life appear to indicate that as a group the gifted are less vulnerable to mental illness, suicide, divorce, and mental deterioration than the general population (Terman & Oden, 1947, 1959). Increases in mental ability were found through middle age, and longevity was much more prevalent than early death, particularly for high-achieving males. "There is no shred of evidence to support the widespread opinion that typically the intellectually precocious child is weak, undersized, or nervously unstable" (Terman, 1925, p. 634). Terman was joined by Cox (1926), Witty (1930), Hollingworth (1926), and a host of other researchers in his crusade to vanquish prejudice against the gifted.

The genius-equals-madness contention has been disputed repeatedly in recent literature (e.g., Rothenberg, 1990; Schlesinger, 2009), but some seem to find it compelling (e.g., Panter, 2009; Simonton, 2009). Simonton (2009) depicts the relationship between "genius" and "madness" as "fraternal twins" (p. 121). Martin, Burns, and Schonlau (2010) were surprised to find that the vast majority of literature reviews on mental disorders in the gifted had no comparison groups of nongifted children. They found no studies that compared rates of bipolar disorder or attention-deficit/hyperactivity disorder (AD/HD) among gifted and nongifted youth. Their meta-analysis of nine studies of children enrolled in gifted programs compared with nongifted controls revealed no differences in depression, anxiety, or suicidal ideation.

Modern research in child development and intelligence has thoroughly discredited the "law of compensation." On the contrary, "Correlation and not compensation is the rule in development" (Lefrancois, 1981, p. 88). Development generally proceeds at a uniform rate, and those who have high aptitude in one mental sphere tend to be high in all mental abilities (Gottfredson, 2003; Lefrancois, 1981). There is ample empirical evidence of these principles in studies of the gifted. Nancy Robinson (1993) concluded, after reviewing an extensive number of studies, "Advanced ability tends to maintain its rapid pace of development. This evidence substantiates the notion that early giftedness, or rapid development, also *predicts* the subsequent rate of development" (p. 511). The Fullerton Longitudinal Study, in which a cohort of 130 1-year-olds was assessed 23 times, in 6-month intervals, until adulthood, serves as an excellent example. "The differences between gifted and nongifted children were significant at 1.5 years and every age thereafter" (A. W. Gottfried, A. E. Gottfried, Bathurst, & Guerin, 1994, p. 56).

> Significant differences between the gifted IQ group and their cohort peer comparison emerged on the psychometric sensorimotor tests of intelligence beginning at age 1.5 years. The difference between the groups was maintained throughout the course of investigation, indicating parallel continuity. ...virtually all children who emerged as gifted at age 8 revealed a developmental index score of 130 or greater during infancy... further indication of early cognitive acceleration. Parents also observed the early advancement of the children. (A. W. Gottfried, A. E. Gottfried, & Guerin, 2006, p. 441)

But the myths endure and appear to procreate.

The New Myths

The new myths are not as overtly psychologically damaging as the old ones, but they negate the existence of giftedness, deny parental concerns, rationalize ignoring these children's differences, and neglect their needs. Parents are bombarded from all sides with misinformation about their gifted children (Alsop, 1997). Teachers, doctors, relatives, neighbors, the press, and mental health professionals perpetuate negative stereotypes, leaving parents raggedly confused.

- "All children are gifted."
- "Giftedness isn't real. Isn't it just 'hothousing' by helicopter parents?"

- "All parents think their child is gifted."
- "He isn't even reading yet. Be happy that he's 'average.'"
- "Why do you want to have your child tested? That will only make her feel different."
- "Gifted children can make it on their own; they don't need special attention."
- "It doesn't matter if she's reading early; all the other kids will catch up by third grade."
- "Don't put your child in a gifted program. It won't prepare her for the real world."
- "Skipping a grade will hurt his social development."
- "Don't you want your child to fit in socially?"
- "He needs to toughen up. He's too sensitive."
- "Gifted programs are elitist."

These stereotypic attitudes about giftedness disregard individual differences and treat all gifted children as if they were the same. It is important for parents to be able to turn to professionals for clarity about the specific needs of their children. Gifted children and adults need help dispelling the multitude of prejudiced ideas that pass from generation to generation as "truths." Several of the most common myths are discussed below.

"All Children Are Gifted"

*Carli's mother has...informed the teacher that Carli [age 5]...was reading before her third birthday. She also has mentioned Carli's analytical skills, such as how she selects fish for her aquarium, and her understanding of the various extinction theories of the dinosaurs. Carli's mother searches the teacher's face for some acknowledgment that such behaviors are unusual, and finds none. She then poses the question, "Do you think my child is gifted?" There is a smile and a reply, "We like to think that **all** of the children in our school are gifted."*

"All children are gifted" implies that all children are the same—there are no notable differences that need to be addressed instructionally.

> *While this statement is intended to convey the teacher's desire to make all children feel special, it is, in fact, insensitive and abrasive. (Cole & DellaVecchia, 1993, p. 8)*

One of the utmost stressors in the lives of parents of the gifted is the degree to which they are discounted. It is unnerving to approach a school principal with concerns about one's gifted child and to hear, in a patronizing tone, "*All* our children are gifted." All children are special, but all children do not qualify for special education. Children who are significantly below the mean intellectually are entitled by law to special provisions. Children who are significantly above the mean intellectually need to be recognized as having special needs, as well.

Parents frequently are derided for attempting to secure "special treatment" for their children and teachers are advised to ignore these parents' pleas (e.g., George, 1988, 1992). Provisions for the gifted are not advantages in the race for success; they are essential modifications for children who learn differently. On occasion, resistance to meeting the needs of the gifted is couched in the language of multiple intelligences: "We believe in multiple intelligences; we develop *all* children's gifts." Under this façade, little in the way of differentiation is usually seen.

"All Parents Think Their Children Are Gifted." This overworked saw completely discredits parents as a legitimate source of information about their children and it is untrue. It would be unthinkable to be this dismissive to a parent of a disabled child. As giftedness is stigmatized in our society (Coleman, 2012), parents are much less likely to say, "I have a gifted child" than to say, "I have a disabled child." There is too much risk of being perceived as "bragging."

The accuracy of parents as identifiers of gifted children has been found in numerous studies (e.g., Alsop, 1997; A. W. Gottfried et al., 1994; Louis & M. Lewis, 1992; N. Robinson, 2008b; M. Rogers, 1986; Silverman, Chitwood, & Waters, 1986). Martin Rogers (1986) conducted a comparative study of the developmental characteristics of gifted and average children. Many of the parents kept detailed records of their child's early development.

> Contrary to the belief that all parents think their children are gifted, this study indicated that parents of average children do see their children's development differently from parents of gifted children. In addition, the parents of the gifted tended to **underestimate** their children's abilities rather than overestimate them. (M. Rogers & Silverman, 1988, p. 5)

The Fullerton Longitudinal Study of the development of gifted and nongifted children from infancy confirmed these results (A. W. Gottfried et al., 1994). "Parents...are accurate in their ratings of their children's functioning and...perceptive of their children's developmental position as early as infancy. This is supported by...the correspondence of their ratings with the objective developmental test data..." (p. 83).

Another longitudinal study was conducted by Dickinson (1956), who found that only 50% of the children who tested within the gifted range were recognized by their parents as having special abilities. When parents failed to notice their children's giftedness, they made no effort to provide opportunities for its development. Several longitudinal studies were conducted by Nancy Robinson and her colleagues. Among their findings are that parents' perceptions of their children's advancement are accurate, standardized test results correlate with actual behavior, and standardized testing of young children predicts later performance.

> These findings confirm the accuracy of parental descriptions of their children's behavior. They tell us to trust parents who think

that their children's behavior is advanced—whether or not we have seen that behavior in school. But the studies also do something else. They confirm that the results of standardized tests *are strongly correlated with the children's actual behavior at home! They are "for real!"* Furthermore, each of the above studies had a two- to five-year longitudinal aspect, and in each case, the scores initially attained by the children were predictive over time for the group as a whole. (N. Robinson, 2008b, p. 168)

Feldhusen (1998) wrote, "In truth, few parents think their children are gifted and want to label their children as gifted" (p. 194). Afraid that they are overestimating their children's abilities and will be proven foolish, parents feel compelled to amass large amounts of evidence of precocity before they are willing to even begin exploring the possibility of giftedness (Seeley, 1998). Assouline, Foley Nicpon, and Huber (2006) wrote, "It is essential...to listen to parents, because, in almost all cases, parents' instincts about their child's abilities are correct and deserve to be considered in educational decision-making for their child" (p. 22).

"You Have to Be Gifted in Everything." In their zeal to counter the prevailing myths, the early researchers were so successful that they inadvertently created a new illusion of the gifted as superstars (Clark, 1983; Whitmore, 1980). Teachers began to believe that if a child is gifted in one area, he or she should be gifted in all areas (Sankar-DeLeeuw, 2004; Webb, Gore, Amend, & DeVries, 2007), and perfectly well behaved. This is the myth assumed by teachers when they say, "If you're so gifted, why are you running down the hall?" "Why can't you tie your shoes?" "Why don't you have straight A's?" "How can you say Sallie is gifted when she spells so poorly?" These arguments humiliate gifted children and negate their intelligence. This myth has made it difficult to identify twice exceptional children.

"Gifted Kids Can Make It on Their Own." The modern iteration of the cream inevitably rising to the top is that gifted children do not need any special provisions (Assouline et al., 2006). Research indicates that the gifted do not always make it on their own. Estimates of the numbers of gifted students who drop out of school range from less than 1% to 5% of the gifted population (Matthews, 2009; Renzulli & Park, 2000) amounting to a conservative estimate of 200,000 gifted students nationwide. The exceptionally and profoundly gifted may be at higher risk of dropping out of school (Gross, 2009). Depression and suicidal ideation are not uncommon in the gifted (Jackson & Peterson, 2003). A considerable number of gifted youth find their way into juvenile courts (Harvey & Seeley, 1984; Seeley, 2003). Underachievement is a pervasive problem (Rimm, 2008). The number of twice exceptional children is increasing (Silverman, 2009b). And then there are countless cases of vanishing giftedness—those children whose talents are lost through lack of detection and nurturing (J. Gallagher, 1979; M. Lewis & Louis, 1991).

"The Others Will Catch Up Anyway." Many believe that when children are developmentally advanced in early childhood, and come to school already knowing how to read, the other children will eventually "catch up." Again, just the opposite proves to be the case. When educated appropriately, the gap between the gifted and their age mates widens with age (Martinson, 1974; Silverman, 1998a). Gifted children have a different trajectory of development from average learners. Their minds are like new high-powered computers that process greater amounts of information at a more rapid rate, organize that material more efficiently, integrate it with other information more systematically, and retrieve it more easily. The only way a newer computer can appear to have the same capabilities as an older, less powerful one is by using only a fraction of its capacity.

The goals of the educational process are not the same for all students. One student needs to master enough basic mathematics to be able to balance a budget in adult life, while another needs to understand enough advanced mathematics to be able to discover a new source of energy. If the educational goal of one student is to be able to read books and the goal of another is to be able to write them, there is no point in keeping both of these students at the same level of instruction. This prevents the natural progress of the rapid learner and frustrates the slower one.

"Acceleration Is Socially Harmful." Education is notoriously anti-acceleration, on the grounds that it is will create social misfits (Geake & Gross, 2008; Jones & Southern, 1991). "Psychological suspicion of outsiders,..." as described by Wilson (1956) in *The Outsider*, could explain why the most cited reason by teachers for not accelerating a gifted child is that the child is "not fitting in socially" (Geake & Gross, 2008, p. 226). Sankar-DeLeeuw (2002) reported that 93% of teachers in her study were against early entrance due to concerns about social and emotional development. In a recent survey of school counselors, 71% indicated that they would be concerned about recommending acceleration due to its impact on social and emotional development (Wood, Portman, Cigrand, & Colangelo, 2010).

Actually, it is socially harmful for a child who is light years beyond his or her age mates to be locked into a grade placement that serves neither academic nor social needs (Gross, 2009; Neihart, 2007; Wood et al., 2010). When children are too advanced, they are shunned by their classmates. Gifted children often have older friends. They tend to make friends with those who are closer to their mental age (Hollingworth, 1926).

Allowing them to learn with older children increases their chances of making friends and reduces the likelihood of social isolation (Colangelo, Assouline, & Gross, 2004). "Those who experienced social isolation earlier say it disappeared after the first grade-skip" (Gross, 2006, p. 416).

For the first half of the 20th century, it was common for gifted children to be placed with children 1 or 2 years older than themselves. Terman (1925) found that the youngest child in the class was more likely to test in the gifted range than the children the teacher identified. The term "acceleration" was only applied to 3 years of advancement or more—what we would call "radical acceleration" today. Acceleration is "the most documented, supported and cost-effective method" of accommodating the needs of the gifted (Wood et al., 2010, p. 169). A considerable amount of research has been conducted over the last 80 years on the effects of acceleration (Boazman & Sayler, 2011; Colangelo et al., 2004; Gross, 2006; Lee, Olszewski-Kubilius, & Peternel, 2010; N. Robinson, 2004), all of which supports it as a viable option, socially as well as academically. Accelerants are more likely to feel socially accepted than equally gifted students not permitted the opportunity to accelerate. In addition, they tend to be more ambitious, earn more graduate degrees, have higher achievement, and feel more challenged and less bored (Wood et al., 2010) (see http://www.nationdeceived.org/ for more information).

An important criterion to consider is whether the child wants to be accelerated. A child who is eager to skip a grade usually needs a more advanced peer group. Social adjustment difficulties usually occur in children who were grade-skipped without being given a choice. While there have been scores of studies indicating that even radical accelerates enjoy excellent social adjustment (e.g., Boazman & Sayler, 2011), there are no studies that indicate that gifted children have better social adjustment when they are kept with their age peers.

"Gifted Kids Need Socialization." The myth of the gifted child as a social misfit was debunked by Terman (1925). Extensive modern research confirms Terman's findings:

> Perusal of a large group of studies of preadolescent children revealed [that] ... as a group, gifted children were seen as more trustworthy, honest, socially competent, assured and comfortable with self, courteous, cooperative, stable, and humorous, while they were also seen as showing diminished tendencies to boast, to engage in delinquent activity, to aggress or withdraw, to be domineering, and so on. (N. Robinson & Noble, 1991, p. 62)

It is interesting that the context of most of these studies was some form of special provision for the gifted, such as special classes or acceleration. Clearly, these provisions are not harmful for social development. Many children claim that this was the first time they formed real friendships.

In general, gifted children are well adjusted, but making friends becomes more difficult the further the child's abilities veer from the norm. It is more challenging for children above 160 IQ to find others to relate to, than children at 130 IQ, who are closer to the norm. Hollingworth (1942) considered IQ scores around the 125 to 145 range to be "optimal" for leadership, since these children are more likely to share the vocabulary and interests of their age mates. Recent support has been found for Hollingworth's contention that the lower range of the gifted spectrum is the optimal level of intelligence (S. Shaywitz et al., 2001). Highly, exceptionally, and profoundly gifted children may actually be socially advanced, but they have little in common with average children their age. When they are placed in programs with true peers—that is, children who are their mental equals and who share their interests and values—they make friends easily, keep those friends indefinitely, become elected as leaders, show social awareness, and have positive views of humanity.

"Special Programs Are Elitist." The most emotionally charged myth is the one that asserts that grouping gifted children is elitist. Elitism runs against the very fiber of our democratic system; however, no research supports the fear that gifted programs create elitism (Marland, 1971/1972; Newland, 1976; Silverman, 1992). And these programs are not just advantages for the advantaged (McCoach & Siegle, 2007). Though percentages of gifted students in affluent schools may be higher, a much greater number of gifted children come from the lower classes, because the poor far outnumber the rich (Zigler & Farber, 1985). When provisions are denied to the gifted on the basis that they are "elitist," the poor suffer the most. The rich have other options.

More elitism is fostered by keeping gifted children with their nongifted age mates than by grouping them with one another. Students who are the smartest in their class for 12 years, never crack a book or take home homework, and ace all the tests without studying, often get a ballooned sense of their own importance and place in the universe. They think they are always supposed to be in first place, and they have difficulty coping with a challenger for their top-dog position. They are unprepared emotionally to go to an Ivy League college and discover that they are not the brightest star in the sky. These students are at great risk for breakdowns and suicide attempts in college.

When gifted students are placed in classes together, they do not conclude that they are "better than everyone else." Rather, they are *humbled* by finding peers who know more than they do. Hollingworth (1930) wrote, "Conceit was corrected, rather than fostered, by the experience of daily contact with a large number of equals" (p. 445).

This is just a sampling of the innumerable myths that exist about the gifted and provisions for them. These myths are more than just inaccurate—they are destructive. They prevent the gifted child from being understood, accepted, and served appropriately by the school system. Some humiliate the child personally. Others are used as an excuse for negligence. Parents need to be taken seriously. Thankfully, 21st-century parents are able to connect with each other through Internet and gain a reality check from others who understand the prejudices they face. In order to serve the gifted population in a healthy manner, mental health workers need to guard against their own prejudice, the prejudice of the press, and the common misperceptions in society.

Life at the Extremes

The world is always ready to receive talent with open arms.
Very often it does not know what to do with genius.
Oliver Wendell Holmes

n the preceding chapter, the folklore that enshrouds giftedness was discussed, as well as historical attempts to shatter the myths. In this chapter, the rich heritage of the discipline comingles with new research, as we explore the incidence of giftedness, the parallels between degrees of delay and advancement, giftedness as an organizing principle, different levels of giftedness, typical characteristics throughout the lifespan, and why it is important to recognize advanced development as early as possible.

The psychologists who pioneered the study of giftedness were interested in atypical development at both extremes (e.g., Binet, Stern, Goddard, Terman, Hollingworth). They understood the wide-ranging psychological implications of developmental differences. But the yellow brick road taken in the

20th century diverted this discipline further and further away from psychology. Educators forgot the integral role of psychologists in the development of the gifted, and psychology abandoned the gifted. The 21st century holds promise of reconnecting gifted education with its psychological roots. It is time for psychology to reclaim its lost child.

PARALLELS AT THE EXTREMES

Giftedness is a psychological reality—the opposite end of the spectrum from Intellectual Developmental Disorder, as it is referred to in the *Diagnostic and Statistical Manual of Mental Disorders* (5th ed., *DSM-5*) (American Psychiatric Association [APA], 2013). This term replaces the *DSM-IV* diagnostic category of Mental Retardation. According to the *DSM-5*, Intellectual Developmental Disorder requires an intellectual deficit of at least two standard deviations in IQ below the mean for a person's age and cultural group (approximately 70 IQ or below), as measured on an individualized, culturally appropriate, and psychometrically sound test.

The *DSM-5* also requires significant impairment of adaptive functioning, in areas such as communication, socialization, and personal independence. These limitations cause the need for continuous support in all activities of daily life. Intellectual Development Disorder has its onset in the developmental period of one's life.

This description in the *DSM-5* highlights the psychological differences in those who differ from the norm by 2 or more standard deviations (SD) in IQ. While the concept of IQ and IQ testing remains controversial (A. Kaufman, 2009), it is fundamental to our recognition, understanding, and support of those in the extremes of the distribution of intelligence. Two SD from the mean in either direction theoretically represent 2.14% of the population. The two extremities of the curve combined comprise

approximately 5% of society. In our mushrooming populace, over 3 million Americans and approximately 70 million
global citizens are *highly* gifted or beyond (99.9th percentile).
And highly intelligent individuals seem to be more likely to
voluntarily seek mental health services than those closer to the
average range. The further individuals veer from the norm in
either direction, the greater their psychological differences, and
the greater the need for professionals who have had specialized
training in working effectively with special-needs groups.

Alienation is a serious risk at both extremes, but it is experienced more intensely at the upper echelon, because the individual
has more awareness. Hollingworth, who wrote leading textbooks
on both exceptionalities, recognized their analogous social difficulties. "The farther a person diverges from medium ability, in
either direction, the less frequently will those like him occur in the
world" (Hollingworth, 1942, p. 5). In 1940, she noted that psychological isolation tends to occur at 30 points below the norm, when
inadequacies are perceived by others, and at 50 points above the
norm, when feelings of inadequacy are experienced by the self.
Recent research on the social adjustment of the highly gifted confirms Hollingworth's earlier findings (J. Cross, 2012; Dauber &
Benbow, 1990; Gross, 2009; N. Robinson & Noble, 1991).

For this group, social alienation is a function of the lack of a
suitable peer group, rather than emotional disturbance (Gross,
2009; Hebert, 2011). Even those highly gifted children who are
accepted by others feel lonely for true peers:

> "Mom," he said, "It's like I'm a duck and all these chickens want
> to play with me. Where are all the other ducks? I can play chicken
> games forever and it's fun and all, but none of them understand
> what I like to do." Like Patrick, many highly gifted children feel
> like ducks out of water, pretending to be chickens to get along.
> (Lovecky, 2011, p. 147)

Those in the very highest ranges are at the greatest risk
(Hafenstein & Honeck, 2011). The higher the individual's IQ, the
more intense the struggle for identity, meaning, and connection.

The definition of Intellectual Development Disorder includes the requirement of significant adaptive difficulties that limit communication, social adjustment, functioning at school or work, and independence. These difficulties result in the need for ongoing support.

Adaptive or adjustment difficulties become more apparent in the higher ranges of giftedness (J. Cross, 2012; Lovecky, 2011; S. Shaywitz et al., 2001). Communication failure is common when a person's vocabulary or humor is not understood by classmates or colleagues. Highly gifted children are often shunned by others, which limits their social participation. It can be difficult to succeed in school when the student embarrasses the teacher by correcting the information that the teacher is imparting. Gifted adults applying for positions may not be able to secure a job if they are perceived as "too intelligent." Some gifted individuals are more comfortable in the role of student and fearful of their inability to negotiate the world of work; their extended years of schooling may compromise their independence.

While the early psychologists worked feverishly to verify the positive social adjustment of the gifted, they could not ignore the stumbling blocks exceptionally gifted children encounter in developing interpersonal relations with their age peers. Terman (1931) wrote:

> Precocity unavoidably complicates the problem of social adjustment. The child of eight years with a mentality of twelve or fourteen is faced with a situation almost inconceivably difficult. In order to adjust normally such a child has to have an exceptionally well-balanced personality and to be well nigh a social genius. The higher the IQ, the more acute the problem. (p. 579)

An IQ score of 160 or above is hazardous to social adjustment. Hollingworth (1939) asserted that children in this IQ range played little with other children "because the difficulties of social contact are almost insurmountable" (p. 588). Children with IQ scores above 180 face even greater obstacles. In "The Child of Very Superior Intelligence as a Special Problem in Social Adjustment," Hollingworth (1931) reported that only one in six related well to other children. The other five "were unpopular with children of their own age because they always wanted to organize the play into a complicated pattern, with some remote and definite climax as the goal" (p. 7).

Wasserman (2007) has noted difficulties in "functional living skills" as well as "social competencies" in some exceptionally gifted children (p. 61). These issues may continue into adulthood. There are anecdotes of brilliant men who become so preoccupied with their mental life that they forget to bathe, brush their teeth, or flush toilets; insist on being right at the expense of others' feelings; have hair-trigger temper outbursts; leave guests at the dinner table in their home without saying goodbye; or who have no idea when others are no longer interested in what they are saying.

"Onset during the developmental period" also fits both ends of the spectrum. Developmental differences in either direction become apparent by 18 months (A. W. Gottfried, A. E. Gottfried, Bathurst, & Guerin, 1994) and are fairly stable throughout the lifespan. In the Fullerton Longitudinal Study, the earliest predictor of giftedness appeared at 1 year: receptive language ability (A. W. Gottfried, A. E. Gottfried, & Guerin, 2006). Other studies report that parents of gifted children observe accelerated development within the first year of life (Alomar, 2003; Gogel, McCumsey, & Hewett, 1985; Kaufmann & Sexton, 1983; Louis & M. Lewis, 1992).

Parent education and counseling take on increasing significance as the child's development moves deeper into the extremes. Children whose abilities are 2, 3, 4, or more SD higher or lower than the norm require adaptations in family life and parental expectations. "The parent responses provide indications that parenting highly gifted children may be a difficult experience" (S. Shaywitz et al., 2001, p. 20).

> This life is not what I expected....The intensities, the insatiable curiosity, the stubbornness, the sensitivities, the asynchrony, the sensory issues, the over-excitabilities, the questioning of every single thing, the constant demands on every cell of my being...and that doesn't even take into consideration the challenge of advocating for them outside the house. (J. Merrill, 2012, p. 43)

While it may be exciting for parents to learn that their child is talented (e.g., "America's Got Talent!"), parents of gifted children usually experience anxiety. Most parents of exceptionally gifted children report feeling "overwhelmed" by the test results (Silverman & Kearney, 1989).

Similar to learning about any exceptionality, parents go through a period of adjustment. They mourn the loss of their fantasy of having a "normal" child (Meckstroth, 1991, p. 98) whose needs will be taken care of easily within the regular classroom. Parents often feel inadequately prepared to meet the needs of the child and lack information about resources. They worry that "more will be expected of them. They wonder if they can measure up. Since their child's abilities are now recognized and valued, they feel that the job of parenting must now be taken much more seriously" (Meckstroth, 1991, p. 98).

> *It seems that everything about raising a highly gifted child is harder. It's all so complicated and there's always the fear that I'm not doing enough for her. I can't just kiss her goodbye and send her off to school. I have to be involved in all aspects to see that her needs are met as best as can be.*

How will this information affect our family? What impact will it have on our other children? What should we tell our child? How will we explain this to our relatives? To our child's teacher? What should we do about school? How will we handle the extra financial burden of special programs?

Mothers frequently cry, and fathers often question the validity of the test results. All parents feel an overwhelming responsibility for these children, and some feel inadequate to the task of meeting their needs. … Limited finances are usually a major concern.

Some parents react in a straightforward, problem-solving mode. … Other parents, however, have been filled with dismay at the results. Most parents who bring their children for testing hope that the neighborhood schools will be able to serve their children's needs, and an astronomical test score can throw off all of the family's plans. One mother even worried herself into an ulcer over the situation.

Integrating the information that one has a child with exceptional needs takes a period of adjustment (Dirks, 1979). For some families, this can be a long, drawn-out period, as they try to balance the child's greater need for stimulation, the needs of other family members, and financial considerations. (Silverman & Kearney, 1989, pp. 48–49)

Support from psychologists is needed to obtain documentation of abilities and needs, to help parents understand the implications of their child's developmental differences, locate available resources, guide them through the complex bureaucratic maze to obtain services, help them advocate effectively at school, and deal with family dynamics. Parents need practitioners who not only care about their children, but also care about them and understand their challenges. They do not need to be advised, "Remember that she is a child first."

More than one parent has heard, "Let's take giftedness out of the equation," from a well-meaning psychologist. You cannot buy pants without knowing the child's height any more than you can deny the role that giftedness plays in one's difficulties. (Amend & Beljan, 2009, pp. 133–134)

Parents of the gifted should not be advised to teach their children to "just play the game." Instead, like parents of other exceptionalities, they should be given negotiation tools to help them work effectively with teachers to develop accommodations to meet the needs of their children.

Psychologists and counselors are needed for children at both extremes to identify the degree of atypicality, document strengths and weaknesses, create individual education plans, generate recommendations for home and school, monitor implementation of plans, guide families, advocate for children in school, and teach specific adaptive and social skills. Assistance is available to parents and children at the lower end of the spectrum to cope with the adaptive difficulties of exceptionality. Similar support is needed for children and their families at the upper extreme of the curve to prevent loneliness and isolation. Adults at the extremes continue to need psychological services to deal with the specific issues they face as society's outsiders.

Correspondence at the extremes breaks down when it comes to funding and legal rights. Moreover, the field of psychology has paid much more attention to those significantly below the norm. "The substantial attention lavished on the lower end of the intellectual continuum remains unequaled. No parallel effort has been directed toward unraveling the mysteries of the opposite end of the scale, intellectual giftedness" (Zigler & Farber, 1985, p. 388).

GIFTEDNESS AS AN ORGANIZING PRINCIPLE

Much wisdom can be gained about giftedness from closely examining the way we view the opposite end of the intellectual spectrum (Zigler & Farber, 1985). *Intellectual Developmental Disorder* is an organizing principle—a unique trajectory of development with atypical characteristics. The *DSM-IV* recognized this by adding the caveat in several diagnoses, "If Mental Retardation . . . is present, the . . . difficulties are **in excess** of those usually associated with these problems" (American Psychiatric

Association, 1994, p. 58, emphasis added).[1] A similar caution should be considered in working with the gifted (Amend & Beljan, 2009). If giftedness were understood as an organizing principle, behaviors would be perceived within the context of those with similar abilities, rather than viewing them as "aberrant" in relation to those in the average range. "It is intensely bittersweet to find out that these traits that brought so much shame are normal for the gifted" (Wallach, 1995, p. 37).

School psychologists would strongly advocate for the re-establishment of their central role in identifying this population. Until now, they have been virtually silent about their gradual exclusion in the identification process. Children whose IQ scores fall 2 or more SD below the norm (below 70 IQ) are protected by federal and state mandates. They must be assessed by certified or licensed professionals "on an individualized standardized, culturally appropriate, psychometrically sound test" (American Psychiatric Association, 2013). The top 2% roughly corresponds to the group whose IQ scores fall 2 SD below the norm. Individuals at the 98th, 99th, or 99.9th percentile also warrant assessment by knowledgeable professionals.

It would be apparent that a person does not "outgrow" giftedness, no more than anyone outgrows significant intellectual disability. The issues faced by this group in childhood simply morph into new variations in adulthood. Fitting-in is still a problem. Advanced vocabulary still hinders communication. Difficulties coping with authority increase rather than decrease. Some gifted adults have not mastered the skill of telling "white lies" to protect someone's feelings. Their need for logical consistency outweighs their inclination to purposely distort the truth.

Traits such as introversion, perfectionism, sensitivity, complexity, emotional intensity, intuitive awareness, outrage at injustice, and difficulty with authority, typical of the gifted, would be normalized. Misdiagnosis of the gifted is common (Amend & Beljan, 2009). "When giftedness is denied or ignored, the gifted individual is unable to integrate it into her understanding of who she is" (Amend & Peters, 2012, p. 594). Perhaps the most misunderstood trait of the gifted is perfectionism. As it appears to be a suspect in so many disorders, therapists are tempted to try to cure it. In this population, however, perfectionism is intertwined with the drive for self-actualization (Maslow, 1971) (see Chapter 5 for more information on this topic).

Depression in the gifted would be viewed differently as well, and solutions sought outside the confines of medical interventions. For example, the term "postpartum depression" has been used to describe the typical let down that is experienced by highly creative individuals upon the completion of a creative undertaking in which the individual invested excessive energy (Gowan, 1980). Frequently, it can be resolved by resting the mind and body, and then taking on another demanding project. Gifted teens often become depressed when they don't feel that they can make a difference in a world filled with inequities. This should not be confused with endogenous depression. Books such as *The Kid's Guide to Social Action* (B. Lewis, 1998) may do more good than medication.

Schechtman and Silektor (2012) wrote, "Loneliness is one of the most common characteristics associated with gifted children" (p. 63). They compared a large group of gifted children in Israel who were enrolled in gifted programs to a group of non-gifted students; there were no differences on scores on a loneliness scale. One implication of their study is that the antidote to loneliness and isolation is finding true peers with whom to connect. Practitioners can assist gifted individuals in locating friends.

Gifted traits are often misjudged; in addition, psychological disorders can be missed in the gifted (Amend & Peters, 2012). Not frequently acknowledged, there are greater risks with missed diagnoses than with misdiagnosis. High levels of intelligence can mask disorders, and the gifted often exhibit *atypical* manifestations that are difficult to interpret. Some highly gifted adults with bipolar disorder experience only the lows without apparent highs. Manic phases might look like periods of high energy, enthusiasm, enormous creativity, motivation to begin new projects, and less need for sleep. But when the depression hits, the individual is unable to move forward on these projects, and lethargy sets in. Underachievement is typical. Medication may be needed to break this cycle and to prevent a major manic episode, which could be cataclysmic. Highly creative individuals often experience highs and lows. If there are recognizable cycles, or if there is any suicidal ideation, manic depression needs to be ruled out.

Attention deficit disorders, although often thought to be overdiagnosed in the gifted (e.g., Probst & Piechowski, 2012), can also be missed. Underachievement, a typical symptom of attention-deficit/hyperactivity disorder (AD/HD), may not be present in this population. The gifted—even those with AD/HD—can concentrate for incredibly long periods of time on areas of interest. "In addition, individuals diagnosed with ADHD frequently exhibit a tendency to hyperfocus, particularly on activities that require little mental control and provide immediate feedback" (Mika, 2006, p. 239).

Gifted children with AD/HD only experience attentional issues when they are not engaged. The endless "either-or" debates, especially regarding the overlapping characteristics of giftedness and AD/HD and the possibility of misdiagnosis, could be resolved with a greater appreciation of dual diagnoses. Diagnosticians need to have grounding in the characteristics of giftedness in order to understand the interaction effects of giftedness with various disabilities and disorders. Treating the presenting symptoms of a disorder is often ineffective if the person's giftedness is not addressed (Amend & Peters, 2012). However, while attending to the individual's giftedness often proves ameliorative, it is likely to be insufficient if dual issues are present (Mika, 2006).

It would be far easier for professionals to extricate the symptoms of a disorder from the manifestations of giftedness if they viewed giftedness similarly to the way they view developmental disability—as an organizing principle. Currently, practitioners receive no training in the characteristics of the gifted that would enable them to sort through these complex variables (Amend & Beljan, 2009). "Well-meaning professionals—with limited or no knowledge about gifted individuals—do not have a framework from which to view the behaviors of gifted children as 'typical' for them, thus resulting in misinterpretation" (Amend & Peters, 2012, p. 586). Gifted individuals experience indescribable injury when their typical reactions are seen as personality defects. In addition, lives can be lost when serious disorders, masked by high intelligence, fail to be recognized and treated. The gifted should be compared to the norms for their own group, rather than with societal norms. This caveat will not appear in the *DSM-5*; however, knowledgeable practitioners working with the gifted can ask, "Are these symptoms *in excess* of the traits typically found in the gifted population?"

LEVELS OF GIFTEDNESS

Although much has been written about all the ways people can be gifted, little attention has been given to different levels of giftedness. In some school districts, children are divided into two groups—gifted and nongifted—and those in the gifted group are treated as if they are all alike (Gross, 2009). Giftedness occurs in degrees. Extent of giftedness is as critical to consider as extent of disability. "The range of scores of children in the top 1% on IQ—from 135 to more than 200—is as broad as the range of scores from the 2nd percentile...to the 98th (Gross, 2009, p. 338). The boundaries of both giftedness and intellectual disability are debatable, but at the furthest edges, differences are more readily acknowledged. Unless they have been completely hidden, a child who reads before age 4 and a child who is not communicating by the age of 4 readily capture attention.

It is at the margins of exceptionality where the battle lines are drawn. The overrepresentation of ethnic minorities and multilingual children in programs for the milder range of intellectual disability has been an ongoing source of concern. The underrepresentation in gifted programs of culturally diverse groups, children for whom English is a second language and those of low socioeconomic status, has also attracted considerable attention (e.g., Esquierdo & Arreguín-Anderson, 2012; Ford, Moore, & Scott, 2011; Latz & Adams, 2011).

Broadening the selection criteria for gifted programs has not appreciably increased the percentage of these underrepresented groups. Changing "gifted" to "talented" and identifying the top 10% instead of the top 5% is not likely to be the magic bullet that changes the distribution. State classifications of giftedness were broadened from 1% to 2%, and then to 3%, and then to 5%; however, inequitable ethnic, linguistic, and socioeconomic distributions persist (Matthews & Kirsch, 2011). "Some of the states with high placement rates for minority students also have high placement rates for white students" (National Research Council, 2002). All percentages are arbitrary. It would be unconscionable to categorize the lowest performing 10% of the school as having "Intellectual Developmental Disorder."

The fact that there are degrees of intellectual disability is widely accepted. Labels for various gradations of intellectual disability have changed swiftly due to the speed with which they turn into pejoratives. The *DSM-IV* (American Psychiatric Association, 1994) specified degrees of severity as *mildly, moderately, severely,* and *profoundly,* roughly equivalent to the standard deviation (SD) from the mean.[1] Each SD denotes a different level of intellectual and adaptive functioning, requiring increasing degrees of support, from intermittent to pervasive.

There is no consistent nomenclature to represent different degrees of intellectual ability. For decades, IQ and achievement test manuals have used the term "superior" to designate children from 120 to 129 IQ and "very superior" for children at or above 130 IQ (2 SD above the norm). Negative connotations of these terms, and the logical conclusion that children at the opposite end of the spectrum are "inferior" (Dai, 2009), has

TABLE 4.1 **LEVELS OF INTELLECTUAL GIFTEDNESS**

Descriptive Term	Composite Scoring Range	Normal Curve Score Range
Profoundly gifted	175+	+5 SD and above
Exceptionally gifted	160–174	+4–4.99 SD
Highly gifted	145–159	+3–3.99 SD
Gifted	130–144	+2–2.99 SD
Advanced (superior)	120–129	+1.33–1.99 SD
High average	110–119	+.067–1.32 SD
Average	90–109	–0.67–+0.66 SD

Note: SD means standard deviation(s). The descriptive terms and corresponding ranges vary among systems and tests. These are intended for a test with a normative mean of 100 and standard deviation of 15.

Source: Wasserman (2007, p. 60, used with permission).

not led as yet to new terminology. However, in 1999, in his role as Project Director for the fifth edition of the *Stanford-Binet Intelligence Scale* (SB5), John Wasserman requested that an international committee of over 20 diagnosticians and experts in the field of gifted education collectively determine nomenclature for the different levels of giftedness. After a full year of deliberations, the above descriptors were established (Wasserman, 2003, 2007). Table 4.1 describes the psychometric designations at different levels of giftedness, the IQ or composite score range, and the SD from the norm. It would be helpful if these designations were codified in new IQ test manuals.

Inconsistent terminology is a serious issue. At this juncture, the term "profoundly gifted" can refer to children of at least 180 IQ, or 175 IQ, or 160 IQ, or 145 IQ. The thought processes of children in the exceptionally and profoundly gifted ranges are very different from children in the moderately gifted range (Gross, 2009; Lovecky, 1994).

> A striking characteristic of exceptionally and profoundly gifted children is their capacity for "dual processing"—the seeming ability to process two sets of information simultaneously and in parallel. ... Both the prevalence and quality of this are significantly more marked in ... children of IQ 175 or above. (Gross, 2009, p. 339)

I tested a 9-year-old boy who attained an IQ score of 237+. He had an extraordinary mathematical mind. Upon meeting me, he inquired how old I was and the highest IQ score ever attained. When he was in kindergarten, his mother would reward him for getting along with the other children by reading him a chapter in a college physics book. He was asked how he solves math problems, and replied that he can do two mathematical operations at the same time, and on a good day, he can do three. His mind was quite different from that of a child with a 145 IQ.

In research conducted with gifted populations, the sample is most often defined as those who have been placed in a gifted program. Criteria for selection to gifted programs can range from 115 IQ to 140 IQ or bypass intelligence scales altogether, with achievement tests, portfolios, checklists, grades, or recommendations. The gifted population in one study bears little resemblance to the gifted population in another study, which leads to conflicting results and confusing interpretations.

> The challenge with having multiple definitions, ways to interpret those definitions, and methods to identify gifted children who meet criteria outlined in those definitions, is that it results in tremendous heterogeneity among the gifted populations under study. As such, results of research ... are less generalizable, and replication of findings becomes more challenging. (Martin, Burns, & Schonlau, 2010, p. 33)

Until recently, there has not been a perceived need for terms that distinguish highly from exceptionally from profoundly gifted. For the last 50 years, the highest IQ scores generated by modern tests made it virtually impossible to differentiate levels of giftedness beyond the highly gifted range. As a result, most exceptionally and profoundly gifted children were never identified.

Wasserman set the stage for the testing industry to develop methods of identifying individuals at the higher regions of giftedness. In addition to creating a forum to establish consistent terminology to represent extreme levels, Wasserman assembled a group of examiners of exceptionally gifted children and asked what they needed in an IQ test, he arranged for extensive validation studies to be conducted on the SB5 with exceptionally and profoundly gifted children, and, in July of 2000, he organized a "Gifted Summit" with test constructors and key members of the gifted assessment community to discuss the necessity of raising ceilings on IQ tests (Silverman, 2007). As a result, Richard Woodcock extended Woodcock–Johnson test score ranges over 200, and extended norms were devised for the SB5, raising the ceiling as high as 225 (Roid, 2003).

In 2007, data from a nationwide study of 334 gifted children sponsored by the National Association for Gifted Children were submitted to Pearson Assessments. J. J. Zhu used this database to create extended norms for the fourth edition of the *Wechsler Intelligence Scale for Children* (WISC-IV) (Zhu, Cayton, Weiss, & Gabel, 2008). The maximum subtest scaled score was raised from 19 to 28. The maximum Index (composite) and Full Scale scores were raised from 160 to 210. The new norms were posted February 7, 2008, on the Pearson website in *WISC-IV Technical Report #7*: http://pearsonassess.com/NR/rdonlyres/C1C19227-BC79-46D9-B43C-8E4A114F7E1F/0/WISCIV_TechReport_7.pdf.

Currently, Pearson is conducting a validation study with highly gifted children to extend the norms on the fourth edition of the *Wechsler Preschool and Primary Scale of Intelligence* (WPPSI-IV). These new developments have created a need for consistent descriptive labels for higher ranges of intelligence.

There are vast differences in developmental needs at the lower and higher realms of giftedness. "Some of the behavioral characteristics of the highly gifted resemble those found in children with learning disabilities" (S. Shaywitz et al., 2001, p. 21). Exceptionally gifted children are among the highest risk gifted populations (Gross, 2009; Hafenstein & Honeck, 2011; Rimm, Gilman, & Silverman, 2008). When not recognized, these children are in danger of depression, loneliness, misdiagnosis with AD/HD, and even suicidal ideation (Silverman, Cayton, & Raiford, 2008). They are often seen as inattentive and unmotivated. Continuously given schoolwork they have already mastered, they frequently are driven into patterns of underachievement.

Gifted educators have been so focused on the development of talented children (approximately 120 IQ and above) that they have not taken seriously the needs of children in the higher extremes of ability. These children are beyond the radar of teacher training programs in the field and outside the range of typical provisions for the gifted. Many parents of exceptionally and profoundly gifted children have found schools to be so unresponsive to their children that they have had no choice but to homeschool them (Goodwin & Gustavson, 2011; Lovecky, 2011). There are numerous cases of profoundly gifted children who refuse to go to school. One 6-year-old told her parents, *"I'm not going back there. They aren't teaching me anything new."* Gross (2009) describes "Australia's youngest school dropout at age 5 years after 2 weeks of stultifying boredom being 'introduced' with the other 5-year-olds to 'reading readiness' although he had been reading since age 2" (p. 348).

Parents of exceptionally gifted children often select homeschooling from the beginning as the best educational option, as it enables their children to progress at their own rate. One consequence of the burgeoning homeschooling movement (Kearney, 2011) for exceptionally gifted children is that it has rendered these children invisible to public school educators. Few educators are aware that they exist, the incidence of them in the population, or their educational needs. On the grounds that there are "so few of them," they have been considered of little consequence.

There are far more exceptionally gifted children in the population than anyone realizes. Several investigators have discovered bewilderingly frequent scores at the upper end of the IQ distribution (e.g., J. Gallagher & Moss, 1963; McGuffog, Feiring, & M. Lewis, 1987; H. Robinson, 1981; N. Robinson, Zigler, & J. Gallagher, 2000; Silverman & Kearney, 1989; Terman, 1925). Jensen (1980) reported, "there is an excess of high IQs about 150. ... It is generally not statistically detectable in samples numbering fewer than two or three thousand" (p. 84). Terman (1925) disclosed:

> The group contains an unexpectedly large proportion of cases in the upper IQ ranges. ...there is an appreciable excess of 150 IQ cases, or better, and over and above the theoretical expectation. Above 160 the number of cases found increases out of all proportion to the theoretically expected number and by IQ 170 exceeds it several times. (p. 633)

Over a 33-year period, the Gifted Development Center (GDC) has identified approximately 1,000 children with IQ scores at or above 160. This represents 18% of the children referred for assessment. And 97 of these children scored above 200 IQ. In a study of 47 children assessed at Children of High Potential (CHIP) in Australia, 38% were above 160 (Alsop, 1997). Support groups for "PG" (profoundly gifted) children and their families were formed in the 1980s in Maine and Colorado. In 1989, 15 of the families in Maine and 23 of the families in Colorado were compared on a number of variables (Silverman & Kearney, 1989). Data on the first 241 exceptionally gifted children (160+ IQ) brought to GDC for assessment were analyzed and presented in 1997 (K. Rogers & Silverman, 1997) and compared with studies of moderately gifted children (K. Rogers & Silverman, 2001). More extensive studies of this population will be forthcoming. Extended norms on intelligence scales are likely to increase the visibility of, and research on, this neglected population. Hopefully, it will rekindle psychology's interest in the development of these outliers.

CHARACTERISTICS OF GIFTEDNESS

Working effectively with gifted populations of any age requires knowledge of the traits associated with giftedness. The *Characteristics of Giftedness Scale* was originally developed in 1973 (Silverman, 1978) and consisted of 16 items. Since 1979, it has served as a screening tool in clinical practice to ascertain the likelihood of a child testing in the gifted range on an individual, standardized intelligence scale. For 20 years, it was administered to parents in a phone interview, and parents were asked to provide examples of each characteristic. The instrument is now a 4-point Likert scale, ranging from *Not True* to *Very True* that is sent to parents electronically. It has been expanded to 25 traits reported consistently in the literature and found to be predictive of gifted IQ scores throughout 33 years of clinical practice ($N > 6,000$). The instrument has been used in several clinical and school settings worldwide; there is also a teacher version. It has proven useful for children between the ages of 3 and 18. The descriptors were selected to meet the following criteria:

1. Representative of the majority of gifted children assessed
2. Applicable to a wide age range
3. Generalizable to children of varied socioeconomic, ethnic, and cultural backgrounds
4. Gender fair
5. Easily observed in the home environment
6. Brief and clearly worded for ease of interpretation by parents
7. Valid at the lowest and highest levels of giftedness
8. Able to discriminate between gifted and average children
9. Supported by clinical and empirical research

Several studies of the instrument were conducted with gifted samples (e.g., K. Rogers & Silverman, 2001; M. Rogers & Silverman, 1988; Silverman, Chitwood, & Waters, 1986). In the largest study ($N > 1{,}000$), 84% of the children whose parents endorsed 75% of the characteristics achieved IQ scores in the superior and gifted ranges (>120 IQ) (Silverman, 1978, 2003). Parents of 241 exceptionally gifted children (>160 IQ) endorsed at least 80% of the characteristics (K. Rogers & Silverman, 2001). The 17 *italicized* items in the scale below clearly differentiated (<.01) between 38 gifted and 42 average third and fourth graders (M. Rogers, 1986).

CHARACTERISTICS OF GIFTEDNESS SCALE

Compared to other children your child's age, to what extent do these descriptors fit your child?

- Reasons well (good thinker)
- *Learns rapidly*
- *Has extensive vocabulary*
- *Has an excellent memory*
- *Has a long attention span (if interested)*
- Sensitive (feelings hurt easily)
- Shows compassion
- *Perfectionistic*
- Intense
- Morally sensitive
- *Has strong curiosity*
- *Perseverant in areas of interest*
- Has high degree of energy
- *Prefers older companions or adults*
- Has a wide range of interests
- *Has a great sense of humor*
- *Early or avid reader (if too young to read, loves being read to)*
- *Concerned with justice, fairness*

(continued)

> ◉ *Judgment mature for age at times*
> ◉ *Is a keen observer*
> ◉ *Has a vivid imagination*
> ◉ *Is highly creative*
> ◉ Tends to question authority
> ◉ *Has facility with numbers*
> ◉ *Good at jigsaw puzzles*
>
> (Silverman, 2003)

Some of these items are stronger indicators of giftedness than others. Extensive vocabulary, excellent memory, speed of learning, interest in books, asks probing questions, and math understanding were all highly significant (<.001) discriminators of gifted versus average children (M. Rogers, 1986). Compared to samples of moderately gifted children, exceptionally gifted children (>160 IQ) preferred older friends, were more emotionally sensitive, were more frequently reported to have excellent memory, were more intensely interested in reading, and explored a wide variety of interests (K. Rogers & Silverman, 2001).

EARLY INDICATORS OF ADVANCED DEVELOPMENT

How early can developmental delay be detected? Within the first months of life. How early can giftedness be detected? Earlier than we would suspect. Many educators staunchly believe that gifted children cannot be identified with any accuracy until around third grade. But psychological investigation of infant development tells an entirely different story. These indicators of advanced development in infants are well documented by decades of research:

◉ High newborn cry count (N. Robinson, 1993)
◉ Alertness (Gogel et al., 1985; Louis, 1993; M. Rogers, 1986)

- Rapid habituation to visual stimuli (M. Lewis & Louis, 1991; N. Robinson & H. Robinson, 1992)
- Preference and longer attention span for novel stimuli (Fisher, 1990; M. Rogers, 1986; Storfer, 1990; Tannenbaum, 1992)
- Faster progression from reflexive to intentional behavior (Berche Cruz, 1987)
- Curiosity (M. Lewis & Louis, 1991)
- Unusual memory (Parkinson, 1990; M. Rogers, 1986; Tannenbaum, 1992)
- Awareness and interest in the world (Louis, 1993; Maxwell, 1995)
- Early receptive language skills (A. W. Gottfried et al., 2006)
- Early attempts to communicate (utter sounds, first words, and speech) (Louis, 1993)
- Early smiling (Henderson & Ebner, 1997)
- Responsiveness (Gogel et al., 1985)
- Intensity (Maxwell, 1995)
- Reduced need for sleep (Gaunt, 1989; Henderson & Ebner, 1997)
- Intense reactions to frustration (M. Rogers, 1986)
- Rapid learning rate (Louis & M. Lewis, 1992; M. Rogers, 1986; Tannenbaum, 1992)
- Advanced progression through the developmental milestones (Alomar, 2003; Henderson & Ebner, 1997)

She was alert at birth, and smiled within 24 hours thereafter.

B has always been developmentally ahead since she was newborn. On the warming table she would turn and focus at our voices calling her name when she was only 15 minutes old. We started to read to her right away when she was 2 days old and she would focus at the books and be very content for long periods of time that increased as she got older.

She held her head up at 2 days. She made direct and purposeful eye contact before she was a month old. She disassembled the humidifier in her room, lined parts up in the order in which they came out at 10 months.

Michael Lewis and Barbara Louis (1991) conducted numerous studies of gifted and average preschoolers, investigated parental perceptions of their gifted children's early development, and reviewed existing studies of gifted young children. They concluded that the primary signs of giftedness noted by both researchers and parents of gifted children were "early verbal ability, strong memory skills, and abstract reasoning" (p. 377). One surprising observation was that an infant's pleasure in learning was highly predictive of later cognitive scores. Advanced language development was the strongest determinant in the identification of young gifted children. Ranking in first place, over 60% of 276 parents queried endorsed *expressive and productive language* as the most prominent signifier of their child's giftedness. Nancy Robinson (1993) concurred that precocious verbal abilities are more likely to be recognized in young children than unusual visual-spatial abilities.

> During the early years (perhaps throughout childhood), parents tend to do best at identifying precocious children in domains in which there are distinctive milestones and normative expectations, as there are for the emergence of language and reading. Parents are, for example, quite good at identifying toddlers with broad vocabularies and complex sentence structure and better at identifying preschoolers who reason well mathematically and read early than those who exhibit precocious spatial reasoning and memory, areas in which adults typically do not possess such informal timetables. (N. Robinson, 1993, p. 510)

Martin Rogers (1986) asked parents of 39 gifted and 38 average children to describe their children's development during the first 36 months. Nearly two-thirds of each group had kept baby books as records. The groups were matched by socioeconomic level and geographic location. Differences between the achievement scores of gifted and average children were highly significant ($p > .001$). As with other modern studies (see N. Robinson, 1993), no differences were found between the two groups in physical development. Activity level of the samples was nearly identical. One of the earliest signs of giftedness differentiating the groups was alertness ($p < .006$). One parent said that when her child was seven months old "he was watching Sesame Street so intently that when he finally fell asleep he was still watching and just fell over backwards" (M. Rogers & Silverman, 1988, p. 5).

Attention span ($p < .002$), powers of observation ($p < .001$), memory ($p < .001$), age at which the child showed interest in time ($p < .009$), interest in puzzles and mazes ($p < .009$), and age the child could put together a 20-piece puzzle ($p < .006$) were all significantly different between the groups. Over 90% of the parents of the gifted saw their children as having excellent memories and advanced vocabulary development. Over 60% found their children to be curious, creative, imaginative, and observant. They asked "probing" rather than simple questions. At the age of 18 months, one child wondered, "What is air? How high up does it go? Why doesn't it all float away?" (p. 16). Imaginary playmates showed up in both groups, but only one child in the average group had more than one of these playmates, while gifted children often had several of them.

> As a newborn, he didn't want to sleep, and he could hold his head up early. But it was his eyes: you could just see him looking and drinking it all in. Strangers would comment on how preternaturally alert he was. He inhaled books, both read to him and paging through them on his own. On his third birthday he got one of those large floor puzzles. Straight out of the box he had it assembled inside of 15 minutes—with the image facing the floor. He was a Lego maniac from the moment he could handle a Duplo. He rarely asked, "Why?" It was always, "How's it work?" He was "incessant curiosity in Crocs." (J. Merrill, 2012, pp. 1–2)

Gogel et al. (1985) polled 1,039 parents to determine how early they suspected that their children were gifted. Seven percent noted differences in their children's alertness and responsiveness within the first 6 months. Fifteen percent recognized the signs of giftedness when their children were between 6 and

12 months of age. Nearly half the sample observed developmental differences before the age of 2. Most parents saw clear signs of giftedness well before school age (Gogel et al., 1985; Kaufmann & Sexton, 1983). Studies in other countries have produced similar results. Alomar (2003) reported that some parents in Kuwait became aware that their infants (3 to 12 months) were progressing through the developmental milestones at a faster rate.

Some additional signs of giftedness in preschoolers, beyond the general traits in the *Characteristics of Gifted Scale* and the indicators of giftedness in infants include:

- early and extensive language development
- enjoyment and speed of problem-solving
- early use of symbol systems and capacity for symbolic thought
- more complex play patterns
- personal maturity
- heightened concentration
- intuitive insights
- early interest in time (e.g., clocks, calendars)
- recognition of letters before age 2
- ability to count to 10 by age 3
- ability to put together a 20-piece puzzle by age 3
- ability to sight read an easy reader by age 4

A mother of a profoundly gifted child reported how astonished she was to discover that her daughter could read at the age of 3.

> She was reading a package label and asked me, "Mom, what does 'Not recommended for children under the age of three' mean?" We've been struggling to keep up with her ever since. She has always asked unusual questions—she once wanted to know why time doesn't run backwards.

Considerable research has been conducted with gifted and nongifted preschoolers (e.g., A. W. Gottfried et al., 2006; Louis & M. Lewis, 1992; N. Robinson, 2008b; White, 1985). Louis and

M. Lewis (1992) studied 118 preschoolers in two ranges of intelligence. The mean IQ score of the gifted group was 149 and the mean for the average group was 118. Parents of the gifted group described their children's abstract reasoning, memory, and creative imagination significantly more often ($p < .05$) than parents of average children, whereas parents of average children were much more likely to describe their child's abilities in terms of factual knowledge (body parts, alphabet, numbers, special knowledge). White (1985) provided an interesting list of characteristics from the Harvard Preschool Project that differentiated the gifted group from those who were less advanced:

- advanced capacity for language;
- an unusual ability to detect discrepancies and errors in logic;
- the ability to anticipate future events;
- advanced abstract reasoning abilities;
- ability to take the perspective of others;
- original associations;
- planning and executing complex activities;
- effective use of resources;
- exceptional concentration;
- the ability to process large amounts of information.

Knowledge of the research on young children should dispel the myths that giftedness cannot be identified in young children. It also challenges the perception that parents are poor informants about the early development of their gifted children. Now that we know gifted children can be recognized in early childhood, should we do so?

THE IMPORTANCE OF EARLY DETECTION

At what age should exceptional children be identified? When we look at every other exceptionality, the answer is quite clear. The earlier the better. Early identification permits early intervention.

Early intervention is necessary for optimal development. This is common knowledge throughout the world. What is not common knowledge—even in the field of gifted education—is that the same principle applies to giftedness (Witty, 1958). Hollingworth (1942) reported that the earlier highly gifted children were identified, the more favorable their development.

Those who passionately believe that giftedness is the result of environmental opportunity should be equally passionate about locating children of promise in the early years. Giftedness can be found in young children, and, without appropriate stimulation, it can also be lost (J. Gallagher, 1979; Henderson & Ebner, 1997; M. Lewis & Louis, 1991). From their research, Michael Lewis and Barbara Louis (1991) contend that stability of IQ scores in the gifted is maintained only in appropriately nourishing environments. Children of poverty are offered less stimulation than those from affluent families. "If the environment were to remain optimal during the preschool period and beyond, gifted status would remain stable. This is the most influential argument for early enrichment programs for young gifted children" (p. 377).

Much has been written about the neural plasticity of the brain: the capacity of the brain to change structurally and functionally through environmental stimulation. Kalbfleisch (2009) perceives giftedness as "a type of neural plasticity that we do not yet fully understand" (p. 276). "Environmental and sensory stimulation from birth onward lays the wiring and develops the mechanisms for a child's ability to learn information and develop skills throughout life" (Henderson & Ebner, 1997, p. 63). Development is a continuous, dynamic interaction of heredity and environment. In their article, "The Biological Basis for Early Intervention with Gifted Children," Henderson and Ebner (1997) offer a strong rationale for stimulating early childhood programs for the gifted.

> The developing brain [is] extremely sensitive to its environment.
> ...The period from 1 to 3 years of age is especially critical for typically developing children, as well as those with developmental

delay. We suggest that the critical time frame for gifted children may begin even earlier, and if this is the case, adjustments may be needed to accommodate the precocious developmental time line many gifted children follow. (p. 59)

The most effective way to increase equitable distributions of culturally diverse gifted children, multilingual gifted children, rural gifted children, and economically disadvantaged gifted children is to find them as early as possible and enhance their abilities before they fade. Every year the environment exerts a heavier hand on the life of a child. Children are much less likely to underachieve if they are placed, from preschool on, in environments that relish their aptitudes. The research has clearly demonstrated that early enrichment enables low-income gifted children from diverse backgrounds to maintain their high abilities (see Feiring, Louis, Ukeje, & M. Lewis, 1997, for a review).

Early identification and intervention are particularly important for twice exceptional children. The greater one's abstract reasoning abilities, the easier it is for the brain to design strategies that camouflage the problem. For example, gifted children with serious hearing impairments have been known to read lips so well that the hearing loss was not discovered for many years. Many children with visual weaknesses use verbal reasoning to talk their way through visual tasks. Such compensation strategies cover up the difficulties temporarily, but they do not resolve the issues. At a later point in development, early strategies may fail.

Gifted children often are allergy-prone, may be colicky babies, and may sustain repeated infections, particularly if they are in day care. Toddlers who have experienced chronic ear infections (more than nine in the first 3 years) are at risk for central auditory processing disorder (CAPD) and attentional issues (Feagans, 1986). Early detection and treatment of ear infections can reverse or prevent conductive hearing losses. Infant screening for hearing impairments and amplification of sound (hearing aids) can also prevent cognitive delays (Yoshinaga-Itano, Sedey, Coulter, & Mehl, 1998).

Fine motor weaknesses are common in gifted boys (Terrassier, 1985). They may appear as clumsiness, lack of coordination, poor balance, delayed choice of handedness, poor pencil grip, slow handwriting speed, inability to cross the midline of the body without switching hands, difficulty cutting or drawing simple figures, and avoidance of motor tasks. Parents are often told that their children are so smart that they will "outgrow" these problems. When any of these difficulties are observed, it is important for the child to be evaluated by a pediatric occupational therapist as early as possible. A program of exercises before the child is 7 is likely to prevent problems with handwriting and underachievement down the road (Silverman, 2009c).

Preschool and primary years are the most critical in the development of a child's self-concept. There is that moment of truth when the young gifted child discovers that he or she is different from other children.

> One mother reported that her 4-year-old son wrote a note to hang on the front door, telling his friends that he did not want to play. He then crumpled the note, and sadly explained to his mother, "I can't hang this note up, Mom. They can't read!" (Roedell, 1988, p. 7)

It is important for young gifted children to have the opportunity to find true peers—children with similar abilities and interests. Asynchronous gifted children whose intellectual development far exceeds their physical development may have different sets of friends for different types of activities: "one set of peers for reading and discussing books, and another set for riding tricycles and playing ball" (Roedell, 1988, p. 7). The ability to adapt to less advanced age mates is useful, but it is insufficient to be emotionally fulfilling. Without true peers, young gifted children may hide their abilities or withdraw or be seen as strange.

> One 4-year-old boy was diagnosed as emotionally disturbed by his preschool teachers because of his tendency to withdraw from social interaction. His worried parents enrolled him in a program

113

for highly gifted children, where his friendly, outgoing manner demonstrated that his withdrawn behavior had been the result of having no intellectual peers with whom to interact. Without someone he could talk to, he stopped talking.

When a gifted child finds a real friend, the child's personality will blossom. Ronald, a gifted 5 year old, explained it well when he commented, "Do you know why Bill is my best friend? Because he's the only one who understands the kind of guy I really am." (Roedell, 1988, p. 7)

Some think about gifted children as a nation's most precious resource and recommend that society provide early environmental stimulation to conserve this national treasure. But the most compelling reason for early intervention is to protect the children themselves. "Children who are out of step with their peers may be denied a happy, healthy childhood" (N. Robinson, 1993, p. 508).

The field of psychology demonstrates social responsibility to those who are disabled. We are strong advocates for early intervention to assure optimal development. Early identification of the gifted should be seen as rivaling in importance the early identification of all other exceptionalities. Optimal development of the gifted is at least as valuable as optimal development of any other special-needs group.

GIFTEDNESS IN ADULTS

I frequently ask audiences, "How many of you used to be gifted?" This would be a rather absurd question in the context of any other exceptionality. Stephanie Tolan (1994/1995) uses the label, "the gifted ex-child." It is problematic to have been identified for a gifted program as a child and then learn that you can only be a gifted adult if you're eminent. If you aren't eminent, does that mean you were never gifted in the first place? The idea that you can "outgrow" giftedness makes very little sense (Fiedler, 2012). The characteristics of giftedness do not disappear in adult life. Some actually intensify. Some become disguised. Giftedness is a different way of experiencing (Piechowski, 1991b).

> The unusual developmental trajectory of the gifted creates an extraordinary experience of life for the individual at any age, whether or not that individual is able to achieve in ways society recognizes and values. The achievement orientation that has always existed for adults and is now taking over the field of gifted education makes it difficult for the gifted to understand the qualities of mind that make them different. (Tolan, 1994/1995, p. 13)

> If giftedness is merely an artifact of rapid progress through normal developmental stages, it could be destined to fade when others "catch up" or even move beyond. If, on the other hand, it is a quality of mind that creates a genuinely unusual developmental trajectory, it would be a stable attribute, remaining with the individual throughout life whether outwardly evident or not. (p. 14)

High ability may or may not translate into high achievement in school or in life. There are brilliant volunteers, cooks, parents, teachers, therapists, and so on, who devote themselves to helping others rather than to achieving lasting recognition. The delight with learning that has been documented in very young children (M. Lewis & Louis, 1991) is a lifelong quality of giftedness. However, it does not necessarily translate into "task commitment" to perform to others' expectations. Wallach (1995) maintains that asynchronous development in childhood leads to pronounced strengths and weaknesses in highly gifted adults and that asynchrony often exists between the highly gifted person's needs and the expectations of the environment. Since they think so differently from the decision makers in their fields, the highly gifted may not rise to the top.

The majority of gifted adults were never identified as gifted in childhood (Stalnacke & Smedler, 2011) and do not recognize their giftedness (Kuipers, 2010). They have no positive way to describe the feelings and attributes that make them feel like outsiders. They only know that they don't fit in. They often assume that there must be something wrong with them—that in some mysterious way they are deficient. Fiedler (2012) describes "The Invisible Ones" (p. 38) who move so far into denial that their giftedness vanishes from sight. Many gifted adults seek therapy to try to gain a better understanding of their differences. And many gifted individuals enter the profession of psychology for the same reasons, as well as to help others (Silverman & Conarton, 2005). Empathy, a quality that draws many psychologists into this practice, is one of the hallmarks of giftedness in adults (Perrone-McGovern, Boo, & Vannatter, 2012).

Giftedness is the capacity for high abstract reasoning and greater awareness. It bestows on its bearer overexcitability, intensity, complexity, and idealism. The complexity of gifted minds is mirrored in the complexity of their emotions. These individuals tend to be emotionally sensitive, empathic, compassionate; they have a difficult time accepting criticism; and they often feel isolated and misunderstood (Perrone-McGovern et al., 2012). They need therapists who can deal with their complexity and intensity.

> "Gifted people are like high wattage transmitters that emit very powerful signals. In order to pick up the transmissions and decode them the sound system needs to be able to operate on the same frequency." If the intensity of the "transmitter" is much greater than the intensity of the "receiver," the receiver will be overpowered and the message will not be understood. This principle also applies to complexity, speed, use of metaphor, multiple layers of meaning, processing several ideas simultaneously, synthesizing, etc. (L. Azpeitia, as quoted in Leviton, 1995)

"Gifted adults do not make decisions easily. With every step they take, they are aware of a multitude of available alternatives, as well as the possible unexpected consequences that could occur because of their decision" (Roeper, 2011b). Highly intelligent people see so many connections between seemingly unrelated events and so many potential outcomes that they may not be able to sort through all of the information to find an appropriate path. Decision-making is simpler when one has less information. If one is petrified of making a mistake and sees infinite options, but believes that all but one will be a dreadful error, life becomes a perilous walk on a tightrope with no safety net below.

Greater awareness and insightfulness, combined with honesty, often gets gifted individuals in trouble. They see through hypocrisy; they sense hidden agendas; they see the essence of a situation (Roeper, 1991/1995). But their truth-telling is unwelcome. And they are unwilling to play the game of pretending things aren't happening when they see quite clearly what is really going on. They alienate people until they learn that they can't always say what they see. They need guidance in determining when and how to share their perceptions.

> An ability to view several aspects of a situation simultaneously, to understand several layers of self within another, and to get quickly to the core of an issue are characteristic of gifted adults with the trait of perceptiveness. ...The gifted adult must come to understand that the question is not whose world view is more accurate but how to use disparate views in ways that enhance connectedness to others and further understanding of the self. Neither the self nor the other is defective or stupid. ...The dilemma for the perceptive gifted adult is how and when to use the gift with self and others. (Lovecky, 1990/1995, pp. 76–79)

The need for mental stimulation that is so apparent in gifted infants and toddlers is a stable characteristic throughout the lifespan. My father lived a long life—98 years—but he probably died of boredom. He lost his sight to macular degeneration of the retina and he lost most of his hearing. The decline of his sensory equipment left him without sufficient stimulation of his fine mind to make life worth living. At the age of 93, Annemarie Roeper found the lack of intellectual stimulation in a retirement home for the elderly stifling to her spirit. She craved the companionship of gifted peers with whom to exercise her quick wit and sharp intellectual fencing skills. To the very end of her life, she continued to contribute books and professional articles. Roeper (2011a) shared:

> Much has been said and written and researched about gifted children. Gifted adolescents also have a place in the consciousness of researchers. But it seems that there is a dearth of information when it comes to the gifted adult and giftedness in old age has not, as yet, caught our attention as a worthwhile subject of investigation. (p. 23)

Fiedler (2012) has begun to explore this uncharted territory with a stage theory of adult giftedness that extends beyond 80 years of age. One of the earlier phases, The Explorers Stage, from 35 to 50, is described in the following passage:

> The image of a kaleidoscope probably most accurately depicts what life is like from the ages of 35–50 for a gifted adult in the 21st century. The brightly colored bits and pieces of their lives consist of thoughts, feelings, interests, and experiences from before, along with new insights, understandings, and internal urgings toward generativity—all of this swirling into place and then recombining periodically into new patterns. Furthermore, because of their asynchronous development, they may actually seem to be different ages simultaneously—very young and childlike in their joyful delight at the world and all it offers while also being highly concerned with significant issues such as war and poverty—issues usually associated with mature minds. (Fiedler, 2012, p. 30)

In Roeper's (1991/1995) oft-cited essay on "Gifted Adults: Their Characteristics and Emotions," she discussed 23 characteristics of this population, such as being driven by their giftedness, feeling overwhelmed by the pressure of their own creativity, enjoying intense intellectual discussions, searching for meaning, needing solitude and time for contemplation, developing their own methods of grasping concepts, being able to predict trends, seeing relationships, reacting to image-making at the expense of truth, perfectionism, sense of humor, multipotentiality, dismay with the short-sighted behavior of others, recognizing the difference between justice and equality, difficulties with authority figures, strong moral convictions, and the need to make a difference in the world. In a recent essay on this topic, Roeper (2011b) elaborated on some of these themes:

> All of their lives, the gifted live with a sense of isolation because of their greater intellectual power, greater awareness of why things are happening, and greater capacity for logical conclusions that don't always coincide with the way other people see reality. Their ability to predict certain events frequently meets with general disbelief by others. Often they realize that some plan is bound to end in failure because certain aspects are not being considered.... (p. 1)

When a psychologist evaluates a child and concludes that the child is gifted, it often has a ripple effect on the parents' self-perceptions. Even grandparents wonder if they were gifted, too. Parents of gifted children are usually gifted as well. They are often "casualties of a childhood where their needs as gifted children were misunderstood, pathologized or unmet" (Wallach, 1995, p. 37). Parent forums and support groups prevent isolation and enable parents to share solutions to common problems. "Gifted people need to talk to each other because their development, experiences and needs are radically different from the norm" (Wallach, 1995, p. 38).

The most precious goal for the gifted is finding meaning. They are meaning-makers. Skilled, knowledgeable, intelligent mental health workers provide the safety net that enhances their self-awareness and allows them to embark on their quest to make a difference in this world.

> Gifted adults, perhaps more than any other group, have the potential to achieve a high degree of self-actualization. Despite

the problems that being gifted can bring, the positive social and emotional aspects of giftedness can more than compensate for the problems. To continue to hear the flowers singing and to turn visions and dreams to reality throughout an entire lifetime is a goal to be desired by every gifted adult. (Lovecky, 1986, p. 575)

NOTE

1. It is unclear at this time if the *DSM-5* will be worded similarly.

The Psychology of Giftedness

*Great minds have always encountered violent opposition
from mediocre minds.*

Albert Einstein

t is time for a psychology of giftedness—time to recognize the developmental differences, personality traits, lifespan development, particular issues and struggles of the gifted, as well as the consequences of not being acceptable. The norm, the average, is still revered, and those who are dissimilar are marked by society as *"ab*normal." It is painful to be called a "freak," or to be treated as one, even if there is no name-calling involved. The field of psychology has always been the champion of marginalized groups. Through our efforts, slurs against racial and ethnic minorities and the disabled are no longer tolerated. The gifted are still fair game.

Precious few psychology books have been written on the topic of giftedness, and those that exist often blur the distinction between eminence and giftedness. The focus on eminence ignores the exceptionally gifted, the twice exceptional, underachievers, gifted preschoolers, women who chose parenting as the main expression of their gifts, gifted teachers, gifted elders, self-actualizing volunteers—the gifted whose names shall never be known. When only those who transform domains are acknowledged, the psychological needs of the gifted are invisible. Gifted individuals have deep, complex inner lives that deserve exploration. It is time to "unravel the mysteries of...giftedness" (Zigler & Farber, 1985, p. 388).

FEELING DIFFERENT

Gifted individuals feel different from everyone else because they *are* different. Their differences are apparent from the beginning to the end of their lives. At birth, these intense balls of energy crave incessant stimulation, may be colicky and have a penchant for not sleeping. Despite never-ending sleepless nights, parents of gifted children, by and large, cherish their children. Gifted babies tend to be responsive infants, sometimes smiling early, which elicits the best from their parents (Morrissey & Brown, 2009). (In her diary, Leta Hollingworth's mother recorded that Leta smiled at 2 days old!) Due to similarities in intelligence and personality, gifted children and their parents often have a great deal in common (Bouchard & Lykken, 1999). Some parents find their precocious children deliciously fascinating and document all their amazing accomplishments. This parental delight, which onlookers may find annoying, is actually quite healthy for the child. It serves as a strong foundation for the child's self-esteem. But there are definitely times when the child's precocity is embarrassing. A case in point:

> At a time when most two year olds are content to name items in the supermarket, Andrew had already initiated extensive

discussions with his mother at home about the nutritional value of various products. As they were proceeding down the cereal aisle, Andrew, seated in the grocery cart, spied three middle-aged women selecting sugared cereals with artificial colors. Before Andrew's mother knew what had happened, three startled women turned around to see the two year old standing up in the grocery cart, shaking his finger, and lecturing, "Put those back! Put those back! Don't you realize that cereal is bad for you? It is mostly sugar, and contains artificial flavors and colors!" (Kearney, 1992, p. 9)

The first few years of life are demanding, but strong parent–child bonds are fashioned during this period, which sustain the adults as well as the children. The following era takes much greater fortitude for both. These are the years when gifted children start to interact with other children their age and are required to adapt to group norms. The drama may begin in the playgroup or at the park or in day care programs or in preschool. "Playgroups, pre-schools and primary schools are contexts especially sensitive to unorthodox or unusual behavior, which in many cases becomes labeled as social-emotional immaturity" (Alsop, 1997, p. 31). Preschoolers define themselves according to their first social interactions, and social adjustment issues are inevitable when the gap between the gifted child's development and the development of others in the playgroup is too generous. Parents, too, are judged by their child's ability to play well with others in their age group.

Early childhood educators generally hold the belief that children are only capable of socializing with others close to their age. They receive no training about the advanced development of gifted children or the fact that they play best with older children. As the concept of mental age has been abandoned in psychology, there is little awareness that gifted children's friendship patterns and social conceptions are more related to their mental age than their chronological age (Gross, 2009).

Stages of Friendship

Gross (2009) proposed a model of age-related stages in the development of expectations about friendship; at each stage, the degree of conceptual complexity increases:

- **Stage 1.** *"Play partner"*: A friend is a playmate who shares toys.
- **Stage 2.** *"People to chat to"*: Shared interests take the place of shared activities.
- **Stage 3.** *"Help and encouragement"*: A friend is someone who offers assistance and support, but the child does not see the need to reciprocate.
- **Stage 4.** *"Intimacy/empathy"*: True reciprocity develops, along with affection, bonding, emotional sharing, and intimacy.
- **Stage 5.** *"The sure shelter"*: Faithful friends develop deep and lasting relationships involving trust and unconditional acceptance (pp. 343–344).

Gross conducted studies of the conceptions of friendship held by average, moderately gifted, exceptionally gifted, and profoundly gifted children. She found strong correlations between intellectual development (mental age) and conceptions of friendship. Differences between gifted and average samples were much greater in the preschool and primary years than in the later years of elementary school. Significant differences were even observed between exceptionally and profoundly gifted children.

> Some profoundly gifted children in the early years of school had expectations of friendship that normally do not appear until the years of early adolescence. These children face almost insurmountable difficulties in their search for friendship, at an age when most children view a friend as a companion for casual play....
>
> This study suggests that it is in the lower, rather than the upper, grades that placement with chronological peers, without regard to intellectual ability or emotional maturity, is more likely to result

in the gifted child experiencing loneliness or social isolation. (Gross, 2009, p. 344)

Opportunities to relate to gifted peers in the early, formative years lay the foundation for positive social development.

Mental Age

Though no longer popular, mental age puts in perspective the advanced development of gifted children and helps parents and teachers understand their needs. Mental age predicts:

- the sophistication of the child's play,
- the age of true peers,
- maturity of the child's sense of humor,
- ethical judgment,
- awareness of the world.

A 5-year-old boy who thinks like an 8-year-old will be more interested in chess, monopoly, and more sophisticated games than activities that are of interest to children his age. Young gifted boys appear to have greater difficulty than girls relating to children who are not at their own developmental level. They think the games of average children are "silly," "babyish."

Average 5-year-olds are not yet ready to grasp the concept of rules. They exclaim, "I win!" after each game. That's the whole point of playing for them. A gifted 5-year-old with a mental age of 8 comprehends rules, and is probably rule bound, which is typical for 8-year-olds. The average child and the gifted child are at two different stages of intellectual development. When the average child squeals, "I win!" the gifted child retorts, "He cheats! I'm not playing with him anymore." Gifted preschool and primary children relate much more easily to children who are similarly advanced or to older children who are close to their mental age.

CHAPTER 5

Gender Differences in Socialization

Young gifted children may shut down emotionally if they cannot connect with the others in their class. By the age of 5 or 6, the once-confident gifted child may be filled with self-doubt and have acquired cumulative layers of protective defenses. Being different is a problem in childhood. Young children—even gifted ones—do not have the capacity to comprehend differences. They have difficulty understanding why other children do not think like them or talk like them or respond to their friendship in a predictable manner. They may try to imitate others their age, hiding their true selves, or they may withdraw. They notice how different they are from others their age and they begin to feel "strange" and unacceptable. Parents report that their buoyant, confident, exuberant toddler gradually becomes subdued and uncertain during the preschool and primary years. One parent wrote:

> Alice is doing all she can to blend in and not stand out as different. She does not ask all the questions she used to. Alice is not the same person she was before she started going to school. Before she started kindergarten she had an insatiable quest for more knowledge. We are concerned because we think she is a bright child who is turning off.

Profoundly gifted preschoolers are bewildered by the mismatch between their interests and those of their classmates. Antoine's teacher discouraged him from bringing his favorite video, the ballet of "The Nutcracker Suite," to share with the other 3-year-olds. When he was 4, he made a model of Mars for Show and Tell, and the following week he discussed black holes, implosion, and explosion. He couldn't understand why his classmates weren't interested.

Alice and Antoine exemplify the gender differences observed in social responses of young gifted girls and boys. Alice sought to blend in with other children her age. Her need for affiliation triumphed over her intellectual curiosity. She

126

readily stopped asking questions and slowed down her natural learning trajectory in order to have friends. Antoine pursued his desire for knowledge at the expense of social connection. Undaunted by his classmates' indifference to the two moons of Mars, Antoine followed up with a dissertation on black holes. Staying true to himself, Antoine chose his need to learn over his need for friends, and eventually insisted that his mother home-school him.

Because they refuse to sacrifice who they are for the good of the group, gifted boys are considered poorly socialized. By way of contrast, gifted girls are socially adapted at the expense of their giftedness (Kerr, 1994). Gifted girls are chameleons. They have enhanced ability to perceive social cues, making it easier for them to modify their behavior to fit into a group. They frequently don the mental attire of the other girls in their class, and soon become imperceptible from them. They receive daily practice in sliding by without stretching themselves, hiding who they are to make everyone else comfortable, and being less than they are capable of being. Eventually, they trade their dreams for simpler, less demanding goals.

The antidote is early contact with others like themselves. Girls who have a gifted peer group in a context that supports diversity do not hide their abilities (Eddles-Hirsch, Vialle, McCormick, & K. Rogers, 2012). Gifted peers normalize boys' and girls' experience and they do not come to see themselves as "weird." They make friends easily with others with similar interests, values, vocabularies, and levels of development. Interaction with true peers who are mental equals facilitates social development and prevents social isolation.

Many place a premium on gifted children learning to get along with others who are different from themselves. Wendy Roedell (1989), a developmental psychologist who has studied the social development of young gifted children, has found that getting along with those who are different depends on opportunities to interact with true peers. "While adaptation is important, gifted young children also need the give-and-take of interactions with others of equal ability, where they can find acceptance and understanding, the keys to the development of successful social skills and positive self-concept" (p. 26). Similarly, Miraca Gross and her colleagues in Australia note that gifted children who do not have access to others like themselves face a "forced choice" between their intellectual needs and their desire for acceptance by less-advanced classmates (J. Jung, McCormick, & Gross, 2012, p. 15).

Socialization in Adolescence

Feelings of alienation intensify with maturity. The concept of mental age illumines the progressive degree to which gifted children diverge from average children throughout their school years. The 5-year-old with an 8-year-old mind becomes a 10-year-old with a 16-year-old mind. Unless they find others with whom they have something in common, gifted students may experience intense loneliness all through school.

The gifted are one of the few stigmatized groups that can camouflage their differences in order to gain acceptance. Even when they are being bullied, the gifted tend to remain silent, rather than sharing what has happened with peers or teachers (Coleman, 2012; Peterson & Ray, 2006). Acceleration and homeschooling can ameliorate the social alienation of exceptionally gifted children. Homeschooled throughout high school, Ely Alexander (1992) provided a compelling retrospective view on his socialization.

> Most public schools provide an unrealistic and frequently a harmful social environment for their students. The familiar specter of peer pressure is difficult to exorcise and dangerous to ignore— assaults on a student's integrity and self-respect occur with alarming regularity. Many of the friendships and relationships that develop among public school students are associations of convenience only, and rapidly fail when graduation renders them unnecessary. Furthermore, the world at large is simply not composed entirely of anyone's age peers. If a child learns to relate

only to others of the same age from the same town, he or she is likely to encounter difficulties when adulthood and its challenges approach....

I can say with confidence that I did not miss public school socialization...and I was certainly happy not to be forced to spend half of each day with a group selected for age and not compatibility. (p. 13)

WHO WOULD YOU LIKE ME TO BE TODAY?

The *"I can be anything!"* of early childhood gives way to "I can be anything you want me to be." Multifaceted, complex little beings—unless they are too far off the charts—are quintessentially adaptable. "I can adapt. I can adapt right out of who-I-was-meant-to-be." They quickly learn what is expected of them and how to elicit the responses they desire from adults. They can imitate the word choices, the tone of voice, the facial expressions, the body language, and the belief systems of those in their world.

> *I spoke in complex sentences by seventeen months. However, still today, he will gauge the extent of a child's language development and model that style when he is with that child. I noticed this as early as seventeen months. When kids couldn't talk or didn't talk much or only sang, he did whatever they did. I asked why and he said, "I try to figure out what they know and then I act like they do so I can be their friend."*

Those who keep up this façade win favor at home and with peers and at school. We love these kids. They are mini-us and they will grow up to be just like us, confirming and recreating our worldviews. And our hearts go out to those who do not master skills and keep pace with the rest. But we have trouble with the ones who defy us, who say, "I've got to be me—no matter what you think of me." We suspect that these children have sociopathic tendencies that we need to curb. Admittedly, there are oppositional defiant children who take this to the extreme, but it is psychologically healthy to have a "Me" and internal locus of control. And gifted children demonstrate higher intrinsic than extrinsic motivation (Coleman, 2012; Gross, 2009; Kanevsky, 1994).

Inside every gifted child there are two loud voices: "I can be anything you want" and "I've got to be me." Most of the time, most of them listen to the first voice and try to suppress the second. But the subjugated voice never completely disappears; it just stays hidden in a secret compartment, waiting until it is safe enough to be heard. "Can you love me for who I am or only if I become what you want me to be?"

Betty Meckstroth once said, "You remind me of an old Victorian dresser. You open different drawers for different people." A Victorian dresser is an apt metaphor for the life experiences of adaptable gifted people. They have as many drawers as they need to portray the different selves required of different relationships. That works well as long as they are not interacting with too many different kinds of people at the same time. When too many drawers are pulled out simultaneously the dresser becomes imbalanced and topples over.

Layer after layer after layer of selves created in the service of "Who do you want me to be today?" buries "I've got to me" deeper in the recesses of the unconscious, where it smolders. With each passing year, the rewards of fulfilling others' expectations seduce the gifted further from awareness and connection with their own inner beings. "Even your own voice shouting, hollering your individuality out loud, results only in inward echoes" (Alexander, 1992, p. 1). Eventually, after years of working overtime to give everyone exactly what they want, the question, "What do *I* want?" tentatively bubbles into consciousness, only to receive the hollow answer, "I want the least number of people to be angry with me." The *I* has been effectively silenced—at least for now.

This is but one facet of the inner experience of the gifted—the unseen world that the psychologist may be allowed to visit.

It isn't a world of products, performance, skills, prizes, academic propensities, career choices, hard work, and perseverance. These are only the outer trappings of a much more intricate inner landscape. By their productivity shall they be known to the world, but their interior is opaque.

THE INNER EXPERIENCE OF GIFTEDNESS

The inner life or personal experience of being gifted has been underemphasized in the literature (Coleman, 2012). In his therapeutic practice with exceptionally and profoundly gifted adolescents and adults, Grobman (2009) has found that the majority of psychological symptoms are related to "unresolved conflicts about their inner experience of giftedness" (p. 122). These include guilt for being given extra abilities and the belief that others must somehow have been given less because they have more: "a gigantic zero sum game" (p. 117). "Different parts of their remarkable endowment could *simultaneously* feel like strengths and weaknesses. It was this phenomenon that was at the heart of many of the conflicts within their inner experience of giftedness" (pp. 107–108).

Poised and confident on the outside, fearful and self-reproaching on the inside. Here is a poignant glimpse of the inner world of gifted teens:

> We are not "normal" and we know it; it can be fun sometimes but not funny always. We tend to be much more sensitive than other people. Multiple meanings, innuendos, and self-consciousness plague us. Intensive self-analysis, self-criticism, and the inability to recognize that we have limits make us despondent. (American Association for Gifted Children, 1978, p. 9)

Excitement with new insights is dampened when there's no one with whom to share them. Social exchange becomes a minefield when one is attuned to a symphony of nuances. The gifted are hard on themselves. "Why did I say that?" "What was I thinking?" "What kind of person am I?" Constantly analyzing their thoughts and behavior, and coming up lacking. The inner pressure to do it all, and do it all well, against the backdrop of a mocking clock that smirks, "You're late...again."

It isn't funny and it isn't fun to be laughed at for who you are. The dread of being "abnormal" impels the gifted to lead a double life. They feign normalcy, attempting to mask their vulnerability. In Elizabeth Drews' (1972) words, "Our children are taught to don masks before they recognize their own faces. They are made to put their tender, pliable forms into prefabricated shells" (p. 3). During middle school and high school, gifted teens often camouflage their differences to protect themselves from ridicule (Coleman, 2012; Gross, 1998).

> Some kids really don't have much Me at all. They truly are part of the group. But a lot of them just act—pretend—the way I tried to. Their heart isn't really in the groups, but still they get along, they get by. I wish I could. I honestly wish I could be a good hypocrite. It doesn't hurt anybody, and it sure makes life easier. But I never could fool anybody. They knew I wasn't interested in what interested them, and they despised me for it, and I despised them for despising me....
>
> Since I was trying hard not to be different, I didn't want to be a straight-A type...
>
> But—this is important—I never talked back. I never said anything.
>
> ...I can't do it. I haven't got it. I don't get into fights.
>
> I stand there and take it, till I can run. And then I run.
>
> Sometimes I not only stand there and take it, I even smile at them and say I'm sorry.
>
> When I feel that smile coming onto my face, I wish I could take my face off and stamp on it. (*Very Far Away from Anywhere Else*, LeGuin, 1976, pp. 4–6)

The complexities of being gifted involve the interaction of external and internal factors. Anti-intellectualism, under the guise of egalitarianism, is pervasive worldwide (Colangelo,

2002; Geake & Gross, 2008; J. Jung et al., 2012; Tannenbaum, 1983). The popular name for the gifted in Australia and New Zealand is "tall poppies." The tall poppies syndrome is a social phenomenon of attacking those of exceptional ability. The symbolism of cutting off the heads of "tall poppies," so that none is elevated above the rest, has a grisly history. There are real dangers in distinguishing oneself from one's peers. Intelligence represents a social advantage that may appear threatening to the group. "It could be in the group's self-interest to cut such a precocious tall poppy down to size" (Geake & Gross, 2008, p. 220). True egalitarianism—providing equal opportunity for all—is an ideal that gifted individuals throughout history, such as Jefferson and Lincoln, fought to uphold. Equal opportunity is not obtained through prejudice against outstanding individuals. Bringing the top down cannot bring the bottom up.

> In conversations with teachers and administrators one often senses a virtual prejudice against bright students. There is at times an underlying feeling, never articulated, that such children start off with too many advantages, and that it would be just as well to hold them back until their less fortunate contemporaries catch up with them. (Singal, 1991, p. 67)

Benign neglect of the gifted is customary, with the rationale that they can take care of themselves and other students are more in need. But verbal and physical hostility toward the gifted is intolerable. J. Jung et al. (2012) noted that Westerners have been known "to show rejection and hostility toward students engaging in intellectual activities with high levels of success...; this may take the form of indifference, stereotyping, taunting, and/or intimidation" (p. 16). In discussions with groups of elementary-aged children in United States and Australia, one-third of the boys described being physically attacked for being smart. Latent hostility toward the gifted is demonstrated in accusations that start with, *"If you're so smart, why..."* "can't you tie your shoes?" "don't you try harder?" "aren't you rich?" "aren't you famous?" The host of taunts is demoralizing.

One issue that the gifted face stems from a personality characteristic that is taken advantage of by the unkind. The gifted are gullible. Their first inclination is to be truthful, so they tend to believe nearly anything anyone tells them. In this way, they are similar to those at the opposite end of the spectrum. Their gullibility makes them easy to fool and some delight in making them appear foolish. Early humiliations leave deep scars.

A second trait is what Betty Maxwell, a counselor who specializes in the gifted, has dubbed "gaslighting" (after the 1944 movie, "Gaslight"). The movie portrays an insidious attempt to drive a woman crazy by telling her that what she sees and believes to be true is not. In the lives of the gifted, this occurs unintentionally because others do not observe, apprehend, feel, experience, or intuit in the same manner. When gifted individuals cannot find anyone who understands their reality, they begin to doubt their sanity. This can be compounded if others in their world call them "crazy" or treat them as if they are mentally imbalanced. A major role of the therapist of the gifted is to provide them with a reality check.

Another observation of Betty Maxwell's is that gifted individuals have a "logical imperative." While many people seem blithely unconcerned with contradictory elements of themselves, the logical imperative of the gifted causes them extreme discomfort in the face of incongruities in their belief systems, and between their beliefs and their actions. They are embarrassed by inconsistencies in their thoughts, even if no one else notices. Psychic life is full of wrestling matches between parts of themselves that are at odds. Much of their time with a therapist is spent clarifying things they have shared that are "not exactly true," because they can think of counter-examples.

A typical experience of the gifted has been labeled, "The Imposter Syndrome" (Clance, 1985). In 1970, I spoke to a group of teens involved in the California Scholarship Federation, and referred to these feelings as "The Great Con Game." Compared to average students, gifted students appear incredibly smart. But the gifted don't compare themselves with the average. Instead, they compare their knowledge with all there is to be known about a subject. They soon become aware that they've barely scratched the surface. Every book has a list of references. All those references have more lists of references. The problem is even more acute today, when Google instantly presents several million resources related to a single term or a question. Where does the search end? The gifted often feel like they've just fooled everybody into thinking that they are smart, and at any moment they will be found out. Every term paper, every presentation, every article is an opportunity to be exposed as a fraud by someone who knows something about the topic that the gifted person failed to uncover. When giving a professional paper in an area in which they have developed expertise, they still sweat, "What if they ask me something I don't know?" The belief that one has to know *everything* about a topic before discussing it is another "gifted problem," although Olsen Laney (2002) also identifies it as an issue for introverts.

Inner life of the gifted is marbled with piercing sensitivity, deep moral concerns, passionate convictions, idealism, feelings of inadequacy, relentless self-criticism, perfectionism, and intensity. The gifted hate hypocrisy and they have uncanny perception, which often puts them at odds with bosses, co-workers, teachers and parents who sport inauthentic façades. They are paradoxical: self-assured and insecure, bold and timid, idealistic and practical, compassionate to others and unkind to themselves, mature and immature. An 11-year-old insisted vehemently to his parents that he was too old to be told what time to go to bed, but wanted to be tucked in at night. A 12-year-old stepped off an airplane with his calculus book in one hand and his Curious George in the other.

My son is a study in contrasts. He can be rough around the edges but charming and well-liked. He is able to concentrate and be totally absorbed by some things while at other times completely without focus or attention. He can also be open and forthcoming with what is going on in his life while at other times more reserved.

In childhood, the gifted pay a heavy toll for society's confusion about the nature of giftedness. Definitions are so variable that children come to believe that their abilities are situational. "I don't get to be gifted until third grade." "I used to be gifted in my last school district, but not in this one." "I was in a gifted program in elementary school, but I'm not gifted anymore." A resource teacher for the gifted shared this story:

> A seven-year-old girl identified as gifted in first grade approached the Gifted/Talented resource teacher with some trepidation at the end of her second-grade year. Knowing that the promotion from 2nd to 3rd grade involved going to a new school, she anxiously asked the resource teacher, "Will I still be gifted and talented next year?" The teacher's reply of "yes" apparently did not satisfy her. Her response was, "Are you **sure** I will be gifted and talented next year?" The teacher finally was able to assure her that she would, by explaining that "it doesn't go away."

From the time a child is identified as gifted, a series of questions plague him or her: "What is my 'gift'?" "Where did it come from?" "Will it go away?" "What will be expected of me now?" "What if I fail to live up to these expectations?" "Why me?" They need counselors who explore with them what giftedness means, as well as the feelings related to being different, and help them develop coping strategies.

Two characteristics of giftedness appear with such astounding regularity in descriptions of gifted children and adults that we may almost think of them as synonymous with giftedness: sensitivity and perfectionism. Many of the psychological issues of this population can be traced to these two traits. Gifted individuals are frequently called "overly sensitive" and "too perfectionistic." But asking them to be less of these traits is asking them to be less gifted. They are the emotional correlates of giftedness; they differentiate the gifted from others as strongly as their cognitive qualities. Dabrowski (1964, 1967, 1972) constructed a window into the inner world of the gifted that gives us a deeper appreciation of their sensitivity, intensity, perfectionism and inner conflicts.

DABROWSKI'S THEORY OF POSITIVE DISINTEGRATION

Kazimierz Dabrowski [1902–1980] was a Polish psychiatrist and psychologist who studied the psychological makeup of artists, actors, writers, dancers, and intellectually gifted youth. The theory gets its name from the basic tenet that a rudimentary level of development has to deteriorate in order for a higher level, multifaceted organization of the psyche to emerge. Crises and periods of disequilibrium are perceived as positive growth spurts. Five levels of development were hypothesized, from pervasive egocentrism at Level I ("Primary Integration") to empathic altruism at Level V ("Secondary Integration"). The levels in between represent various degrees of disintegration. Group consciousness dominates at Level II, and the individual experiences a great deal of ambivalence. Level III is the beginning of multilevel development, in which the person develops an internal hierarchy of values. Level IV is more autonomous and development is self-directed. Each level is its own world— dramatically different from the other levels. This part of the Theory of Positive Disintegration (TPD) is useful in therapy with the gifted, as it offers a positive framework for dealing with crises, and provides landmarks by which individuals can monitor their progress toward becoming their ideal selves.

This is not an age-related stage theory. A child doesn't start out delighting in pulling the wings off of butterflies and evolve to Mother Teresa. It is possible to stay at the same level throughout life or to climb—with considerable effort, discomfort and inner conflict—to a higher level. The lower level is not absorbed within the higher level as it is in Piaget's stages. In Piaget's theory, once children are capable of concrete operational thought, they no longer have access to the pre-operational thought process of the previous stage of development. In Dabrowski's theory, however, one's inner milieu can house two different levels of development simultaneously, with the accompanying tension between these clashing households. Vacillations in behavior and self-recrimination are understood as manifestations of this struggle. Developmental potential for multilevel awareness is stronger in the gifted population, but its realization may take a lifetime. Bailey (2011) found that 70% of the gifted adolescents in her study were at Level II (unilevel development). (See Mendaglio, 2008, for an in-depth discussion of Dabrowski's theory.)

Success is a widely-coveted goal that has attracted a great deal of study. Fewer are interested in investigating the factors that lead to universal compassion. And fewer still choose this life path. Those who are called to embark upon such an inner journey have extraordinary potential of a different kind: potential for higher level development.

> Developmental potential for multilevel development takes this form:
>
> 1. Talents, special abilities, and *g* (intelligence)
> 2. Overexcitability: psychomotor, sensual, intellectual, imaginational, and emotional.
> 3. Capacity for inner transformation.
>
> Overexcitability means that reality is experienced in a *qualitatively* different manner. Not just more of curiosity, sensory enjoyment, imagination, and feeling, but added dimensions of depth, texture, acuity and perception. It implies an intense aliveness and a neural processing very different from the norm. (Jackson, Moyle, & Piechowski, 2009, p. 438)

Overexcitability (OE) is a translation of the Polish term, "nadpobudliwosc," which means "superstimulatability"—the capacity for stronger neurological reactions (Falk, Piechowski, & Lind, 1994). Dabrowski originally noted these expressions of emotional tension in gifted and creative youth enrolled in a school for the arts in Warsaw. "Enhanced excitability is thus a means for...a wider range of experiencing" (Dabrowski, 1972, p. 7). Like variables of temperament, the OEs are thought to be innate, and appear to be stable characteristics throughout the lifespan.

The five overexcitabilities are Psychomotor OE, Sensual OE, Imaginational OE, Intellectual OE and Emotional OE. Dabrowski considered Emotional, Imaginational, and Intellectual OE powerful contributors to higher level development. Psychomotor OE and Sensual OE are thought to contribute only if the other three OEs are stronger (Mika, 2006). Gifted individuals resonate strongly to descriptions of the OEs. Considerable research has been conducted showing more overexcitability in gifted than nongifted samples (Jackson et al., 2009), although a recent study of adolescents demonstrated significant differences only in Imaginational and Intellectual OE for gifted males (Piirto & Fraas, 2012). (For reviews of the research, see Falk & N. Miller, 2009; Silverman, 2008.)

Psychomotor OE is an unusually strong physical response to stimulation. It is marked by a surplus of physical energy, high activity levels, love of fast games and sports, competitiveness, compulsive talking, and pressure for action. Psychomotor OE can be seen in children who always seem to have a body part in motion—drumming fingers, a shaking leg, etc. Teens high in Psychomotor OE are often involved in high-risk, adrenaline-pumping activities. Adults may be workaholics or action-oriented; at a meeting, they are the first to say, "We've talked about this long enough—now what are we going to do?" While Psychomotor OE is often perceived negatively in children, high energy levels in adults lead to greater productivity, and it is a boon to the elderly.

Highly under-rated (in my opinion), Sensual OE involves heightened senses and sensuality. Those with Sensual OE love textures, tastes, aromas, sounds, sunsets, nature, dessert, music, art, words, beauty, cuddling, bubble baths, chocolate, back rubs, shopping, sex, and being the center of attention. They are the aesthetic specialists, with fine-tuned abilities to discriminate wines, sound systems or works of art. Some enjoy the aroma of hardware stores as much as the smell of flowers. They would probably be the first to detect a gas leak. They are really fussy. As babies, they hate being wet or dirty. The labels have to be cut out of their clothes. Socks have to fit identically. Super aware of their environment, things have to be "just right" for them to be comfortable: the proverbial Princess and the Pea.

Imaginational OE manifests as vivid imagery, inventiveness, dramatic perception, poetic inclinations, love of fantasy, humor, creative imagination and low tolerance for boredom. Children who are sure that during the night their socks in the closet can turn into vampires have high Imaginational OE. Science fantasy attracts these children as they get older. Sometimes, one's imagination is so much more interesting than reality that truth and fiction become intertwined. (Think of the movies, "Don Juan de Marco" and "Big Fish.") Visionaries envision the world the way it might be; thus, Imaginational OE plays a role in inspiring the individual to undertake the arduous journey toward higher level development.

Intellectual OE enables the person to see another's perspective. Curiosity, asking probing questions, searching for truth, avid reading, love of learning, thinking about thinking, passion for precision, analyzing and problem-solving are all facets of Intellectual OE. As young children, those with Intellectual OE are independent thinkers (Falk, N. Miller, & Silverman, 2009). "Me do it!" may be among their first words. As adults, they love learning new theories and analyzing and solving problems. Intelligence and Intellectual OE overlap, but they are not identical. Intellectual OE in children correlates with IQ scores (Falk et al., 2009). However, in adult life, some individuals with very high intelligence do not show intellectual interests. They show little affinity for reading; they would rather go to a baseball game than a play. They may use their intelligence in practical, financial or artistic realms.

Essential to higher level development, Emotional OE is the heart of Dabrowski's theory. Emotional OE is multifaceted, including emotional sensitivity, empathy, fear of death, capacity for strong attachments, somatic expressions (flushing, blushing), inhibition, extremes and complexity of emotion, depression and loneliness, and more. Individuals with high Emotional OE are tender and care about others' feelings. In childhood, they often come to the aid of children who are being teased by others or stand up to a teacher if they think another child is being treated unfairly (Probst & Piechowski, 2012). They experience a vast range of emotions. Some feel opposing emotions simultaneously, such as laughing and crying. They are often responsible for the emotional well-being of a group or a family. (For a comprehensive list of the Forms and Expressions of Overexcitability, or to examine the *Overexcitability Questionnaire*, see Piechowski, 2006, reproduced in Daniels & Piechowski, 2009; and in Probst & Piechowski, 2012.)

Emotional OE ranked highest of the overexcitabilities in 15 of 19 studies reported in the literature (Falk & N. Miller, 2009). The total sum of ranks ranged from Sensual (29) to Emotional (90). The sum of ranks for Intellectual OE (70) was considerably lower than Emotional OE. This may seem surprising, since most of the studies were conducted with gifted samples, and the characteristics of giftedness overlap with the descriptors of Intellectual OE. However, the research indicates that Emotional OE differentiates gifted from average development to a greater degree than Intellectual OE. Emotional OE also ranked first in the Grand Harmonic Means of 9 international studies using the *Overexcitability Questionnaire II* (OEQ-II) (Falk & Miller, 2009). Falk (2012) analyzed the data on the *Overexcitability Inventory for Parents* (OIP), a parent version of the OEQ-II, with 512 gifted children, and found that Emotional OE split into two factors: emotional intensity and empathy. Empathy is a powerful indicator of giftedness.

Emotional Overexcitability, manifested in the range of emotions and feelings, tends to be wide and multifaceted in gifted children, both in intensity and in sensitivity. Besides compassion, caring, and responsibility, the significance of deep and perceptive feeling lies in *empathy as a way of knowing,* another unexplored ability of the gifted (Jackson et al., 2009, p. 239)

Empathy is more pronounced in gifted than nongifted samples and has been documented in gifted children in many countries (Pramathevan & Garces-Bascal, 2012; Schechtman & Silektor, 2012). Their empathy renders the gifted vulnerable. They have difficulty with the cruelty portrayed in movies, television programs, commercials, books, and children's games. There is a permeable membrane between real and imagined experience, particularly if both Emotional and Imaginational OE are strong. When they watch brutality on the screen or read about it in a book, they respond viscerally as if they had witnessed the acts in reality. Easily overwhelmed by the cruelty in the world, they find it difficult to remove disturbing images from their minds.

> *Has extreme reactions to stories, movies, events witnessed; feels things deeply and expresses profound sadness, excitement, fear. Refuses to go to the movies. Will not watch Disney movies (DVDs at home) as there is always a character that gets harmed. Will not watch most movies/shows other kids watch—simply refuses, she says they are "too scary."*

Counselors may need to intervene with these children's reading assignments. The intensity of their emotional responses may seem exaggerated to mental health professionals who are not familiar with overexcitabilities.

"Being intense is an ineradicable part of the gifted self" (Jackson et al., 2009, p. 443). Overexcitabilities provide the rich texture of the lives of the gifted. Frank (2006) suggests that intelligence enables the gifted to solve problems, while overexcitability supplies the passion for solving them. Overflowing with energy, excitement, enthusiasm, imagination, ecstasy and agony, the gifted experience life "in a higher key" (Piechowski, 2006, p. 266).

PERFECTIONISM

Hard work and effort are applauded, but "working too hard" is considered a personality flaw. These competing societal messages are a double bind for the gifted. Perfectionism is the life partner of giftedness. It takes an abstract mind to strive for an ideal that is seldom, if ever, found in concrete reality. Frequently maligned in psychology, there is more to this characteristic than meets the eye.

Dabrowski's theory offers a template for perceiving the positive value of perfectionism in the development of the personality. It can be seen as a manifestation of Emotional OE; the drive for self-perfection that undergirds the entire developmental process; the capacity for inner transformation; and as a personality function that varies dramatically according to the person's level of development. Higher level development is only accessible to those who are capable of recognizing their potential for growth, yearn to become their ideal selves, and mobilize the will to overcome the inner obstacles to their transformation. This is perfectionism in the service of development.

Perfectionism is a completely different animal at each level of development. It stems from a different source and has a significantly different impact on the personality. Most of the popular discourse on this topic focuses on the expressions of perfectionism at Levels I and II.

At Level I, perfectionism is tyrannical. Without the development of empathy, individuals are essentially narcissistic. Others are expected to live up to their expectations. They are harsh task masters who do not tolerate mistakes. Their affection is contingent upon their ability to control others. In the absence of self-reflection, individuals at Level I can always find reasons to blame others. They are never at fault. Difficult to satisfy, their approval has a short shelf life. "What have you done for me lately?" This type of perfectionism has been labeled "Other oriented" in Hewitt and Flett's (1991)

Multidimensional Perfectionism Scale (MPS). No correlations have been found between giftedness and "other oriented" perfectionism (Chan, 2007).

Perfectionism is usually portrayed as feeling that no matter what one does, it is never good enough (Greenspon, 2012). Such feelings are typical of unilevel (Level II) development. At Level II, individuals suffer from low self-esteem and feelings of inferiority toward others. Their stereotypic values are introjected from family, friends, church, television and movies. They compare themselves with others and find themselves lacking. Others are smarter, wealthier, luckier, more attractive, happier, etc. Desperately needing validation from others, they are excessively anxious about other people's opinions of them. Their days are spent fretting, "What will people think of me if I...?" With no internal hierarchy of values, those at Level II have no inner compass to guide them. They have ambivalent feelings and ambitendencies (contradictory actions), and are easily led by unscrupulous people (at Level I) who have more self-assurance. Unilevel development is fertile soil for the insecurities measured by most perfectionism scales.

Multilevel development gives rise to a different type of inferiority: inferiority toward one's own ideals. An inner hierarchy of values gives depth to the personality. Individuals at Level III start to envision what might be, what ought to be, and they begin to recognize their own potential to actualize that vision. But they live in the painful gap between "what ought to be" and "what is" in themselves. No longer at the mercy of groupthink, they begin to apprehend higher ideals and reject the less evolved parts of themselves that do not fit these ideals. They become excruciatingly self-aware of parts of themselves that are selfish, petty, impulsive, vengeful, imitative, competitive, etc.

Inner transformation requires complete commitment, nothing held back. Pouring oneself into projects is the first step of the journey. Multilevel individuals become totally absorbed in their work, striving to do their very best. They are not trying to gain approval. Unfettered by the judgments of others and

144

their own inner critic, they are capable of entering into a state that Csikszentmihalyi (1990) calls "flow." This perfectionistic zeal was identified earlier by Maslow (1971) as indispensable to the process of self-actualization. The struggle to perfect one's capabilities is a necessary step in the full realization of one's potential.

> Self-actualization means experiencing fully, vividly, selflessly, with full concentration and total absorption. It means experiencing without the self-consciousness of the adolescent. At this moment of experiencing, the person is wholly and fully human. This is a self-actualizing moment. This is a moment when the self is actualizing itself. As individuals, we all experience such moments occasionally. As counselors, we can help clients to experience them more often. We can encourage them to become totally absorbed in something and to forget their poses and their defenses and their shyness—to go at it "whole-hog." (Maslow, 1971, p. 45)

Perfectionism in the service of the personality ideal fuels the process of self-actualization. As development proceeds, the focus of perfectionism changes from manifesting a perfect something in the world to perfecting the self. There is an emerging sense of the purpose of one's existence, an awareness of one's potential, and a dedication to bringing one's life more and more in tune with the personality ideal. Perfectionism catalyzes the work of inner transformation.

The potential for multilevel development can be seen in some gifted children when they are very young. This is a conversation a mother had with her 2 ½-year-old son, while the radio was playing, "If I Could Rule the World."

> *"Mommy, what is he saying?" W asked.*
> *"Oh, that he would like to rule the world," I replied.*
> *"Why does he want to do that?" he asked.*
> *"Well, I guess he wants power and control over others."*
> *"He should know that will not make him happy," W replied.*

And some feel that perfectionism is innate:

> Although the commonsense notion of the causes of perfectionism tends to lay the blame for the perfectionistic child squarely on "pushy," exacting parents, clinical experience shows this conclusion to be unwarranted. Many perfectionistic gifted children are the products of relaxed, easy-going parents with realistic expectations.... It seems possible that certain children are simply *born* with the combination of temperaments that create a need for an orderly environment, or conversely, an aversion to chaos. (Kerr, 1991, p. 141)

> When asked to describe how their perfectionism developed, the group of participants...found the question difficult to answer, for they could never remember a time in their lives when they were not perfectionistic. For that reason, they were quick to note that it seemed to be a tendency they had had since birth, an inborn characteristic. (Speirs Neumeister, 2004a, p. 266)

This perspective is in sharp contrast with the view that parents are to blame for their children's perfectionism. Burns (1980) contended that perfectionism is a learned trait from perfectionistic parents, who are bent on having successful children for their own self-aggrandizement. Greenspon (2012) also traces the origin of perfectionism to conditional acceptance from significant others. These assumptions are not supported in research with the gifted. Parker and Stumpf (1995) reported that parental expectations accounted for less than 4% of the variance in their gifted children's scores on a perfectionism scale. Schuler (2000) found that healthy perfectionists perceived themselves as more perfectionistic than their parents, while the opposite was true for unhealthy perfectionists.

As positive aspects of perfectionism are not admitted in some conceptions of perfectionism, another construct was needed: "the pursuit of excellence" (Greenspon, 2012, p. 600). This desirable trait is distinguished from perfectionism, which is cast as an undesirable trait. The distinction is very popular in gifted education. One wonders how U. S. Olympic champion figure-skater, Evan Lysacek, would be perceived through this lens; it has been said that his coach had to beg him to stop practicing. It is difficult to imagine an Olympic contender who is not perfectionistic.

Increasingly, researchers are finding evidence of healthy perfectionism in the gifted (Chan, 2012). Hamachek (1978) suggested that there are two sorts of perfectionists: healthy and neurotic. Healthy perfectionists derive pleasure from accomplishing difficult tasks, whereas neurotic perfectionists are never satisfied that their accomplishments are good enough. Over 40% of the 400 gifted sixth graders in Parker's (1997) study were healthy perfectionists. He concluded that "the overriding characteristic of perfectionism in these talented children is conscientiousness, not neurosis" (p. 556). In 2000, Parker found similar results with a larger sample of 820, using several instruments. These children were described as "organized, dependable, and socially skilled. Their ACL [Adjective Checklist] scaled scores indicated students who were conscientious, achievement-oriented, well-adjusted, and socially at ease" (pp. 176–177). Schuler's (2000) findings with gifted adolescents in rural settings echo these other studies. Here are her descriptors of healthy and unhealthy perfectionists.

HEALTHY PERFECTIONISTS

- Strong need for order and organization
- Accepted mistakes
- Enjoyed their parents' high expectations for them
- Had positive ways of coping with their perfectionism
- Had adults who modeled doing their best
- Viewed effort as an important part of their perfectionism

UNHEALTHY PERFECTIONISTS

- Were continuously anxious about making mistakes
- Held extremely high standards for themselves
- Perceived that others held excessive expectations for them
- Internalized negative remarks from others
- Questioned their own judgments
- Lacked effective coping strategies
- Exhibited a constant need for approval (Schuler, 2000)

Speirs Neumeister (2004b) found that self-oriented college students had high intrinsic motivation, set high standards for themselves, had a strong work ethic and tried to do their best, but they were not overly concerned about grades or fear of failure. However, in a more recent study, Angie Miller and Kristie Speirs Neumeister (2012) report that self-oriented perfectionism is negatively correlated with creativity.

Chan (2007, 2009, 2010, 2012) has translated the existing scales of perfectionism and constructed his own instruments, such as the *Positive and Negative Perfectionism Scale (PNPS-2)*. He found more positive than negative perfectionism in large samples of gifted children in Hong Kong. Positive perfectionists hold high personal standards and have a realistic striving for excellence. In 2010, Chan conducted a study of late teens, using several different instruments, including a self-report technique. Seventy percent of his sample endorsed a healthy form of perfectionism: "I strive to be perfect in my work, and I feel I can accept limitations and imperfections if I have tried my best" (p. 91).

Nancy Robinson (1996) regards perfectionism in the gifted as a potentially healthy trait, and urges mental health professionals to support positive perfectionism.

Some therapists would label as neurotic those characteristics that are quite typical of bright youngsters. Indeed, therapists are trained to look for psychopathy rather than health in people who are "different." ... Counselors tend, in particular, to see perfectionism as a neurotic trait. Although, in general, high degrees of perfectionism may be associated with lower degrees of self-confidence (Flett, Hewitt, & Davidson, 1990), supportive adults can enable students to practice "positive perfectionism" (i.e., setting high standards for oneself, working to meet those standards, and taking joy in their attainment). (pp. 133–134)

Recently, I happened to look through some magazines such as *Architectural Digest*, and I found it curious that the terms *perfectionism*, *perfectionist*, and *perfectionistic* showed up frequently in the advertisements. It made me wonder if you're allowed to be a perfectionist if you're rich. In this context, perfection is artistry, beauty, craftsmanship—and within reach. When Mary makes her famous pecan pie, she arranges all the pecans in perfect symmetry at the bottom of the pan, where no one sees them. As Mary is the only person who knows that they are perfectly arranged, she must derive some satisfaction that is unrelated to the approval of others. One may be motivated to strive for perfection simply because it is aesthetically pleasing.

One major facet of perfectionism is related to personality type. Concern with mistakes is characteristic of introverts. As a significant portion of the gifted population is introverted, this leads to another area of potential misinterpretation of the gifted.

INTROVERSION

D accomplishes physical tasks by watching and perfecting them in his head before he'll try them independently. He is acutely aware of looking foolish, falling, or getting hurt.

D is a gifted child who is both introverted and perfectionistic. The gifted tend to be perfectionists and introverts tend to be perfectionists. A gifted introvert is a perfectionist squared. Many of the clients that Dabrowski described as multilevel were gifted introverts. Here are some introverted traits that overlap with perfectionism:

- Easily humiliated
- Embarrassed by mistakes
- Cautious
- Mentally rehearse
- Prefer to show their finished products rather than their steps
- Learn by observing
- Have doubts about their abilities

Both perfectionism and introversion have been patholo-gized. In the DSM-5, they are associated with personality dis-orders. A great outcry from leaders in the fields of temperament and personality types led to the term "introversion" being replaced with "detachment." "**Detachment** involves withdrawal from other people and from social interactions.... **Withdrawal:** Preference for being alone to being with others; reticence in social contacts and activity; lack of initiation of social contact" (American Psychiatric Association, 2013). In our extraverted American society, preferring one's own company is apparently a mental disease.

> And if We see You standing alone by yourself, if you're lucky we'll ignore you. If you're not lucky, we might throw rocks....
>
> I tried. I really did. I tried so hard it makes me sick to think about it....But none of it worked. I don't know why. Sometimes I wonder if introverts have a peculiar smell, which only extraverts are aware of. (*Very Far Away from Anywhere Else*, LeGuin, 1976, p. 4)

In Europe, where the construct of introversion and extra-version originated, there are much more favorable attitudes toward introversion. Carl Jung (1923/1938), who invented the terminology, saw it as an inborn characteristic. Jung described introverts as individuals who conserve energy as a means of adaptation, in contrast to extraverts, who expend energy freely and indiscriminately. An introvert himself, Jung considered these basic orientations to be biological, rather than environmentally induced. "In the same family one child is introverted, and another extraverted" (p. 414). Jung felt that individuals who are forced to behave in a manner counter to their natural disposition become neurotic, and that therapeutic intervention must be geared toward enabling them to develop their natural personality type. Jung's classification has been supported in empirical research on high- and low-reactive subjects (Kagan, 1998; Kagan & Snidman, 2004). No one is purely one type or the other. It is possible to be an "ambivert," one who is both introverted and extraverted (Cain, 2012, p. 14). For me, "introvert" is a verb. I am a rabid extravert, but I "introvert" when I write.

Introverts are oriented inward toward the subjective world of thoughts and concepts; they get their energy from inside themselves; and they are inclined toward reflection. Extraverts are oriented outward, become energized through interaction with people and things, and are directed toward action. Whereas introverts feel drained by too much interaction with people, extraverts are energized by interaction—the more, the merrier.

> J is quick to tire when around people too much, and insists that weekends be kept as free of planned activities as possible. She seems very refreshed if she can spend a couple of uninterrupted hours in her room drawing or reading.

At least 50% of the gifted population is introverted (Delbridge-Parker & Robinson, 1989; S. Gallagher, 1990; Hoehn & Bireley, 1988; M. Rogers, 1986) and much higher proportions of introverts have been found among the highly gifted (Silverman, 1986b), particularly those who have extremely advanced verbal abilities (Dauber & Benbow, 1990). The proportion of introverts increases with educational level (Myers & McCaulley, 1985).

Introversion needs to be distinguished from shyness. Introverts are often called "shy," but this is an initial reaction to new situations that usually wears off when they feel comfortable.

> Shyness is a state of anxiety wherein a person is afraid of rejection, ridicule, or embarrassment. Some shy children have poor social skills. They avoid social situations, whether it's with one person or twenty, because they are afraid of being rebuffed or rejected. Social activities are very painful for them. They often attack themselves for everything they do or say in social situations.
>
> Introverted children usually have good social skills and often enjoy social situations. They may need to ease into social engagements, and they become tired if they have to deal with too many people for too long. (Olsen Laney, 2002, p. 156)

Creative people tend to be socially poised introverts (Cain, 2012).

Introverts have high emotional overexcitability—very powerful emotions—that can quickly overwhelm them. Because they have so much internal stimulation, introverts are not stimulation-seekers. They are cautious in new situations until they are sure of what to expect so that they feel in control of their emotions. When they are bombarded by too much stimulation, they feel out of control and want to escape. "Just being around people and activity drains introverts' batteries. . . . Introverts cannot generate new energy unless their external environment is shut out" (Olsen Laney, 2002, p. 138).

There are many benefits to introversion. More National Merit Scholars are introverted than extraverted, and they usually carry higher grade point averages because they are less distracted by their social lives (Myers & McCaulley, 1985). Leaders in academic, aesthetic and technical fields are often introverts (Cain, 2012; Silverman, 1993a). Leadership is not just the charisma to lead groups; it also occurs in more solitary forms in scientific breakthroughs, the creation of philosophy, and the writing of profound works. Introverts tend to have more successful marriages, fewer conflicts with others, and they may even live longer than extraverts (Olsen Laney, 2002). "Introverts think before they act, digest information thoroughly, stay on task longer, give up less easily, and work more accurately" (Cain, 2012, p. 168).

The personality profile of introversion, less focused on the values and attitudes of the mainstream, allows for creative introspection. Introverts are able to develop a personal philosophy, to know what they stand for, and to be self-determining. They also have an advantage at midlife in that long, inward journey to find oneself, which heralds the second half of the life cycle. They are more capable than extraverts of retreating from the world, going deep into themselves, and handling the reflective tasks involved in personality integration.

Giftedness, overexcitability, perfectionism and introversion very often co-exist. Each of these, independently, is frequently misunderstood. Their combination leads to life experiences, feelings and ways of being in the world that are frowned upon, particularly in Western societies. These characteristics are psychologically healthy and describe many psychologists. To work with the gifted effectively, it is necessary to understand and honor the qualities and characteristics that differentiate the gifted from other members of society throughout the life cycle.

Comprehensive Assessment of Giftedness

There is nothing of which every individual is so afraid of as getting to know how enormously much he or she is capable of doing and becoming.

Soren Kierkegaard

omprehensive assessment enables us to recognize, document, and understand atypical development. It involves evaluation of intelligence, achievement, affective development, and various other elements, depending on the presenting issues. Assessment is indispensable for measuring the extent of learning disabilities. It is the foundation upon which programs of intervention are based. Early identification permits early intervention. This is true for all exceptionalities, including giftedness. Evaluation kindles aspirations, helps gifted children and adults believe in their abilities, and changes lives.

Once upon a time, the need for assessment was understood in public schools. But something went awry in the 21st century. The anti-testing undercurrent that has always lurked in dark hallways suddenly erupted and took control of federal legislation. Now everything is supposed to be handled in the regular classroom. Regular classroom teachers have been given the responsibility of recognizing any type of exceptionality, fixing it themselves, and bringing all children to grade-level standards (Assouline, Foley Nicpon, & Whiteman, 2010). "We put extraordinary pressure on individual teachers with heavy class loads, assign them a wide variety of children with special needs, provide little available support, and then complain about them if their students perform poorly on tests" (J. Gallagher, 2004, p. 123).

Instead of being the basis for intervention, assessment is considered a last resort, after the patient fails to thrive with all the remedies available in the classroom. This is a lot like treating a rash with any lotion in the house before going to see a specialist to determine the cause. The wrong treatment can make it spread, and even prevent its cure because the critical period for intervention was lost.

Robertson, Pfeiffer, and Taylor (2011) found that a very small percentage of school psychologists, approximately 6%, assess gifted students more than once a month. While giftedness was acknowledged in the *No Child Left Behind Act* (2002) and the *Individuals with Disabilities Education Improvement Act of 2004* (IDEA, 2004) was the first federal law to recognize gifted children with learning disabilities, the implementation of these laws has neglected both of these groups (Assouline et al., 2010; J. Gallagher, 2004). They must look to psychologists outside the school system for identification, support, and advocacy (Assouline et al., 2010).

WHAT IS THE PURPOSE OF ASSESSMENT?

Testing should be tailored to address the specific needs of the case. Parents of gifted children decide to have their children assessed for a wide variety of reasons. In answer to the question, "Why would you like to have your child tested?" some parents who sought assessment at the Gifted Development Center (GDC) responded briefly, for example, *to confirm our suspicions that she is gifted.* Other parents wrote lengthier responses, revealing more about their children and the issues they faced.

> *I feel that M is capable of doing better than he does in school. I have watched him lose his enthusiasm for learning at school through the years. I would like to find that spark that was evident when he began his school career.*

> *A is miserable at school. She loathes homework and repetitive activities and she is disillusioned about the pertinence of her school experience. She recently announced that she was no longer going to attend school or do schoolwork of any variety.*

> *Although he is very intelligent and does very well on achievement tests, he struggles with written work and also has much difficulty with organizational activities. He was able to compensate in elementary grades, but when he entered middle school, it became more and more obvious that he was not able to keep it all together.*

> *(1) to determine whether she has special educational requirements; (2) to get help in developing an educational plan and identifying options/ resources; (3) to get help dealing with the emotional ramifications of giftedness.*

> *The typical 7-year-old world doesn't seem to entirely fit him; no age-level really ever has. He seems as though he has too much to fit into it, and we'd like to find out as much about him as possible, to help him get the most possible out of his life, both now and for later.*

> *We know J is gifted, but would like to have a sense of how gifted she is in order to help us make appropriate educational decisions for her and*

help provide some explanation for her sense that she "doesn't fit in." We also hope this information will provide the basis for us to find a support network for her, where she can find other kids like her.

A study of 241 exceptionally gifted children revealed that 82% of the parents who brought their children for testing to GDC wanted aid with decisions regarding educational placement (K. Rogers & Silverman, 2001). Alsop (1997) reported that 80.8% of the parents sought assessment at CHIP in Melbourne, Australia, to confirm their belief that their child was gifted. Parent judgment was found to be accurate. A more recent study of 60 cases uncovered 33 different reasons for seeking assessment, including the following:

- Understand their child
- Learn more about giftedness
- Advocacy
- Admission to schools and special programs
- Understand strengths and weaknesses
- Discover the degree of giftedness
- Learn about resources
- Determine appropriate grade placement
- Make decisions regarding acceleration
- Parent more effectively
- Advice about the child's intensities
- Understand the child's learning style
- Diagnosis of twice exceptionality
- Reverse underachievement
- 504 accommodations or accommodations on College Board examinations
- Information about homeschooling
- Retesting after a child has had interventions
- Retesting on a test with a higher ceiling (Silverman, 2012c)

As odd as it may sound, many gifted children do not feel smart. Some cannot concentrate on work that is too easy, some cannot cope with drill and repetition, and some have suppressed their abilities so well in order to gain acceptance that their gifts are no longer discernible to themselves and others. I have worked with exceptionally gifted teens who found the "pile-it-on-higher-and-deeper" philosophy of homework in their advanced classes so oppressive that they sit in class seriously thinking about blowing their brains out. Twice exceptional children, who have difficulty with reading, handwriting, memorization, spelling, or calculation, often have no idea that they are highly intelligent. These skills define what it is to be smart in school, and children who do not develop the required skills on schedule feel inadequate. Assessment is life changing for those who doubt their abilities. One twice exceptional high school student we assessed at the GDC said to his mother after the testing, "Now we both have something to live for." Assessing giftedness is not just about pursuing success; it's about preserving lives.

Intelligence testing is also an important lifelong safeguard in the event of an accident or a head injury, as it provides proof of the existence of high abilities prior to the insult. Unless pre-injury test scores exist, most insurance companies treat average scores attained in post-injury testing as evidence that no damage has occurred. For example, after sustaining a closed-head injury, a gifted therapist was unable to remember the details each of her clients had shared with her—an ability she relied on prior to the accident. IQ testing ordered by the insurance company indicated that she had average working memory. As she had no previous test results to prove exceptional memory, she received no compensation. In addition, she was treated as if her perception of her previous abilities was inflated and she was accused of being an "overachiever."

Comprehensive assessment of giftedness is an essential first step for advocacy. Parents who approach the school with their observations and intuitive appraisal of their children's giftedness are quickly dismissed. They cannot wait for school testing, which may never come, or may involve only group measures. They need to be armed with objective evidence from an independent source that their child tested in the gifted range on a standardized intelligence scale. But a set of scores is insufficient. They need recommendations, guidance, and, sometimes, intervention by a psychologist, in order to be taken seriously.

USING TEST RESULTS TO SUPPORT CLINICAL JUDGMENT

Medical doctors order tests, but they don't base their diagnoses solely on results of those tests. They require a complete medical history of the patient's family, as well as the patient, and analyze test results in conjunction with other information obtained, such as presenting symptoms, medical history, family history, and patient interview. Test results are of limited value unless interpreted by a skilled clinician who has had experience with the presenting problem.

Yet, in the diagnosis of giftedness, high stakes decisions frequently are made on the basis of test scores alone (sometimes even from group-administered tests). Scores become the definitive arbiters of children's qualification for placement, often determining their futures. Clinical judgment, if employed at all, tends to be subservient to the numbers. Similar to the medical field, accurate assessment of giftedness is dependent upon the skill and experience of the examiner in interpreting protocols of gifted children within the context of all the other information obtained.

The best evaluators of gifted children utilize some aspects of *qualitative assessment*. With sufficient experience, they can accurately estimate a child's level of intelligence through clinical observation, a brief discussion with the child, an interview with the parents, developmental milestones, family history, or some combination of these sources.

> Those of us experienced in testing the gifted can usually make close estimates of the scores that children will earn based on our initial conversations with the child.

> Once we begin the IQ test, I am observing verbal abstract reasoning, spatial reasoning, general knowledge, vision, audition, memory, motor skills, processing speed, attention, and a host of subtle cues that help to further explain the scores that the child earns. (Gilman, 2008a, p. 59)

Test results are interpreted within this broader framework and judged to be valid only if they conform to the clinical picture that has emerged from a more comprehensive appraisal of the child. If the test results fail to support the examiner's clinical judgment, further evaluation is sought to determine the cause of the discrepancy.

The more experience an examiner has with gifted children, the more effective his or her clinical judgment will be. This type of assessment is more time consuming, and, therefore, more costly than simply determining whether or not a child qualifies for a gifted program with a specific cut-off score. Examiners who assess gifted children need grounding in the developmental and psychometric patterns of the gifted, as well as knowledge of assessment; otherwise, boilerplate analyses are likely to ensue in which numbers take precedence over clinical judgment. Such interpretations are often inaccurate.

Traditional test interpretation involves averaging of subtests measuring verbal ability, perceptual or visual-spatial reasoning, working memory, and processing speed, from which a Full Scale IQ is derived. Relative strengths and relative weaknesses are reported based on the degree of discrepancy between specific subtest scores and the subject's average scores in these areas. The child's scores are compared to standardized norms to determine if they are above or below the average for their age group. This is standard practice.

Normative interpretation may be suitable for assessments with 95% of the population; however, it is likely to underestimate the abilities of gifted children—and render acute underestimates for profoundly gifted or twice exceptional children. The assessment issues unique to the gifted population are not commonly understood. Variables such as test ceilings, item difficulty, discontinue criteria (the number of items a child must miss before the subtest is terminated), assignment of credit for all raw score points earned, and environmental factors differentially affect the performance of the gifted due to the small number of items that distinguish the gifted from the average.

SELECTING TESTS

Test selection is more complex for the gifted than other populations. Children in the average range score similarly on different measures of intelligence, whereas gifted children exhibit considerable variability on different instruments (Silverman, 1995a). The situation is compounded by the fact that different IQ tests no longer measure the same basic construct of intelligence. Each intelligence scale identifies a different population as gifted. The Full Scale IQ score has not remained a trustworthy gauge of children's intellectual capacities; it no longer represents a unitary construct. The more factors the intelligence scale attempts to measure, the less cohesive the resulting composite score (R. L. Thorndike, in Thorndike, Hagen, & Sattler, 1986).

There are multiple ways of administering and scoring the new IQ tests. Examiners have a choice of subtests. Score ranges in the upper extremes are not equivalent. While scores of 130 and above on a Wechsler Scale indicate giftedness, scores of 120 or higher on the fifth edition of the *Stanford-Binet Intelligence Scale* (SB-5) are considered gifted (Lovecky, Kearney, Falk, & Gilman, 2005; Ruf, 2003). Wechsler Scales are used more than any other IQ tests in the public schools (Wasserman, 2003, in press); therefore, they are discussed in more detail below.

Test Ceilings

One of the most important variables in selecting a test for the gifted is how much room there is at the top for the child to demonstrate the full strength of his or her abilities.

Most IQ tests suffer from ceiling effects. There are several types of ceiling issues in testing the gifted. First, the highest possible score may be barely in the gifted range, and not able to differentiate children in the higher IQ ranges (e.g., 135 is the highest score possible on *Raven's Progressive Matrices*). Second, the child might answer the hardest problems in a subtest, never reaching discontinue criteria (subtest ceiling). Third, test ceilings differ. The maximum test age on the WISC-IV is under 17, while the maximum test age of the *Stanford-Binet Intelligence Scale (Form L-M)* (SBL-M) is 23. A fourth meaning of ceiling is when the child reaches a point at which the examiner is certain that no further items can be passed.

> A valid measurement of a gifted child's abilities is only possible when both the scoring limits are adequate *and* the child clearly reaches a level of difficulty that is too hard—a true ceiling. Otherwise, we have no idea how much further the child could go. (Gilman, 2008a, p. 80)

If a test does not have sufficient ceiling, it would be like trying to measure a person who is 6 feet tall with a ruler that only goes to 5 feet (Stanley, 1990). Julian Stanley created a 12-foot ruler. To differentiate students with exceptional ability, Stanley employed the *Scholastic Aptitude Test* (SAT), designed for high school students, as an above-level test with junior high school students. This is the "talent search." Stanley's talent search model has served well over 3 million students in the United States, and many others overseas (Lee, Matthews, & Olszewski-Kubilius, 2008).

The talent searches illustrate that what appears as "a relative strength" on one test can turn out to be an astronomical strength on a test with a higher ceiling. Two 7th graders who score at the 97th percentile in mathematics on a 7th grade standardized achievement test may appear to have similar levels of ability. Their achievement tests qualify them to participate in a talent search, and take an above-level College Board exam.

One of the two students may score 350 on the Mathematics section of the SAT, while the other obtains a score of 750—high enough for admission to the finest universities! The grade-based achievement test indicates that the two students are in the top 3% of students their age—"a relative strength," which may earn them places in an advanced mathematics class. But the SAT reveals that one of the two has mastered the math curriculum of the next several years and needs a significantly accelerated math program.

Measuring Abstract Reasoning

Test content also must be scrutinized. An appropriate IQ test for the gifted should be an excellent measure of abstract reasoning. Tests that emphasize working memory, processing speed, and nonmeaningful material are likely to produce less relevant results for this population than instruments designed to measure general intelligence (g) (Silverman, 2009a). Plomin and Price (2003) state that "g is one of the most reliable and valid traits in the behavioral domain" (p. 115), that it has the greatest long-term stability of any trait, and that it has greater predictive validity than any other attribute. Subtests highly saturated with general intelligence are better indicators of giftedness than subtests with low g correlations (Table 6.1).

The g-loadings on the WISC-IV demonstrate why the Verbal Comprehension Index (VCI), composed of Similarities, Vocabulary, and Comprehension, is the best predictor of success in a gifted program. Arithmetic, an optional test, ranks fourth in g-loadings. GDC substitutes Arithmetic for Letter–Number Sequencing or Digit Span, in the assessment of gifted children, unless the child dislikes mental math (Rimm, Gilman, & Silverman, 2008). Arithmetic is a good assessment of Working Memory because it employs meaningful material, documents mathematical talent in the gifted, and ranked second only to Vocabulary for the gifted group in the test manual (Wechsler, 2003). When the primary purpose of the assessment

TABLE 6.1 ℊ-LOADINGS ON THE WISC-IV

Good Measures of ℊ	
Vocabulary	(.82)
(Information)	(.79)
Similarities	(.79)
(Arithmetic)	(.74)
(Word Reasoning)	(.70)
Comprehension	(.70)
Fair Measures of ℊ	
Matrix Reasoning	(.68)
Block Design	(.67)
(Picture Completion)	(.63)
Letter–Number Sequencing	(.60)
Symbol Search	(.58)
Picture Concepts	(.57)
Digit Span	(.51)
Poor Measures of ℊ	
Coding	(.48)
(Cancellation)	(.25)

Note: Items in parentheses are optional tests.

Source: Adapted from Flanagan and A. Kaufman (2004, p. 309). Used with permission.

is to document giftedness rather than disabilities, Arithmetic can be substituted for Digit Span. However, it is not wise to make this substitution if the examiner is trying to diagnose a weakness in Working Memory, so that the child can receive accommodations.

At What Age Should Gifted Children Be Assessed?

The age of the child needs to be considered in test selection, as well as the purpose for the assessment. When testing for giftedness, it is better to test children when they are in the primary grades, as they are less likely to hit test ceilings. An ideal age is between four and eight. Testing children under four can be challenging.

> Young children are often unfamiliar with examiners and assessment settings and the establishment of adequate rapport may require the presence of a familiar adult during the initial stages of assessment. Shy or introverted children may choose not to respond to any novel or difficult tasks. ...The maintenance of appropriate levels of patience and redirection, and extended assessment times (resulting from long, sporadic responses requiring much encouragement) are common concerns in the reliable and valid appraisal of young children. (Sankar-DeLeeuw, 2004, p. 201)

The *Wechsler Preschool and Primary Scale of Intelligence, Fourth Edition* (WPPSI-IV) extends to age 7.5 and the WISC-IV begins at age 6.0. At age 6, gifted children should be tested on the WISC-IV to reduce ceiling effects. The same is true with the overlap at age 16 between with the WISC-IV and the *Wechsler Adult Intelligence Scale, Fourth Edition* (WAIS-IV). Gifted 16-year-olds should take the WAIS-IV. However, the picture gets somewhat muddied when the purpose of the assessment is to establish the need for accommodations. For twice exceptional youth, the examiner needs to determine which takes priority: revealing the child's intellectual capabilities and potential for success in college (WAIS-IV) or documenting the need for accommodations on College Board examinations (WISC-IV).

Individual Versus Group Tests

Individual IQ tests are much more appropriate for assessing giftedness than group screeners and the brief intelligence scales that schools often use. "Group IQ screeners have fewer items at the upper levels and are subject to ceiling effects. Some combine knowledge measures (what children have learned at school) with reasoning" (Gilman, 2008a, p. 62). Scores on individual standardized tests are likely to be more accurate than group measures and to yield higher scores. Group IQ tests underestimate scores for twice exceptional, highly gifted, and highly creative children. They often complexify questions, reading more into them than the test designers had in mind. They may miss multiple choice questions because they see so many possible options. Individual scales enable children to generate their own answers and examiners can see the sophistication of their thought processes (Gilman, 2008a).

Timed Versus Untimed Tests

Test constructors are often surprised to learn that gifted children are not always faster than children of lesser ability (Reams, Chamrad, & N. Robinson, 1990). Processing speed is usually considerably lower than other composite scores in gifted samples (Rimm et al., 2008). (See chart in *Interpreting WISC-IV Scores*.) Bonus points for speed in IQ tests depress IQ scores for children who are reflective or who suffer from slow processing speed or poor motor coordination (A. Kaufman, 1992). Timed tests exact a greater toll on the gifted because of the extent of the discrepancy between their competence and their performance under timed conditions. To improve diagnostic accuracy, gifted children should be allowed to continue after the time limits, and both timed and untimed performance should be reported.

Achievement Tests

IQ tests may not tell the whole story. Achievement tests are needed as well. Most children attain lower scores on achievement measures than on measures of ability (R. Woodcock, personal communication, July 8, 2000). However, as the *Woodcock-Johnson III Tests of Achievement* (WJ-III) has higher ceilings, some gifted children obtain higher scores on the WJ-III than on intelligence scales. When achievement surpasses ability measures, achievement scores offer better estimates of the child's actual capabilities. Individuals can underachieve, but no one can achieve beyond his or her capabilities; therefore, the term, "overachiever," is an oxymoron (Silverman, 1993c).

Here is an illustration. A boy tested at GDC obtained a VCI of 148 on the WISC-IV. His other composite scores were severely depressed by visual, auditory, and motor issues. On the WJ-III, his standard score in Calculation was 180 and his Broad Math score was 172. In this case, the child was able to demonstrate more of his intellectual abilities on the achievement test than on the ability measure. The WJ-III also has diagnostic utility. A girl tested recently at GDC had a very even profile on the WISC-IV. All of her scores were in the gifted range with the exception of Processing Speed, which was high average. Yet, her mother was convinced that her daughter had a learning disability. The WJ-III supported the mother's observations. Her daughter scored 157 in Broad Math, but only 88 in Spelling, a discrepancy of nearly 5 standard deviations.

Achievement tests are the school's report card. When achievement scores approach IQ scores, the child appears to be educated at the level of his or her ability. Achievement tests evaluate the effectiveness of the curriculum, monitor the child's progress in school or homeschooling, and are essential in determining if a child should be accelerated. They are required for some programs (e.g., the Davidson Young Scholar Program) and some private schools for the gifted. School personnel are more familiar with achievement tests than with IQ tests, and are more likely to understand the student's need for acceleration when they are shown grade equivalents attained on an achievement test. Grade equivalents may not be accurate assessments of a student's level of mastery, but they do provide some broad guidelines as to the degree of acceleration needed.

Other Instruments

Other instruments are helpful in examining a child's self-concept, learning style, personality style, overexcitabilities, progression through the developmental milestones, learning disabilities, attention issues, memory, attitudes about school, and social and emotional development. Some of these tools provide a more comprehensive picture of the child's giftedness, while others are important for establishing twice exceptionality or exploring emotional issues. To avoid pathologizing gifted clients, professionals who use emotional inventories and projective tests should be familiar with the typical characteristics of the gifted (Gilman, 2008a).

DISCONTINUE CRITERIA

At the dawn of intelligence testing, Terman and his colleagues endeavored to measure all that a child knew—testing the limits of the child's abilities. This practice was driven by Terman's desire to locate the brightest children. The SBL-M (Terman & M. Merrill, 1973), still in use as a supplementary test for exceptionally and profoundly gifted children (Wasserman, 2007), was based on an entirely different philosophy of testing than modern instruments.

Unlike most scales, where the examiner must discontinue offering items after a child has missed a certain number, with the SBL-M, examinees are shown *all* the vocabulary words in the test and encouraged to attempt to define terms well beyond their age level—even after they have missed several consecutive words. A child only has to pass one item at an age level to be given the opportunity to attempt all of the items at a higher age level. A ceiling is reached when the child fails to answer correctly any items at a specific age level, at which time no further items are presented. Some items score at several age levels, and examinees are given credit for all items passed beyond the ceiling they attained. Gifted children enjoy being offered extremely challenging items, and usually are not daunted by their inability to answer items designed for older children and adults. Examiners are permitted to give test items out of order to maximize the child's engagement (Vernon, 1987). Testing the limits of a gifted child's abilities is exciting, and worth the investment of extra time.

Over the years, interest in the gifted waned and the industry shifted its focus to testing children with much shorter attention spans. Clinical judgment was replaced with standardization. And time became a precious commodity. As school psychologists had limited time allotted for psychological assessment, shorter assessments were prized. To save time, as well as to avoid frustrating less capable children, discontinue criteria were progressively shortened. Short discontinue criteria underestimate gifted abilities.

The *Reynolds Intellectual Assessment Scale* (RIAS) (Reynolds & Kamphaus, 2007) requires examiners to stop after a child has missed only 2 or 3 items. This practice penalizes twice exceptional learners, who often miss easy items and pass more difficult ones (Silverman, 2009b). In addition, it appears to depress scores for culturally diverse children. Two ethnically diverse children applying for admission to a special program for the gifted were administered the RIAS. As they both missed fairly easy items, the examiner chose to continue offering items beyond the discontinue criterion to test the limits of the children's abilities. One child's composite score jumped from 119 to 156, and the other rose from 118 to 153 (Silverman, 2009b). Differences exceeded 2 standard deviations! Had the examiner adhered faithfully to the discontinue guidelines, neither child would have qualified for placement in a gifted program. The WAIS-IV also has shorter discontinue criteria than the WAIS-III. If an examinee can answer items beyond the discontinue criteria, then a true ceiling has not been attained.

Tom Cayton (2008), Clinical Content Director at Pearson Assessments, suggests that good clinicians often go beyond standardization criteria in order to obtain valuable diagnostic information. Since discontinue criteria are critical to standardization, scores obtained under standard conditions must be reported. However, Cayton advises examiners to report two sets of scores, one obtained through standard administration, and a second score obtained under nonstandard conditions, with an explanation in the narrative.

Another issue for the gifted is that subtests frequently lack sufficient item difficulty to capture the full strength of their knowledge. Even young gifted children often go all the way to the end of a subtest, never reaching the discontinue criterion. GDC analyzed the performance of 104 gifted children on the WISC-IV and found that 95 of the 104 children did not reach the discontinue criterion on at least one subtest; 45 met no discontinue criterion on four or more subtests; and 3 children failed to meet discontinue criteria on eight subtests (Gilman, N. Robinson, Kearney, Wasserman, & Silverman, 2010).

Looking at separate age groups, 30 of the 31 children between the ages of 9 and 12 failed to reach discontinue criteria on at least one subtest, and as many as seven subtests, while 24 met no discontinue criteria on four or more subtests. Perhaps the most revealing finding was that 25 of the 33 6-year-olds met no discontinue criteria on at least one subtest, and as many as five subtests. As six is the youngest age group for which the WISC-IV is designed, it is clear that considerably more difficult items are needed for full assessment of the gifted. For 91% of the children assessed, resulting scores were minimal estimates of their actual ability (Gilman et al., 2010).

One might assume that gifted children who go all the way to the end of a subtest earn the highest possible score, but that is not usually the case. They often answer the hardest items on a subtest, while missing several easier items. Even average scores may be underestimates of ability. When a ceiling is never reached, the full extent of the child's ability is unclear. It is important for the examiner to acknowledge the possibility that the child might have scored higher if there had been harder items available. In GDC reports, a plus sign is placed next to subtest scores where the discontinue criteria were not met. An explanatory note appears under the chart: "There was insufficient item difficulty on these subtests. It is possible that X might have scored higher had there been more difficult items to offer. Therefore, X's scores may be underestimates."

EXTENDED NORMS

Until recently, the maximum subtest score on any Wechsler Scale was 19 and the maximum IQ score (although nearly impossible to attain) was 160. Some children barely answered enough items to obtain a subtest score of 19, while others gave many more correct responses, but no higher scores were available. Their extra raw score points were disregarded in the calculation of their subtest and composite scores. Creative practitioners who specialized in testing the gifted developed various methods for indicating that a child's subtest score did not reveal the full picture of the child's abilities. Some examiners put a plus sign next to the subtest score and the resulting composite scores to show that the child achieved additional raw score points. This practice hinted at the limitations of the test ceiling, but did not demonstrate the degree to which the child surpassed the ceiling. Some psychologists used test ages from the manual to provide a better picture of the strength of the child's abilities. The highest test age for WISC-IV subtests is 16 years 10 months, which is certainly impressive when testing a 7-year-old, but not as striking with a 12-year-old.

Betty Meckstroth created a more precise way of representing the strength of the child's abilities. She recorded the raw score points earned beyond the minimum number required to attain the ceiling score of 19 (e.g., 19 + 1, 19 + 2, etc.). GDC adopted this method of tracking extra raw score points earned. One child earned 35 extra raw score points (Silverman, Cayton, & Raiford, 2008). Another scored 13 raw score points beyond the ceiling on Vocabulary (19 + 13) and 8 extra points on Similarities (19 + 8) (Rimm et al., 2008). "Leslie," at the age of 8 years 3 months,

TABLE 6.2 **EXTRA RAW SCORE POINTS EARNED**

Similarities	19 + 8
Vocabulary	19 + 12
Comprehension	19 + 4
(Information)	19 + 2
Picture Concepts	19 + 2

obtained 28 extra raw score points, 26 of which were earned in the Verbal Comprehension subtests (Table 6.2).

Leslie's scores, along with those of 333 other gifted children from eight different sites, were brought to the attention of Pearson Assessment. Some of the children, like Leslie, earned higher raw scores than the publisher had ever seen (Gilman, 2008a). Additional raw score points earned, which never before had been reflected in IQ scores, became the basis of a historical breakthrough in assessment: extended norms on the WISC-IV.

By allowing credit for the actual number of raw score points earned, Pearson was able to raise the maximum subtest scores from 19 to 28 and the composite scores (e.g., Full Scale IQ) from 160 to 210! Extended norms enable children to qualify for programs for the highly gifted and they support acceleration. They are available on the Pearson website (http://pearsonassess.com/NR/rdonlyres/C1C19227-BC79-46D9-B43C-8E4A114F7E1F/0/WISCIV_TechReport_7.pdf). Based on the same measurement metrics used in all Wechsler Scales, the scores are "a smooth extension of the test's normative scaling" (Gilman, 2008a, p. 80); they allow meaningful comparisons of strengths and weaknesses and illuminate the true extent of discrepancies. Leslie obtained the following scores when extended norms were used to calculate her performance (see Table 6.3).

TABLE 6.3 **LESLIE'S EXTENDED NORMS SCORES**

Subtest	Score and Extra Points	Extended Norm
Similarities	19 + 8	23
Vocabulary	19 + 12	25
Comprehension	19 + 4	22
(Information)	19 + 2	(21)
Picture Concepts	19 + 2	21
Index	Composite Score	Extended Norm
Verbal Comprehension (VCI)	155	182
Perceptual Reasoning (PRI)	145	149
Working Memory (WMI)	141	141
Processing Speed (PSI)	128	128
Full Scale (FSIQ)	153	166
General Ability Index (GAI)		180

Leslie did not earn extra points in Working Memory or Processing Speed. Information is an optional test that was not included in Leslie's composite scores. Table 6.4 from Pearson Assessments compares the ranges in the manual with the extended ranges.

TABLE 6.4 **WISC-IV SUBTEST AND COMPOSITE SCORE RANGES**

Scores	Published Range	Extended Range
Subtests	1–19	18–28
VCI and PRI	45–155	150–210
WMI and PSI	50–150	150–210
FSIQ and GAI	40–160	150–210

VCI, Verbal Comprehension Index; PRI, Perceptual Reasoning Index; WMI, Working Memory Index; PSI, Processing Speed Index; FSIQ, Full Scale IQ; GAI, General Ability Index.

Source: Silverman, Cayton, and Raiford (2008). Used with permission.

The extended norms table should be consulted when a child attains ceiling-range scaled scores (18 or 19) on two or more subtests (Zhu, Cayton, Weiss, & Gabel, 2008). The norms can be calculated on prior WISC-IV test results; it is not necessary for the child to be retested.

INTERPRETING WISC-IV SCORES

One of the most interesting facets of psychological testing is interpreting the results. The "practice" of psychology is well named. Each client teaches us something new. "For me, amidst the enjoyment of getting to know them, the pieces of a puzzle are being put into place, and the final picture seems always to be unique from all of the others that I have seen" (Gilman, 2008a, p. 59). Interpretive skill takes time and patience; it helps to have good mentors.

Some are opposed to the interpretation of cognitive test profiles, claiming that analysis of subtest scores within a subject's profile ("ipsative analysis") is not supported by empirical research (e.g., Lovett & Lewandowski, 2006; Watkins, 2000). Studies of the gifted do not appear to inform this perspective. This faction does not acknowledge the existence of twice exceptional children (see Lovett & Lewandowski, 2006), attributing their difficulties to lack of motivation. (Apparently, none of them has held a crying child who could not get his thoughts down on paper.) They hold genuine disdain for clinical observations, seeing them as "unscientific" (Watkins, 2000). They exhort psychologists to paint with broad strokes about global cognitive abilities. They concede that general intelligence predicts school persistence, achievement, and job performance in numerous occupations. Beyond determining how smart a child is, they believe that no additional information of any value can be gleaned from examining subtest profiles. This view makes IQ interpretation quite simple. "Here's your score. Have a nice life."

Rejection of the validity of profile analysis has a longstanding history in school psychology (e.g., McDermott, Fantuzzo, &

Glutting, 1990). Alan Kaufman (1994a, 1994b) has eloquently defended both ipsative analysis and clinical insight. "To prove their point that the ipsative approach should be punished painfully, they stripped the method of all dignity. They gutted it of its heart and soul" (A. Kaufman, 1994a, p. 5). Alan Kaufman (1994b) provides empirical evidence of the utility of clinical analysis in the study of stroke patients, the elderly, Hispanics, Native Americans, depression, epilepsy, fluid versus crystallized abilities, changes in intelligence throughout the lifespan, and so on.

> Wechsler's tests are clinical tests designed to be used to understand the child or adult being assessed. ...Furthermore, I believe the clinical arguments are even more persuasive than the empirical ones to psychologists who engage in individual assessment within the real world. (pp. 200, 205)

Clinical research deserves greater appreciation within the field of psychology as a legitimate source of information. The wisdom that is gained with practice is worth sharing. This section is informed by 33 years of clinical practice with more than 6,000 clients, as well as a PhD in the study of learning disabilities. It would be difficult to ignore patterns that have appeared repeatedly in this many profiles. The analyses and recommendations that have followed from these interpretations have made a difference in the lives of children. Some may be unorthodox, some may lack empirical data to support them, but they work.

General Ability Index

Gifted children are known to be asynchronous in their development (Alsop, 2003; Silverman, 2012a). How does an examiner determine how much asynchrony is to be expected for the gifted population and when the degree of asynchrony is sufficient to suggest the need for further evaluation of a learning disability? This is an important diagnostic question. Greater discrepancies among subtest scores are found for the gifted

TABLE 6.5 **WISC-IV NORMATIVE SAMPLE**

Composites	Gifted Group	Control Group
Verbal Comprehension (VCI)	124.7	106.6
Perceptual Reasoning (PRI)	120.4	105.6
Working Memory (VMI)	112.5	103.0
Processing Speed (PSI)	110.6	102.8
Full Scale IQ (FSIQ)	123.5	106.7

Source: Wechsler (2003, p. 77). Used with permission.

than other groups (Rimm et al., 2008). Composite scores for the gifted sample (*N* = 63) and the control group reported in the *WISC-IV Technical and Interpretive Manual* (Wechsler, 2003) are illustrative (see Table 6.5 above).

The composite scores for the control group vary by less than 4 points, whereas the gifted sample varies by over 14 points. Discrepancies of 1 standard deviation (15 points) among composite scores would be considered typical for the gifted. Note that Working Memory and Processing Speed are in the average range; these do not discriminate the gifted from the control group. The National Association for Gifted Children (NAGC) Task Force study of 334 gifted children from eight sites provides a larger data bank as a basis of comparison (see Table 6.6 below).

The overall pattern is similar, and the mean scores indicate that the NAGC group is somewhat brighter than the gifted group reported in the *Technical Manual*. Working Memory is elevated since one-third of the sample was administered Arithmetic, a more meaningful task, instead of Letter–Number Sequencing. Once again, Processing Speed is in the average range. The composite scores vary by 21 points. This is still considered normal asynchrony. In *Essentials of WISC-IV Assessment*, Dawn Flanagan and Alan Kaufman (2004) suggest that composite scores that vary by 23 points or more (1.5 standard deviations) are significant and render the Full Scale IQ "not interpretable"

TABLE 6.6 **WISC-IV MEAN COMPOSITE/ INDEX SCORES FOR NAGC TASK FORCE DATA (N = 334)**

Verbal Comprehension (VCI)	133.17
Perceptual Reasoning (PRI)	127.84
Working Memory (WMI)	121.58
Processing Speed (PSI)	112.02

Source: Gilman, N. Robinson, Kearney, Wasserman, and Silverman (2010).

(p. 128). Further, if the Verbal Comprehension Index (VCI) and Perceptual Reasoning Index (PRI) scores vary by less than 23 points, the General Ability Index (GAI) "may be calculated and interpreted as a reliable and valid estimate of a child's global intellectual ability" (p. 128). The GAI is an excellent indicator of abstract reasoning ability. It is derived from the six core subtests of the WISC-IV composing the VCI and the PRI. Working Memory and Processing Speed are eliminated in the calculation. The GAI and VCI serve as the best measures of giftedness.

Flanagan and Kaufman (2004) found that the most frequent and pronounced pattern of discrepancy was between the Verbal Comprehension Index (VCI) and the Processing Speed Index (PSI). Gifted samples show the same configuration (Rimm et al., 2008; Silverman, Gilman, & Falk, 2004). In these studies the VCI emerged as the best representation of giftedness and the PSI as the weakest. In the NAGC study, 70% of the sample showed significant enough discrepancies among index scores to render their Full Scale IQ scores uninterpretable. And 78% qualified for the calculation of the GAI (Gilman et al., 2010).

Selection Criteria for Gifted Programs

When the discrepancy between the VCI and the PRI exceeds 22 points, the NAGC recommends that one or the other index be considered acceptable for selection to gifted programs. The NAGC Task Force study was the basis of the position statement on "Use of the WISC-IV for Gifted Assessment," posted on the NAGC website January, 2008.

> When the WISC-IV is used for the identification of gifted students, either the General Ability Index (GAI), which emphasizes reasoning ability, or the Full Scale IQ Score (FSIQ), should be acceptable for selection to gifted programs....
>
> The Verbal Comprehension Index (VCI) and the Perceptual Reasoning Index (PRI) are also independently appropriate for selection to programs for the gifted, especially for culturally diverse, bilingual, twice exceptional students or visual-spatial learners. (NAGC, 2008)

This practice is in concert with test interpretation for developmental disabilities. The *Diagnostic and Statistical Manual of Mental Disorders* (*DSM-IV*) (American Psychiatric Association, 1994) admonishes against averaging significantly discrepant subtest scores. "When there is significant scatter in the subtest scores, the profile of strengths and weaknesses, rather than the mathematically derived full-scale IQ, will more accurately reflect the person's learning abilities" (p. 40).[1] It is only by viewing discrepancies that one can locate gifted children with learning disabilities. A 30-point discrepancy in composite scores (2 SD) or a 9-point discrepancy in subtest scores (3 SD) suggest the need for further evaluation of a possible learning disability. This is well beyond the typical asynchrony of the gifted. Even if the lowest score is in the average range, the child may be experiencing frustration and the weakness needs attention (Gilman, 2008a; Silverman, 2009a).

The analysis of discrepancies as a means of determining learning disabilities has fallen out of favor in public education, but this practice is still very much alive in private and university clinics (Assouline et al., 2010). It allows the detection of weaknesses that can be ameliorated therapeutically. Education's lack of acknowledgement of twice exceptional children does not make them disappear. They need psychologists who are willing to continue to examine closely the discrepancies between their strengths and weaknesses. The child's strengths should be viewed separately from weaknesses, as indications of giftedness. Simply deriving Full Scale IQ scores conceals both the gifts and the learning disabilities, and neither one of them is dealt with appropriately.

What Do *g*-Loadings of Subtests Mean?

Knowledge of *g*-loadings of the subtests enhances the examiner's ability to pinpoint specific strengths and diagnose subtle weaknesses (Silverman, 2009a, 2009b). Gifted children usually perform best on Vocabulary, Information, Similarities, and Comprehension—measures of abstract verbal reasoning. All of these subtests have high *g*-loadings. Even gifted visual-spatial learners often show stronger performance on Verbal Comprehension than on Perceptual Reasoning. This ranking is so robust that when Perceptual Reasoning is higher, it raises numerous questions. Is the child bilingual? Is there an auditory processing issue? A weakness in expressive language? If Vocabulary and Similarities are high, but Comprehension is 9 points lower, does this child have Asperger Syndrome? The subtest discrepancies by themselves are not sufficient evidence of disability, but they provide strong clues for the need for further evaluations.

Whenever one subtest appears to be an outlier, an optional subtest should be administered. Information is a useful subtest for this population, as the gifted often soak up an unusual amount of information from their environment; in addition, Information yields higher extended norms than many of the other subtests. The combination of Vocabulary, Similarities, and Information is usually very high in exceptionally and profoundly gifted children. Leslie, described earlier in the chapter, obtained scores on the extended norms on these three subtests and Comprehension (See Table 6.2).

Children who score in the gifted range on Arithmetic and Block Design often score high on math achievement on the WJ-III and demonstrate math talent. Visual-spatial learners frequently show high performance on Matrix Reasoning and Block Design. They may perform poorly on Picture Concepts, because they associate visual aspects, rather than functional ones. For example, they might pick three objects that are yellow, or that look like teeth, or that could be used together. Picture Concepts is not an assessment of visual-spatial reasoning. It's inclusion in the PRI depresses scores for visual-spatial learners. Picture Completion, an optional subtest, measures visual closure; it is one of the few visual-spatial measures that shows little gender bias. When Picture Concepts is two standard deviations (6 points) below Matrix Reasoning and Block Design, Picture Completion would be a suitable substitute.

On face value, scores on Similarities and Picture Concepts should be similar, since Picture Concepts is a visual similarities task. But the g-loadings on these two tasks bear no resemblance. The g-loading on Similarities is .79, third from the top, and Picture Concepts is .57, fourth from the bottom (See Table 6.1). Gifted children tend to obtain similar scores on subtests that have similar g-loadings. Performance on Similarities is more predictive of performance on Vocabulary and Information than of Picture Concepts.

Matrix Reasoning and Block Design both measure visual-spatial abilities, and they have similar g-loadings. When a child shows visual-spatial interests, such as a passion for LEGOs™, and attains a gifted score in Matrix Reasoning, but an average score in Block Design, the examiner ponders the cause of the discrepancy. Is it a timing issue, because Block Design is timed and Matrix Reasoning is untimed? Is Processing Speed also low? At the GDC, we allow children to complete the block designs after the time limit. They don't get credit for the item, but it is diagnostically important to determine if the child *can* perform the task. Some children give up in frustration. But, because the task involves abstract reasoning, their strong suit, many gifted children keep struggling with a difficult item and feel a sense of accomplishment if they can do it, regardless of how much time it takes. (This takes extra patience on the part of the examiner.)

Visual Processing Issues

Block Design has a fairly high g-loading; thus, it is a decent measure of general intelligence (See Table 6.1). If the child's verbal reasoning scores are high, then the problem cannot be a lack of abstract reasoning. Interpretive manuals note that Block Design has a motor component, whereas Matrix Reasoning does not, but gifted children rarely have difficulties with the physical manipulation of the blocks, even if their score in Coding is low. Are there undetected visual issues? Here are some clues in the way the child approaches the task:

- Not being aware that all the blocks are alike
- Reversing the red and white blocks
- Breaking the set (not creating a square)
- Placing blocks at an angle and then reorienting them at the end
- Not being aware when a block is in the correct position
- Using overt or covert verbal mediation to solve the task
- Becoming angry, and saying the task is "impossible"
- Becoming embarrassed, saying, "I'm not good at this"

Sometimes we use some of the alternate presentations of Block Design in the *WISC-IV Integrated*, such as putting a transparent grid over the design outlining the blocks. Can the child complete the designs easily with the grid, but not at all without the grid? After a child completes a design, examiners frequently ask, "Does this look right to you?" If the child fails to notice when the blocks do not match the design, or other diagnostic signs emerge from observing how the child approaches the task, a vision evaluation is in order.

The Perceptual Reasoning and Processing Speed sections of the test are presented visually. When Matrix Reasoning, Block Design, Coding, and Symbol Search are considerably lower than the VCI and WMI, then vision, visual processing, or visual–motor coordination may be the culprit. Children with subtle visual processing issues have less difficulty with the concrete objects in Picture Concepts than they do with visualizing abstract images. Those who hate handwriting usually have significantly lower Coding scores. Many children with low Coding scores also have difficulty copying from the board; both activities involve vertical tracking. When Symbol Search and Reading Comprehension are both lower than expected, given the other scores, horizontal tracking is suspect. The child's eyes may be jumping from one line to another. This problem is easily corrected with 6 months of vision exercises.

We have seen remarkable improvement and enjoyment of reading after vision therapy. Recent research supports the effectiveness of this intervention in correcting convergence insufficiency (eye-teaming) and improving reading skills (e.g., Borsting et al., 2012; CITT Study Group, 2008; Goss et al., 2007; Shin, Park, & Maples, 2011). Psychologists tend to overlook vision problems. Large discrepancies between VCI and PRI are often misinterpreted as signs of abnormal brain functioning (e.g., Nonverbal Learning Disorder). Visual processing weaknesses need to be ruled out and visual remedies sought before diagnosing a child with a more serious Nonverbal Learning Disorder (Silverman, 2001).

Auditory Processing Issues

At GDC, we collect a great deal of information about ear infection history. If a child has depressed scores in Comprehension and Letter–Number Sequencing, mishears instructions, mispronounces words, asks for many repetitions, or has had more than nine ear infections beginning prior to 7 months of age, we recommend an auditory evaluation. Digits Backward is a good assessment of Working Memory, since the child has to manipulate auditory information, while Digits Forward is a good assessment of auditory sequencing. Most children can repeat two more digits forward than they can backward. Gifted children who have low scores in Spelling often have lower scores in Digit Span (although visual memory may also play a role).

Supplementary Tests

To further explore outlying scores, examiners may select additional subtests from the *WISC-IV Integrated*, which presents many of the same tests in a different format. Results of the *WISC-IV Integrated* subtests are not used to derive IQ scores, but they provide valuable diagnostic information to pinpoint the child's strengths and weaknesses. The SBL-M can be offered as a supplemental test for children who surpass the ceiling scores on the VCI (Gilman, 2008a; Silverman, 2009a; Wasserman, 2007).

These are a sampling of considerations in interpreting WISC-IV profiles for the gifted. The diagnosis of twice exceptional children is far more complex, and requires an understanding of the interaction of giftedness with various disabilities.

BRINGING OUT THE BEST

I love the challenge of molding myself into the kind of person that will bring out the best in each child I test. Close familiarity with the IQ tests and their standardization procedures gives me the freedom to focus on the children's behaviors and patterns. I can go slowly or race along, speak in an animated way or softly, whatever works best....

Why do I do this? I do this because I enjoy watching these kids feel confident, competent, and proud. They are kings or queens for a day. I am amazed by their passion to want to protect the environment, their compassion for people and animals, and their strong need to do something worthwhile in this world. They are positive, excited dreamers, and I am a privileged passenger along for the ride. (Tucker, February 2012, p. 1)

Gifted children are highly attuned to the attitudes of the examiner. If the tester really enjoys gifted children, they know it instantly and respond accordingly. Rapport building is essential and takes time. Children can be asked to bring a favorite toy or a photograph album to share with the examiner (Meckstroth, 1989). If the child becomes afraid of making mistakes, a toy or a hand puppet can help answer the questions. Examiners should encourage guessing, as there are many gifted children (particularly girls) who will not offer an answer unless they are certain. Sometimes practicing simple guessing games like "Guess what I ate for breakfast?" helps the child relax enough to speculate on the more difficult questions. Positive feedback for good guesses increases risk-taking and supports effort over performance.

Unusually sensitive, the gifted may not demonstrate their full capabilities for a variety of reasons:

- *choosing to hide* their abilities out of fear of the consequences of being labeled gifted (e.g., being removed from a current placement and being placed in a new environment, greater expectations of parents and teachers, losing friends, effect on siblings, etc.);
- unwillingness to guess for fear of making a mistake and appearing foolish;
- anxiety at being evaluated;
- feeling uncomfortable with the examiner;
- discomfort with aspects of the physical surroundings.

These factors can affect performance for all examinees, but they exert a greater impact on the scores of the gifted. Some highly gifted children will not respond if a test item is too easy. They think it is a "trick question" and read many deeper meanings into it (Lovecky, 1994). Their IQ scores may be depressed because they know too much about a subject rather than too little. Examiner Melody Wood asked a child she tested, "Who discovered America?" The girl thought for a long time and then said she didn't know. When the test was over, Melody asked her the question again and she replied that she knew it wasn't Christopher Columbus, because that theory had been disproven, but she couldn't remember who it was!

Most important of all, the tester cannot be in a hurry. When they are rushed, these sensitive children shut down. Testing the gifted takes longer due to the complexity of their thought processes, their tendency to be reflective, and their typical pattern of missing nearly enough items to discontinue and then getting some correct—sometimes going all the way to the end of the subtest.

> Many gifted children continue to hone their answers until a point at which they are finally satisfied. However, if the tester rushes to the next item, the child is quickly "trained" to offer the quick, concise answer that may not score as high. (Gilman, 2008a, p. 61)

How the evaluator feels about the child exerts a powerful effect on test scores. Some gifted children are extremely intuitive and pick up on facial expressions, body language, and other signals that the tester is unaware that he or she is emitting. If the examiner is hungry and is annoyed that the child is answering so many items correctly that the evaluation is taking longer than expected (delaying the examiner's lunch), the gifted child is likely to try to get the test over with by giving only minimal responses. On the other hand, if the evaluator thoroughly enjoys the workings of a gifted child's mind and delights in every correct answer, the child responds to the twinkle in the examiner's eye and tries his or her best.

> The sessions are usually very engaging for these children; the inherent challenge of the tests often eclipses what they experience at school. They are usually happy, frequently quite humorous, and virtually always well-motivated to do their best.

... Laughter [is often heard] emanating from a testing room. The tester's enjoyment of these children and comfort with high levels of sensitivity, reflectivity, perfectionism, and curiosity makes for a more comfortable session for the child. (Gilman, 2008a, pp. 59, 65)

A good starting point for locating an experienced tester of the gifted is Hoagies' Gifted Education Page: "Psychologists Familiar with Testing the Gifted and Exceptionally Gifted" (www.hoagiesgifted.org/psychologists.htm). Psychologists cannot refer themselves for this listing. They need to be recommended by families who have had good experiences or by other psychologists on the list.

QUALITATIVE ASSESSMENT

Expert examiners use qualitative as well as quantitative information in creating a cohesive picture of a child. Their judgments are informed by observing the child's behaviors before and during the assessment. Children who say "approximately" or "precisely" demonstrate advanced language development, regardless of their actual scores. The IQ scores of parents or siblings, early achievement of developmental milestones, profound curiosity, deep moral concern, remarkable associations or generalizations, perfectionism, advanced vocabulary, keen attention to detail, unusual empathy, vivid imagination, superb memory, early reading or fascination with LEGOs®, school achievement, reading interests, and parental anecdotes of unusually precocious reasoning are all taken seriously in determining the abilities of a child. A seasoned tester of the gifted uses this information to create a composite picture of the level of the child's abilities. IQ test results, then, are nested into this schema to add further information. "Those qualities that we have learned to recognize as gifted—or highly or profoundly gifted—become recognizable. Likewise, the developmental history of a child is vital information in judging apparent or potential ability levels" (Gilman, 2008a, p. 59).

One type of evaluation, developed by Dr. Annemarie Roeper, relies completely on observations such as these. With her husband, George, Annemarie founded The Roeper School in Bloomfield Hills, Michigan, one of the first schools for the gifted; it has been in operation for over 70 years. The Annemarie Roeper (AMR) Method of Qualitative Assessment (QA) is used as an alternative to, or in conjunction with, traditional testing and offers a unique approach to evaluation for giftedness.

> The human psyche is one of enormous complexity, not fully measurable by standardized psychometric examinations. The only instrument complex enough to understand a human being is another human being. AMR Method practitioners use themselves as the instrument through which to understand the child or adult. AMR Method of Qualitative Assessment offers a broader perspective to the assessment process, revealing the inner world of the individual. (Roeper, 2012)

Psychometric assessments have repeatedly demonstrated the efficacy of this method of estimating levels of intelligence in gifted children. AMR Qualitative Assessment is used independently by several private schools as their method of selecting students. The evaluator experiences the child in an unstructured observation that resembles play therapy. He or she enters the child's world with no preconceived notions. "An essential element of AMR Method of QA is to provide an open and totally non-judgmental atmosphere in which the child has freedom of expression" (Roeper, 2012). The children frequently talk openly about their interests and experiences, their hopes, their disappointments, and their problems. In addition to talking with them, the evaluator plays games with them that require strategies or problem-solving abilities, and allows them to express themselves with building materials, art, or story telling.

QA is an excellent alternative for children who do not perform well on IQ tests or for whom the test ceilings are too low. In addition to yielding information about the child's level of cognitive functioning, QA offers a glimpse at the inner world of the child, his or her emotional functioning, and may reveal issues related to the home, the school, peers, or self-concept. Videotapes of Annemarie Roeper's qualitative method have been created with the assistance of a grant from the Malone Family Foundation. They are available from The Roeper Institute (2012). Anne Beneventi, who worked with Dr. Roeper for 25 years, has become the current Director of the AMR Method of Qualitative Assessment. She writes:

> The goal of QA is to recognize and reflect the inherent value and uniqueness of the individual and encourage a positive esteem and interaction with the world.
>
> The Annemarie Roeper Method of Qualitative Assessment (QA) focuses on intensities and sensitivities, which underlie an individual's cognitive drive. QA does not separate the cognitive from emotional development of the individual but rather endeavors to understand the emotional need behind commonly agreed upon characteristics of giftedness. For instance, if a child has a strong interest in dinosaurs, extensive knowledge is evidence of advanced cognitive ability. Driving the motivation to learn is the individual's need for depth and complexity. The gifted child may be inspired to learn about dinosaurs to better understand the origin of the world in which he has found himself. To recognize a strong interest in dinosaurs as an emotional need expressed cognitively offers a more complex understanding of the child, which includes his or her inner experience. (Beneventi, March 2012, p. 1)

With gifted children, there are many nuances in both testing and interpretation. False positives are very unlikely. Scores in the gifted range do not occur "accidentally," as one cannot fake abstract reasoning (Silverman, 1986a). However, false negatives are abundant. Many more children *are* gifted than test in the gifted range. The common phrase in test reports, "This is a valid estimate of the child's abilities," needs to be reconsidered when assessing the gifted. How can one be certain? Underestimation of gifted children's abilities, unfortunately, is much more common than accurate appraisal.

When the examiner knows enough about giftedness to recognize the pitfalls that may cause underestimates, he or she confirms test results with other data. If, for example, a child's Broad Reading score is 160, but the IQ score is 125, the IQ score is probably an underestimate. It is impossible for a child to achieve beyond his or her capabilities. The highest indicator of a child's abilities *at any age* should be seen as the best estimate of the child's giftedness (Silverman, 2009a). When other measures fall short of this indicator, the evaluator needs to explore carefully to determine possible causes of the underestimate. Accurate diagnosis of the degree of a child's developmental advancement is a worthwhile investment. It should be based upon clinical judgment, rather than psychometric data alone. IQ scores are never an end in themselves; they are simply tools to be used wisely in the hands of professionals who understand giftedness.

NOTE

1. It is unclear at this time if the *DSM-5* will be worded similarly.

Optimal Development of the Gifted

Those who believe in our ability do more than stimulate us.
They create for us an atmosphere in which it becomes easier to succeed.
John Lancaster Spalding

n our success-oriented culture, optimal development of giftedness often is construed as fulfilling one's potential for greatness. As very few of the millions of gifted individuals in the world achieve lasting fame, this is an unrealistic expectation, as well as superficial. In Dabrowski's (1972) theory, the lowest level, most egocentric goals are money, fame, and power.

In humanistic psychology, optimal development has been conceptualized differently. Self-realization can be understood in terms of Maslow's self-actualization, Dabrowski's secondary integration, Jung's individuation, or other theoretical perspectives of human development. Is the individual leading a meaningful life? Does he feel fulfilled? Is she kind and happy? Does he have personal integrity? Is she authentic? Is he altruistic? The goals of inner development involve deepening the personality, overcoming conflicts, and actualizing one's potential for becoming one's best self. Families, educators, and psychologists can support inner development or they can act as agents of socialization, exhorting the gifted to "work harder" to attain external trappings of success.

Psychologists plumb the depths of the interior world. They have seen "successful" adults, dancing as fast as they can, who are suffering miserably because their inner world is in shambles. They understand the value of nurturing a rich inner life from which one's external life unfolds. It is from this core value system that giftedness can enrich the self and society.

HONORING THE IMPORTANT ROLE OF PARENTS VERSUS PARENT BASHING

The role of parents in fostering eminence has been studied for nearly a century (e.g., Bloom, 1985; Cox, 1926; Goertzel & Hansen, 2004). Current research has found parents to be instrumental in the academic, social, and emotional development of gifted children (Campbell & Verna, 2007; Cho & Campbell, 2011; Garn, Matthews, & Jolly, 2010; Hebert, Pagnani, & Hammond, 2009; Reichenberg & Landau, 2009; Wu, 2008). Most of the literature focuses on parents as *instruments* (tools) of their child's success, rather than as individuals who have their own need for support.

Scant attention has been given to the struggles of parents of the gifted, the issues they face when they discover they have a gifted child, or the Sophie's Choice some are forced to make responding to one child's needs at the expense of a sibling's. In his study of young world-class performers, Bloom (1985) honored their parents as:

child oriented and willing to devote their time, their resources, and their energy to giving each of their children the best conditions they could provide for them. Almost no sacrifice was too great if they thought it would help their children's development. (p. 510)

Piechowski also acknowledged the role of nurturers:

Clearly, it is nearly impossible to invest oneself in a demanding career and equally in raising a talented child, unless we view it as a division of labor between the career-absorbed father and the gifted child-centered mother. ... The great achievers and the eminent as a rule have a parent or mentor especially devoted to them (Albert, 1980b). No doubt it takes considerable dedication and integrity to live for the child but not through the child, to cherish and guide rather than to want to own. Thus the nurturing generations appear to be necessary to the achieving ones. The idea behind this view is simply to acknowledge the great importance of those who nurture the talents of their children. (Piechowski, as quoted in Silverman & Kearney, 1989, p. 54)

Sadly, this high regard for parents of the gifted is unusual. When these parents advocate for their children, educators often perceive them as "pushy" (Cole & DellaVecchia, 1993). Although some of the thousands of parents we have encountered in the last 33 years at GDC were anxious and difficult to work with, all were genuinely concerned about the welfare of their children and wanted to understand their needs. Most had faced dismissive attitudes from school personnel. One parent was asked, *"Does your child have to be 'gifted' for you to love him?"* In an Australian study, Alsop (1997) found that 83% of the parents of gifted children were treated by teachers as if they were "pushy" (p. 31). Coleman (2012) sees this attitude as the "conventional view."

The conventional view of adults (teachers, psychologists, and principals) is that the child's drive is generally externally directed, rather than internally; the motivation is a result of her pushy parents, not the child. This view is remarkably resistant to change, although the literature on families and giftedness since early in the last century has repeatedly shown that gifted children do not regard their parents as pushing them forward (Bloom, 1985; Olszewski-Kubilius, 2002; Tannenbaum, 1983; Terman & Oden, 1947). Opportunities are provided, rather than "you must do this" or that. (p. 388)

Are gifted children a lot smarter than their parents? Are parents jealous of their children's abilities? Are they so awestruck by their children's intelligence that they "parentify" their children? Do they become "overinvolved" in their children's lives? Do they put too much pressure on their children? Do they know less than teachers about what is best for their children? Do they make unreasonable demands on teachers? These were some of the unsettling impressions I gleaned from reviewing the literature on parents of the gifted (Silverman, 1993a). One researcher even suggested that mothers label one of their children as gifted—"the star"—for their own narcissistic ego needs (Cornell, 1984).

Shocked by these portrayals, I called Betty Maxwell, the Associate Director of GDC, who had interacted with thousands of parents. "Betty, I need a reality check. Have I been an advocate for parents of the gifted for so many years that I just don't see how dysfunctional they really are?" She laughed and assured me that, on the contrary, she found them to be appropriately concerned about their children and accurate in their perceptions of their children's abilities.

> We feel alone, accused of being "elitist" for advocating for our kids, accused of bragging when simply talking about them, and accused of pushing our kids, when, in reality, they are pulling us behind them at a high rate of speed. It can be lonely. Add in the natural quirkiness and challenges of a gifted or twice-exceptional kid, and even extended family may not believe what you go through. (J. Merrill, 2012, pp. iii–iv)

Many parents of the gifted complain that their children are the ones exerting the pressure. Their speed of learning and quest for knowledge often exceed their parents' comfort level. Cho and Campbell (2011) suggest that gifted children draw more resources from their parents. Rather than the influence going in one direction, from parent to child, they found "bidirectional or reciprocal causal influences" in the development of talent (p. 42). Alomar (2003) arrived at a similar conclusion after studying 246 parents of gifted and nongifted children in Kuwait. The cognitive and affective aspects of gifted children directed the manner in which the parents interacted with their children. "Parents act according to the natural demands of their child, including when giftedness requires more intensive involvement and support from parents" (Alomar, 2003, p. 99).

Negative views of parents of the gifted continue to appear in the literature (e.g., Hermann & Lawrence, 2012; Mudrak, 2011). Parents who observe an "inborn need to learn independently" are accused of having a "reified" view of giftedness that compromises their effectiveness (Mudrak, 2011, p. 206). And some educators view parents as a nuisance. Too many times, I've heard teachers and administrators say, "I love working with gifted kids, if only I didn't have to deal with their parents."

Why don't we hear more about the healthy, functional parents who comprise the vast majority of the 6,000 families who have brought their children to GDC? Or the 535 families deemed to have "healthy family function" who sought assessment at CHIP in Melbourne, Australia (Alsop, 1997, p. 33)? Or the highly supportive, encouraging parents of star performers studied by Bloom (1985)? Or the indomitable parents who have advocated tirelessly for their twice exceptional children (Assouline, Foley Nicpon, & Huber, 2006; Yssel, 2012)?

> Contrary to many negative portrayals of families with gifted children within the psychological and popular literature, researchers have found that the vast majority of families tend to have healthy

interaction patterns, high levels of psychological adjustment and positive coping strategies. (May, 2000, p. 58)

When we have administered projective tests (e.g., Incomplete Sentences), the children consistently indicate that they feel supported by their parents and unhappy at school. Parents have legitimate cause for dismay.

> *Our biggest concern is that . . . the core of this profoundly gifted person will be hidden forever. . . . She appears to be hiding her intellect from her teachers and not advancing intellectually as she was before she began school. . . . Within two short months of starting Pre-K we saw a fundamental shift in how she chooses to use her gifts, and although we are happy that she, unlike many gifted, also seems to have a high social IQ, we are afraid that she is sacrificing her mental abilities for social acceptance. We also know that this "dumbing down" behavior tends to set a precedent for their entire life and, given how quickly it happened, we are highly concerned. Within four months of starting school she started complaining of stomach aches every morning before going to school. She loved the social interaction, but realized the other kids were nowhere near her intellectual equivalents. When we asked if school was hard she said, **"It's hard pretending you don't know anything!"***

The foremost reason that parents of the gifted seek the assistance of psychologists is concern about their children's schooling (Alsop, 1997). School was a major dilemma for nearly all the families of children above 170 IQ in a study conducted in Maine and Colorado (*N* = 38) (Silverman & Kearney, 1989). Over 53% of 241 parents of exceptionally gifted children reported lack of a sufficiently challenging curriculum in their child's current school placement and 35% felt that their child lacked personal attention in school (K. Rogers & Silverman, 2001). This discontent is pervasive throughout the gifted range, not just at the upper extreme (see Moon, 2003, for a summary of studies). In a nationwide survey of parents of moderately gifted children (*N* = 30), "more than half of the parents discussed how school assignments and classroom environments rarely provided appropriate challenge or meaning, hindering the development of academic motivation" (Garn et al., 2010, p. 269). Less than 28% of the 47 parents in Alsop's (1997) study felt that their child was in an adequate educational environment. A larger survey of 385 parents of the gifted revealed that 47% of parents of elementary-aged students and 53% of parents of high school students felt that their children's needs were not being met at school (Feldhusen & Kroll, 1985; Moon, 2003). More recently, Morawska and Sanders (2009) identified "school concerns" as a major need of families of the gifted.

These studies suggest that a large percentage of parents do not feel that schools are adequately challenging their gifted children. Is the appropriate solution blaming the parents? "Blame-the-victim" mentality has been strongly challenged in psychology, but it seems to have escaped notice in education. Yes, some parents of gifted children are difficult and lack social skills. Does this negate their concerns or warrant stereotyping all parents of gifted children? Two decades ago, I labeled this practice "parent bashing" (Silverman, 1993b). The genesis of this prejudice appears to be:

a. the lack of recognition that gifted children have special needs, so parents are perceived as wanting special privileges for their children (e.g., George, 1992);
b. the lack of training that educators receive about giftedness, combined with the assumption of some teachers that they know what is best for all their students;
c. complete lack of exposure of psychologists and counselors to the unique concerns of the gifted, which often leads to the misinterpretation of both the children and their parents (Silverman, 1993a);
d. lack of respect for the intelligence of mothers, who are the main advocates for the gifted (Silverman, 1993b).

"I wanted to go talk to the principal when they gave my daughter a primer to read in first grade," a mother explained to the district's gifted consultant. "She'd been reading the 'Little House' books at home for two years. But I didn't go. I didn't know what to say. After all, I read before I went to school, too. Maybe it doesn't mean that much. They know more than I do about teaching kids. I'm only a parent." (Tolan, 1992, pp. 1, 8)

Schools are more likely to take seriously gifted children's fathers than their mothers. I recommend that both parents talk to school personnel together.

The overt disdain with which many parents of the gifted must cope is more disturbing than the bias against gifted children. At least the children have their parents to advocate for them. Parents of the gifted have little support within the school system (Alsop, 1997). In our cyberspace world, they find and help each other in online communities and support groups. Even this type of support may be scorned by some administrators as "gripe groups."

> Every single one of these kids presents differently, and they are not in parenting magazines or books, mainstream blogs, or general societal acceptance. So when we find other parents in the same leaking boat, bailing water with a cracked Styrofoam cup, we're thrilled. We're not living the same lives, but they are close enough that we can relax a little bit when we all get together, knowing that we're not going to be judged by people who just don't get it. (J. Merrill, 2012, pp. 9–10)

These parents do not deserve ridicule. They need the safe shelter of knowledgeable, parent-friendly psychologists and counselors to turn to for advice, to be their advocates (May, 2000). They deserve to be taken seriously and respected as individuals, as well as for the important role they play in their children's development. Education is focused on children. In the practice of psychology, we can expand the circle of concern to include optimal development of parents as well. Parents of gifted children need professionals to turn to for support in dealing with schools and for guidance in parenting. They need advocates in the field of psychology who see their children as individuals rather than only as members of a group. They need you.

PSYCHOLOGICAL SUPPORT SERVICES FOR PARENTS

Moon (2003) suggests that there are two types of support services needed by families of the gifted. She characterizes them as *parent guidance*, which is preventive, and *family therapy*, which is restorative. The purpose of parent guidance is to foster "optimal development" through early intervention and prevention of social and emotional problems (p. 388). The emphasis of parent guidance is on assessment, test interpretation, and forging recommendations for school and home. In many respects, this is an excellent dichotomy between the functions of psychologists who conduct assessments and therapists who sort through complex relationship issues. But few parents contact psychologists to prevent problems from occurring; most seek services in response to concerns. The exception to this is when parents are trying to enroll their child in a school for the gifted that requires intelligence testing. Broadly speaking, schools for the gifted can be seen as helping to prevent social and emotional problems.

Assessment can be healing, as well as preventive. It can clarify why a child does not relate well with age mates, cannot stand drill and repetition, hates handwriting, sometimes feels smart and sometimes feels dumb—and lead to school modifications that rectify these issues. Sibling rivalry often lessens dramatically when the secondborn sibling discovers that he, too, is gifted. In a one-on-one situation, introverted children show surprising abilities that may be obscured in school. Gifted girls who hide their abilities to fit in with the other girls may reveal gifts during testing of which no one was aware. The *"I won't"* of belligerent children is understood as *"I can't"* when an undetected learning disability surfaces. Underachievement sometimes vanishes when a child has access to a keyboard for assignments. The discovery of giftedness is often ameliorative, kindling aspirations, and healing self-concepts. "I just thought I was crazy!"

In addition to parent guidance, family therapy may be needed to repair relationships, resolve conflicts, model active listening, assist in family transitions, explore roots of underachievement, increase understanding of the complex dynamics of living in a gifted family, and develop new ways of perceiving and interacting (Leviton, in press). Assessment can act as a prelude to family therapy. Parent guidance is focused on the implications of assessment, and it is offered intermittently—before, during, or after assessment. Family therapy usually involves a commitment to several successive sessions to deal with family interactions.

There is a dearth of empirical research on the issues facing gifted families (Morawska & Sanders, 2009; Reichenberg & Landau, 2009) and the effectiveness of different approaches (Moon, 2003), but much can be learned from clinical practice. The issues discussed in Chapter 6 would all be subsumed under parent guidance:

a. understanding the meaning of their child's developmental differences;
b. gaining accurate assessment of their child's abilities;
c. coming to terms with the significance of the test results;
d. determining supportive educational provisions;
e. deciding appropriate grade placement;
f. assisting parents in advocating more effectively;
g. locating available resources (e.g., scholarship opportunities, enrichment programs, special schools, etc.);
h. diagnosing twice exceptionality and obtaining accommodations.

Parents of exceptionally and profoundly gifted children have additional concerns. These children learn at such an astonishing pace that parents often choose to homeschool them, or move their family to a city with more resources, or find a way to afford private school, or use distance learning programs, or accelerate them—sometimes 2 or 3 years. Acceleration speeds up the educational trajectory so that the child is often ready for college courses at a very young age (Solow & Rhodes, 2012). This leads to a whole new set of questions. "Now what do we do? Do we enroll our child in Advanced Placement courses early? Are they sufficiently challenging? Do we let our child have access to college-level information through online courses? Do we go with our child to a college campus and audit courses together? Do we allow our child to enroll in college courses? Do we move to a college town so that our child can be an early entrant while still living at home? Is our child ready to leave home and go to college? Are we ready to have an empty nest after focusing all our energy on this child? What impact do these decisions have on our other children?" (Silverman & Kearney, 1989).

In concert with assessment, parents of the gifted may request assistance with emotional issues that could be considered the domain of family therapy, such as:

a. defusing tension in the family as a result of the special needs of their gifted child(ren) (e.g., conflicting parental perceptions) (Cornell, 1984);
b. dealing with attitudes of neighbors, extended family, and community members;
c. coping with the child's intensity, perfectionism, heightened sensitivity, introversion, or overexcitability;
d. assisting the child in finding friends and developing better peer relations;
e. reversing underachievement;
f. dealing with complex family dynamics;
g. coming to terms with their own giftedness;
h. developing their own aspirations.

Families of the gifted may engage in therapy for more typical reasons, such as stress-related symptoms, divorce, relocation, sibling rivalry, parental conflict, depression, or suicidal ideation, but giftedness must be taken into account even when the circumstances appear unrelated. It is often the elephant in the middle of the living room. Raising a gifted child, or a family full of gifted children, puts extra pressure on parents, and can strain marriages to the breaking point. There is not enough time, not enough money, not enough energy to meet all the demands and one's expectations of oneself. "The needs of gifted children can...strongly challenge the family's financial resources" (Alomar, 2003, p. 96). Brief family therapy has been found effective with therapists who are trained in both giftedness and family therapy (Moon, 2003). A gifted therapist can quickly bring about balance and family harmony, freeing up emotional resources and energy for creative problem solving (Leviton, in press).

Few researchers have attempted to ascertain what parents of the gifted need from psychologists. During an era in which psychologists were more involved in the assessment of giftedness, Dembinski and Mauser (1978) conducted a study of the needs of 105 parents whose children were enrolled in special programs in Illinois and California. Beyond the guidance issues discussed above, 52% inquired about additional support services for their family (e.g., counseling), 67% requested reading material, 82% were curious about the best way to enrich their child's home life, 73% asked about child-rearing practices for gifted children, and 54% wanted to be put in touch with other parents with similar concerns. These needs are still present today. The popular parent forums, conducted by Supporting Emotional Needs of the Gifted (SENG) (DeVries & Webb, 2007), attest to the continued need for parent support groups, parent education, and parental guidance.

AN OPTIMAL HOME ENVIRONMENT

Parents of young gifted children sometimes consult with psychologists for permission to provide home stimulation, as well as advice about how to respond effectively to their child's advancement. This type of early intervention sounds preventive, but the call is usually prompted by maternal angst and insecurity. These young mothers want to do what is best for their children, but receive mixed messages. They may be perceived as "bragging" about their children's abilities, and warned by friends, neighbors, and relatives to minimize their child's differences (Alsop, 1997) so that their child will grow up "normally." Over 20% of the parents in Alsop's study considered the advice they received from their families "hurtful" (p. 30). Mothers trained as teachers dread being perceived as "pushy." Fearing that others will attribute their child's advancement to "overinvestment," they plead nonguilty to charges of home stimulation. "I didn't teach her to read. Honest! She did it on her own when I wasn't looking."

Home enrichment should be encouraged for all children. Most of the variance in achievement is due to the home environment. "Schools can account for as much as 25% of the variance contributing to student achievement" (J. Gallagher, 2004, p. 122). An impressive body of research has accumulated revealing the importance of a rich home environment in the development of gifts and talents (Albert, 1978; Alomar, 2003; Chan, 2005; Feldman, 1986; Kulieke & Olszewski-Kubilius, 1989; N. Robinson & Noble, 1991; Tannenbaum, 1992). In an era in which inherent differences are questioned (e.g., Ericcson, Nandagopal, & Roring, 2009), and in Asian cultures that emphasize effort over ability (Wu, 2008), parents absorb the major responsibility of developing their children's gifts to their fullest. "Giftedness starts at home and develops at home" (Reichenberg & Landau, 2009, p. 874).

While mothers have been recognized as the primary source of the success of highly able Puerto Rican students (Garrett, Antrop-Gonzalez, & Velez, 2010), other studies emphasize the important role of fathers in the development of their sons' gifts. Hebert et al. (2009) summarized research on fathers' roles in their children's development as follows:

"paternal involvement was related to positive child outcomes such as school success, lower instances of behavioral or emotional problems, and positive social behaviors" (p. 243). Utilizing a case study approach, these researchers examined positive father–son relationships of 10 prominent men who had biographies or autobiographies published about them. The men's fathers provided encouragement and guidance, fostered determination, and inspired their sons to do their best in whatever they chose to do. Mutual admiration and respect evolved in these relationships. "Their fathers believe in them unconditionally, serve as models of strong work ethic, maintain high expectations for them, respect them, and take pride in their accomplishments" (p. 269). These are key ingredients in effective parent–child relationships.

Cho and Campbell (2011) conducted a study in Korea of 908 students in gifted education and 866 students in regular education. Results showed that the most influential predictor of mathematics and science achievement was "father's involvement" (p. 45). Parents of nongifted children were less engaged in their education as the children matured. Fathers of youth enrolled in science-gifted centers maintained their involvement with their children's education throughout high school.

The significance of extended family, especially grandparents, should not be overlooked. Grandparents are particularly important in cultures where elders are respected, extended families live in community, or grandparents take a major role in caretaking. In her years of working with gifted children and their families in Israel, Erika Landau noted a steady increase in the influence of grandparents.

In our admittance interview is a question, "Where did you learn the things you know?" Thirty years ago most of them answered "in school"; 20 years ago more children answered "at home"; 10 years ago very few answered school, but many answered, with a warm and nice smile, "from my grandmother/grandfather." (Reichenberg & Landau, 2009, p. 881)

As a result, Landau began offering workshops for grandparents. She finds that children enjoy unconditional love from their grandparents, and that grandparents are more patient than parents. VanTassel-Baska (1989) studied 15 gifted adolescents from economically disadvantaged homes, half of whom were Black. She found that maternal grandmothers were the most dominant figure in the family, and that they provided a stabilizing and nurturing influence on their granddaughters. Garrett et al. (2010) mentioned the positive influence of grandmothers on the high academic achievement of low-income Puerto Rican elementary students. Books are now being written on grandparenting gifted children (Webb, Gore, Karnes, & McDaniel, 2004).

Responsive parenting follows the lead of the child and extends the child's interests. Parents respect their children's individuality and allow them freedom of choice. They expose their children to a variety of stimulating activities and pay attention to what fascinates each child; then they provide intensive enrichment in the child's areas of interest (Munger, 1990). Of critical importance, the focus is on the process, not the product. With no attachment to the outcome, parents enjoy the enrichment they provide for their children. They are building *relationships* with their children robust enough to last a lifetime. Families that spend quality time together form close bonds. When parents enjoy spending time with their children, it is likely that their children will enjoy spending time with their parents when they are adults. I often ask parents, "What kind of a relationship do you want with your children when they are adults? What do you have to do now to ensure that kind of relationship?" (I remind them that the child they hollered at for bringing home a B is eventually going to decide if they go into a nursing home!)

The family climate is suffused with the values of the family. The parents of exceptionally gifted children in Colorado and Maine had well-defined values, held high expectations for their children, spent a great deal of time reading, and modeled the need to know (Silverman & Kearney, 1989). In the Colorado group, mothers' number one personal interest was reading; for the fathers, reading ranked second only to sports. Several mothers mentioned "child rearing" as a primary interest. Parents of the gifted tend to be industrious, and they pass on the value of hard work through example, as well as expectations (Hebert et al., 2009). Mutual respect is mentioned frequently by gifted children. They feel respected by their parents, which enables them to develop respect for their parents. They also describe how much they have benefited from their parents' warmth and affection (American Association for Gifted Children, 1978). Parents demonstrate affection and respect for their children in numerous ways: making time for them in their busy lives, giving them undivided attention, listening, asking questions, approving their decisions, trusting them, encouraging their curiosity, allowing autonomy, supporting their interests, and believing in their children.

How should parents handle precocious children who teach themselves to read at three and beg for advanced mathematics? Children learn at remarkably different rates, and parents should respond accordingly. Parents have more freedom than teachers to follow the natural learning trajectory of their child. Direct parental instruction is perfectly appropriate if the child is eager, interested, and enjoying the activities. The litmus test is if the learning is *fun*. If the parent and child are both enjoying it, it is not harmful. Criticism should be avoided. There is so much to learn in this world and so many ways of learning. Families should be commended for enriching their children's lives in every way possible. Early home stimulation is healthy for children and other living things.

Parents should not be afraid of teaching their child anything the child is interested in knowing. As parents are their children's first teachers, they should be respected for exercising that role effectively. Unfortunately, parents receive more than their share of criticism and very little in the way of acknowledgment for being good parents. With no markers other than their child's achievement (which may or may not reflect the quality of parenting), how are parents to know if they are doing a good job? Psychologists are in a unique position to be able to give parents positive feedback on their effectiveness. Self-concept scales, projective tests (such as incomplete sentences), and interviews with children can provide confirmation to parents that their child feels safe and supported at home. These measures can also reveal areas that need attention. Giftedness in parenting is a precious attribute, one that should be prized.

> All in all, giftedness develops through an array of uniquely exquisite efforts by a caretaker who cares for the child's special qualities and who takes wise steps to accelerate their ripening.... Children with superior inner resources can fulfill their promise only if the nurturance they receive is "tailor-made" to meet their special needs; but without the requisite inner resources in a child, no amount (or type) of nurturance can make the difference between mediocrity and excellence. (Tannenbaum, 1992, p. 128)

OPTIMAL DEVELOPMENT OF GIFTED FAMILIES

Gifted children are not distributed randomly by the stork. Giftedness is a family affair. When one child is gifted, usually all the children are gifted (Silverman, 1988, 2009e). Terman discovered 20 families with three gifted children, 10 families with four gifted children, and 2 families with five gifted children (Terman & Oden, 1959). This comes as no surprise to physicians, who seem to be better trained in genetics. But the similarity of siblings' IQ scores was a revelation for me.

In 1979, the vast majority of children assessed at the GDC were firstborns. This did not capture my attention as it was consistent with Terman's study (1925), where firstborns were overrepresented, MacKinnon's study (1962) of famous architects, and many other studies. Then, two families, convinced that their second child was *not* gifted, came to the GDC asking to have their secondborn tested to gain information about achievement, learning style, and learning needs that they found valuable in the assessment of their eldest. To everyone's astonishment, these secondborns scored within a few IQ points of their older siblings. We were all puzzled because these children did not "act gifted"—they did not behave or achieve like the firstborns, who walked right out of the textbooks. Could a child be average on the outside and gifted on the inside? Taking a closer look, I realized that very few parents had brought their second child for assessment. This prompted a study of IQ scores in siblings. As parents often failed to recognize giftedness in their second child, the GDC had to offer a substantial discount on the assessment of secondborn children in order to gather a large enough sample. Comparing 148 sets of siblings, 73% were within 13 IQ points, 62% were within 10 points, and 36% were within 5 points (Silverman, 1988) (see Table 7.1).

TABLE 7.1 **DISTRIBUTION OF IQ SCORES IN 148 SETS OF GIFTED SIBLINGS**

IQ Difference	Number	Cumulative Percentile
0	3	
1	4	< 5%
2	14	14%
3	11	22%
4	10	28%
5	13	36%
6	6	41%
7	5	45%
8	9	51%
9	13	60%
10	3	62%
13	5	73%

Lack of recognition of giftedness in second children might account for some of the sibling rivalry that occurs in families in which only the firstborn child has been brought for assessment. Undetected gifted children may resent those who are identified. As a group, firstborns tend to be perfectionistic, reliable, well-organized, critical, adult-like, and serious (Leman, 1984), whereas secondborns usually demonstrate opposite personalities, tendencies, and interests. Eldest children usually have a strong need for achievement and conform to adult expectations (Leman, 1984), while secondborns are more likely to march to their own drummer, often rebelling (Sulloway, 1996).

> When first-borns predominate in a sample, we should expect a high percentage of doctors, lawyers, professors, and other professionals (Schachter, 1963), but a low percentage of artists, writers, and others who are less willing to conform to societal definitions of success. (Simonton, 2003, p. 363)

Those secondborn children who live in the shadow of a challenging older sibling often blossom when their giftedness is recognized.

If gifted siblings are close in IQ, could their parents be far behind? When Betty Meckstroth spoke to Kathi Kearney's class of gifted students, 8-year-old Jason asked her where giftedness comes from. After listening to a detailed explanation of sources and causes of giftedness and the effects of environment and heredity, Jason shook his head. "I think that they get it from us: First we're told that we're gifted and then our parents think that they're gifted, too" (Meckstroth, 1991, p. 98).

Parents often sheepishly admit that the characteristics of giftedness that they see in their children fit them as well when they were children. Researchers, such as Bouchard and Lykken (1999), offer "evidence for a very strong genetic influence on intelligence" (p. 92). When IQ scores of parents, or even grandparents, are known, children often test within 10 points (Silverman, 2009e). "Family studies show that *g* runs in families" (Plomin & Price, 2003, p. 115). So much for the oft-repeated tale that parents of the gifted are not as smart as their children. Grandparents don't help either when they jest, "Giftedness skips a generation!" Gifted parents need reassurance that they really are as intelligent as their children and they have the inner resources to raise a gifted child.

Just as fish are not aware of water, gifted families may not apprehend giftedness. Munger (1990) noted that parents often fail to recognize giftedness in their children when they are gifted themselves and most of their friends are gifted. If one's entire clan—parents, grandparents, aunts, uncles, cousins, nieces, and nephews—all are highly intelligent, the child just appears to be developing "normally" for that family.

Why is it important for parents to embrace their own giftedness? Paying attention to their own giftedness increases the likelihood of recognizing atypical development in their children. Denial of such a basic trait can cause a distorted view of themselves and their offspring.

> Gifted children do *not* disappear when they graduate from high school or finish college or graduate degrees. They become gifted adults. If they enter adulthood blind to their unusual mental capabilities, they may go through their lives fragmented, frustrated, unfulfilled and alienated from their innermost beings. (Tolan, 1994/1995, p. 19)

Parents' definitions of giftedness are important to examine. Those who believe that giftedness equals recognized achievement are unable to acknowledge their own giftedness. Even if they were placed in gifted programs as children, they completely deny the possibility that they might be gifted adults. "After all, whoever heard of a 'gifted mommy'?" (Silverman & Kearney, 1989, p. 53). Parents are their children's primary role models. It is difficult for gifted children to wrap their minds around their own abilities if their parents are in denial. This is particularly important for gifted girls. "If my mother cannot be gifted, how can I be gifted?"

Acknowledging one's abilities, at least to oneself, is not lack of humility. It is a positive explanation for the differences that may have plagued one since childhood. "They may have spent their lives assuming that this difference was a deficit, a fault, even a defect of character or a sign of mental illness" (Tolan, 1994/1995, p. 14). Mental health workers who are willing to overcome their own embarrassment and admit they, too, have unusual minds help parents own this part of themselves (Kuipers, 2010). Willem Kuipers (2010) in The Netherlands has created a term that is more palatable than *gifted* to many gifted adults: "eXtra intelligent (Xi)." If individuals are put off by that concept, "Xi" can also stand for "eXtra intense" (p. ix). He describes the particular difficulties that "XIPs" have in the work world when their intelligence and intensity are not understood. He has reframed some of the "nuisances" of gifted adults as "assets" in the workplace (p. 49).

Even the most obviously gifted adults reject the idea that they are gifted, and believe that others with different abilities "are the really bright ones" (Tolan, 1994/1995, p. 17). In 1999, Stephanie Tolan offered an analogy that is helpful to gifted parents. She describes individuals' unusual abilities as "dots" and the things they do poorly as "spaces." We tend to take our dots for granted, as a special knack that is of little consequence. Someone else's dot is considered significant and valuable if it is a "space" for us—an ability that we lack. Two individuals of identical intelligence may see the other person's giftedness, but not his or her own. The creative writer thinks the physicist is the gifted one, and the physicist may think the creative writer is the gifted one. "The combination of focusing on one's spaces, while taking one's dots for granted,...and valuing other people's dots more highly than one's own, can lead an extremely intelligent person to feel 'dumb' or inadequate" (Tolan, 1999, pp. 149–150).

Some who refuse to admit that they are gifted acknowledge that they have a gifted sibling. Learning about similarities in siblings' IQs can change the parents' self-concept. When they discovered that they were as bright as their brothers and sisters, and similar to their gifted children in ability, some parents made major life changes, such as going back to school or entering new professions.

> One father, deeply moved by the testing experience, sought counseling to understand his own abilities. As a child he had shown the same signs of extraordinary precocity as his son, and yet his had never been recognized. His gifts went unutilized. When his son was tested, he realized his own pattern of underachievement and began to set new aspirations for himself. (Silverman & Kearney, 1989, p. 53)

The parents that educators consider "difficult" are often gifted adults who were emotionally crippled by the way they were treated as children (Tolan, 1992). They bring all of the unresolved childhood issues surrounding their giftedness into their adult lives and into their parenting decisions. If they were dumped into a higher grade level without their permission, they may be anti-acceleration for their children. If they were humiliated as children for being smart, they may not want their own children identified as gifted. If they were terrified of teachers, they may have difficulty approaching their children's teachers. If they learned to play the game, and sacrificed their gifts in the bargain, they may expect their children to make the same choices.

Parents who were wounded as children for being too smart may arrive at adulthood with self-loathing. This is not a good foundation for parenting. A family therapist who understands giftedness can help all members of the family see how giftedness has affected the entire family system. The heightened sensitivity, intensity, and overexcitability of family members can be reframed as indicators of giftedness, and dealt with more effectively. Wise therapists explore the childhood experiences of parents of the gifted, the obstacles they faced as gifted children, and their solutions. They help parents separate their own experiences from those of their child. Therapists who understand the importance of giftedness in identity development (Mahoney, 1998) can assist parents in understanding themselves better, appreciating their differences, and integrating their giftedness into their identities.

Hollingworth (1926) acknowledged the conundrum of gifted women who have the major responsibilities of caretaking, and yet yearn to fully develop their own abilities. She called this "the woman question" (pp. 348–349) (see Chapter 3). This is an issue that may need to be addressed in therapy. Some women are very fulfilled in their nurturing role, and some are not. Exceptionally energetic women try to balance a full-time position and motherhood, and may become exhausted. They need to create strong support systems, such as extended family, grandparents who live close by, live-in help, childcare assistance, or a husband who is willing to do a role-reversal. Working from home is an alternative available to many families today. After giving up her career to homeschool her two children, a mother appeared in my office one day and announced, "I put myself on the shelf for 18 years. When is it my turn?"

It is often a revelation to parents when giftedness in adults is defined in terms of the potential for self-actualization. Maslow (1962) studied creative self-actualizers and found that he had to discard his stereotyped ideas that productive, talented individuals were positively healthy, highly evolved, and matured.

> ...I soon discovered that I had, like most other people, been thinking of creativeness in terms of products, and secondly, I had unconsciously confined creativeness to certain conventional areas only.... Theorists, artists, scientists, inventors, writers could be creative. Nobody else could be. (p. 135)

Maslow found self-actualizers among parents, among poor people, and among those who had not distinguished themselves through their productivity.

Optimal development of all family members requires appreciation of giftedness throughout the entire family system.

This awareness shifts the emphasis from supporting the gifts of one child to supporting everyone's abilities. Intensity is to be expected. So are bumps in the road (J. Merrill, 2012). But the gifted family also has an inherent capacity for empathy and problem solving. The process of growth and development of the family can enrich the lives of all of its members.

> My all-time favorite Disney movie is Pixar's *The Incredibles....* They are a gifted family. The entire Parr family is odd, different, complex. They have to hide their greatest abilities, for the supposed benefit of society. They all have a hard time out in the real world, because hiding their abilities is not something they can do easily. But at home, where they are safe and accepted for who they truly are, they can relax and be themselves. Sound familiar? (J. Merrill, 2012, p. 53)

"One of the best things about raising gifted children may be the selves we discover along the way" (Tolan, 1992, p. 10).

AN OPTIMAL SCHOOL ENVIRONMENT

In order to guide gifted children and their parents in making informed decisions about school, psychologists need to be aware of the types of environments to recommend in which giftedness can blossom. When the child's school is resistant, the psychologist may need to coach parents on how to advocate effectively (Gilman, 2008a); write letters supporting grade advancement; observe the child in the school setting; assess the child's intellectual, academic, and emotional functioning; and, at times, intervene with school personnel on behalf of the child. It is clear that there are some teachers who genuinely dislike gifted children (Geake & Gross, 2008; McCoach & Siegle, 2007). No child should be forced to remain for a full year with a teacher who resents the child's giftedness. On occasion, the psychologist may need to recommend placement of the child with a more supportive teacher. He or she also may be asked to write recommendations for gifted students to win scholarships or gain acceptance to special programs or colleges.

Professionals who are aware of the teaching strategies and provisions most effective with the gifted can also support school districts and individual teachers. Expert teachers of the gifted develop some of the repertoire of counselors (Silverman, 1993a). They facilitate learning, ask provocative questions, and withhold feedback, asking instead, "What do you think?" Mental health workers can model these approaches and assist teachers in developing skills as a teacher/counselor.

Gifted children respond to roles in a qualitatively different manner from average children; they are likely to want to know more about the personal lives and beliefs of those who work with them. When I taught sixth grade, one of my students saw me in the grocery store and stopped dead in his tracks—shock written all over his face. I had to resist the urge to say, "Yes, I shop. I eat, too." A gifted student in the same class wanted to know where I was born, how many siblings I had, my birth order, whom I voted for in the last election—and why.

What Do Gifted Students Want?

To teach and counsel gifted students effectively, the most important principle is, "Ask the child." Even young gifted children are excellent informants. A coordinator of gifted services in Dallas asked a gifted first grader, "What do you need?" He replied, "More books. I've read every book in this classroom." An exemplary high school teacher wrote, "I sit with each student individually and I will say, 'What is it you want?'" (Gentry, Steenbergen-Hu, & Choi, 2011, p. 118). Harrison (2004) succinctly describes the needs of young gifted children as "the search for complexity and connection" (p. 78). Older gifted children have similar yearnings.

One summer, when I worked with a group of fourth through eighth graders in Vermont, I asked, "What do you wish your teachers knew about you?" Hear their voices.

- Some teachers make everybody do the same work. We want harder work. We don't want hard work that's beyond our knowledge. We want challenging work that stretches the edge of our knowledge.
- We aren't bored when the teacher lets us do harder work and doesn't hold us back.
- We don't want extra work. We want challenging work instead of lots of easy work. Lots of easy work gets boring. Challenging work is work we know it's possible to do—it just takes longer.
- It's not the quantity of the work, it's the quality that counts.
- We don't get the same amount of attention as students who are having trouble learning or making trouble for others. Teachers don't realize we need help, too.
- We don't like being singled out and treated differently from the other students. If we have different work in the regular classroom, the other students make fun of us.
- We often feel like outcasts.
- When we're placed with other gifted students, we feel more normal, but it's harder to be special.

These students resented being given extra work that was too easy. They wanted challenging work that stretched their knowledge, yet felt within their grasp. Finding what Vygotsky (1962, 1978) called the student's "zone of proximal development"—the cutting edge of the student's level of mastery—is the artistry of teaching. Gifted students thrive on challenge, abstraction, and complexity; however, the difficulty of the task must not exceed the child's level of confidence. The students also expressed feeling like outcasts and getting less attention from teachers. Another Vygotskian principle is the inseparability of cognition and emotion (Coleman, 2012;

Kanevsky, 2011). Gifted students seek a caring relationship with their teachers (Harrison, 2004; Kanevsky, 2011), as well as an emotionally safe, supportive classroom environment, where their vocabulary, complex questions, and creativity won't be mocked. Exemplary teachers of the gifted connect with them emotionally (Gentry et al., 2011).

Another issue that surfaced in the students' list is the dilemma of being singled out in the regular classroom for different work, with the attendant risks of being ridiculed by their classmates, versus being placed with other gifted students and not feeling special. Vygotsky (1978) considered learning a social activity; the student learns best dialoguing with others who are more advanced. This suggests that the gifted student who sticks out like a sore thumb in the regular classroom, feels like an outcast, and does not receive an equitable amount of teacher attention, will learn less than a student who can collaborate with other gifted children in a stimulating and supportive environment (French, Walker, & Shore, 2011). Most gifted students do not like to ask their teachers for assistance (Kanevsky, 2011). Teachers unknowingly reinforce this reticence by conveying to gifted students that they ought to be able to do the work on their own; other students are more in need of teacher attention (French et al., 2011).

> Mental-health professionals, from pediatricians to counselors and school psychologists, should recognize that when children and youth express aversion to school, describe isolation, or express low self-worth or efficacy, they could reflect a lack of perceived support in the classroom.... It can be helpful to ask whether they feel alone in school, whether they would like to work on some activity with some other students, and, if so, to follow this up with the teachers. (French et al., 2011, pp. 155–156)

Lannie Kanevsky (2011) contends that when teachers explore their students' learning preferences, they convey a message of caring; this facilitates learning in the child's zone of proximal development. She found that gifted children enjoy learning about "weird" topics, wrestling with complicated ideas and problems, and finding creative solutions to difficult problems. The biggest discrepancy between gifted and unselected children was the degree to which gifted children dislike "learning small bits of information at a slow, easy pace with lots of practice" (p. 287). They also are not fond of "waiting until everyone in the class or group understands the lesson before going on to a new idea" (p. 287). "The most universal school experience for children who are gifted is sitting and waiting" (Coleman, 2012, p. 382). Kanevsky (2011) described the impetus for her rich study of student preferences:

> One day, early in my work with his class, [Alex] came to me with questions about my research. . . . "Dr. K, why are you having us fill out these forms after we do activities with you?"
>
> "Well, I'm trying to find out the best ways for all of you to learn."
>
> He looked down at the floor. I knew he had more to say and he was trying to find a diplomatic way to say it. He looked out from under the fringe of bangs across his forehead and said, "So why don't you just ask us?"
>
> I did, and now I always do. Alex remains one my wisest teachers and the inspiration for this study. (p. 279)

The Fine Art of Teaching the Gifted

Gifted children blossom when they have the good fortune of being placed with gifted teachers. Effective teachers of the gifted connect with them emotionally. They are often similar to their students in characteristics, overexcitabilities, and personality type (Silverman, 1998b). Gentry et al. (2011) found that over two-thirds of the exemplary teachers they studied sought advanced learning in gifted education. Those who decide to obtain advanced degrees in gifted education usually are sensitive to the burdens of being gifted. They teach from the heart and soul more than from the textbooks, delighting in their students' discoveries. Aware of the teachable moment, they use expert strategies to deepen learning and elevate thinking (VanTassel-Baska, 2012a). They are a very special group of people with deep appreciation of the beauty of the human mind. Regardless of the type of provision, the ultimate goal is to locate teachers who cherish the child.

Several years ago, I conducted a qualitative study of instructional strategies of master (expert) teachers and novices in elementary education, special education, early childhood education, and gifted education (G/T) (Silverman, 1995b). I observed and recorded verbal and nonverbal interactions. These observations fell into four categories: instruction, questioning, feedback, and personal interactions. No differences were found in the actual instructional techniques used in the four groups. However, G/T teachers spent more class time asking questions and less of it in direct instruction. Instead of answering all of the students' questions, they tended to reflect questions back to them or to the class, (e.g., "Would anyone like to comment on Connor's impression?") They attempted to draw the information they wanted to teach from the students themselves. G/T teachers asked more divergent questions (e.g., "Who has a different idea?") than convergent questions. G/T teachers and early childhood educators both tried to understand the student's thought process, asking questions such as, "What made you think that?"

Chan (2011) found that gifted students valued highly their teachers' adeptness with questioning techniques. Questioning skill ranked second only to skill at "teaching higher level thinking abilities, creativity and problem solving" (p. 163). "Question-asking is a critical component of promoting inquiry among gifted learners... it requires being open to the moment, asking the probing question at the right time" (VanTassel-Baska, 2012a, pp. 498–499).

One of the most intriguing differences was the manner in which master G/T teachers acknowledged student responses. Novice teachers offered verbal and nonverbal feedback to nearly every student utterance. Some of their feedback was repetitive, such as head nodding, or "Yes," or "Uh huh," and they would often repeat what the student said. Master G/T teachers responded significantly less often. Some intentionally avoided giving feedback to students. They accepted students' responses, rather than reacting to them. Their behavior was similar to that of a counselor or psychologist: they appeared attentive, interested, and nonjudgmental. This strategy enhanced interaction of the students with each other and promoted self-evaluation. Students were encouraged to comment on each other's ideas. Classroom discussions resembled adult conversations.

Expert G/T teachers responded to the students' feelings, as well as to the content of their responses. When necessary, they found unobtrusive ways of refocusing the students' attention on the task at hand, such as humor and nonverbal cues. The teachers used more "we" than "you" statements. They included themselves among the culprits, with statements such as, "*We* had better get back to the subject or we won't finish this section today."

Personal interactions, which cement the relationship between the student and the teacher, also differed. The relationships between G/T teachers and students were not role-bound; there seemed to be more equality. Master G/T teachers enjoyed discovering with their students; they were not threatened if the students knew more than they did. Some observed the children's interactions with their peers during recess purely out of curiosity. And they laughed a lot! Teachers and students appreciated each other's humor. These teachers enjoyed their students as interesting people and vice versa. This was evident in conversations that occurred before and after class and at transition periods. They often discussed issues unrelated to school, freely exchanging viewpoints. The most significant difference I observed was the extent to which these teachers revealed personal information to their students. Why? Because the students asked them about themselves! There was obviously a high level of trust.

When the gifted are asked what they remember about school, they always talk about the *relationship* they had with certain teachers who made them feel seen and respected. Some teachers had a passion for their fields that inspired the person to enter a particular profession. Some spent extra time getting to know a child who was not performing well and helped that student see the relevance of school in fulfilling his or her ambitions (Emerick, 1992). Gentry et al. (2011) found four themes that distinguish exemplary teachers of the gifted from others: (1) taking a personal interest in students, (2) setting high expectations for themselves and their students, (3) making content and learning meaningful and relevant to the future and students' interests, and (4) clear passion for their students, teaching and content (p. 116).

> I genuinely know my students.

> I...really care about kids. I am interested in them, not just about them learning the subject matter, but actually having a connection with them, the people who they are, and I have an interest in their lives in and out of school.

> When I ask students what their best experience is in class, they indicate a teacher who is engaged, and who has taken the time to connect to them as people...

> Adore them, find every single strength possible...you have to find something they do well, and you have to absolutely strive to make that count for every minute that they're there. Make them special. (Gentry et al., 2011, p. 117)

Lifelong bonds have been forged between teachers and gifted students.

> On a senior's last day...I take them one at a time to the door and tell them that they are no longer welcome to pass through this door as a student, BUT PLEASE KNOW that they are always welcome to return as a friend. My door is open! (Gentry et al., 2011, p. 121)

Teachers change lives. Recently, a high school teacher wrote a lengthy, glowing letter of recommendation for a highly gifted student in his class. Although this veteran teacher had written many recommendations for his high-achieving students, it was clear that he *saw* this student's abilities in a different light.

> *Moreover, he is the rare sort of person whose mind is so extraordinary that he is able to grasp the full continuum of human knowledge. Our AP English teacher has raved to me about his ability to analyze literature. He writes poetry and short stories. He has won awards for his ability in physics. Furthermore, there is a sense that he is not straining to accomplish these things. They seem to grow naturally out of his genuine interest in understanding how things work. I have had no student over the past 14 years who has greater potential for academic achievement in a college setting.*
>
> *Finally (and most importantly) you need to know that this is a really good person. In the often cruel and imitative world of high school students, C stands out for his strength of character and maturity. He is one of the most genuinely tolerant and kind students I have ever come across. He seeks no recognition for his abilities. He never tries in any way to place himself above others or seek attention. He seems preternaturally content to simply be a kind and good person who does his best at whatever challenge he faces.*

The teacher shared his recommendation with the student. The depth of acknowledgment the student felt will never be forgotten. It will not only open doors in higher education, but also inner doors to self-confidence in this highly introverted youth.

Provisions for the Gifted

As is true at the other end of the spectrum, gifted children need more intensive support the further they diverge from the norm. For mildly advanced students, ability grouping in reading and mathematics, enrichment and differentiated instruction are excellent options. Unfortunately, although differentiation has become a buzz word in education, studies have found that relatively few regular classroom teachers make more than cosmetic adjustments to the core curriculum for their gifted students

(Kanevsky, 2011). Group projects are recommended, as children in this range usually enjoy learning with their peers (French et al., 2011). Independent schools serve this population well. This is the level at which talent development opportunities are needed.

Various instructional strategies designed to be useful for all learners become crucial for advanced learners (VanTassel-Baska & Brown, 2007). Higher level inquiry processes, creative problem-solving models, critical thinking, problem-based learning, and other constructivist approaches are critical components for stretching the thinking skills of advanced learners and providing a systematic basis for solving real problems (VanTassel-Baska, 2012a).

At 2 standard deviations above the mean, different developmental needs become apparent. Moderately gifted children (2%–3% of the population) have a more accelerated learning trajectory and require advancement in all subject areas. A differentiated curriculum, tailored to the needs of the group, should be "delivered by a trained educator of the gifted" (VanTassel-Baska & Little, 2011, p. 10). Gifted students need trained teachers, gifted peers, advanced material, opportunity for continuous progress at their own rate, fast-paced instruction, and counseling groups.

All of these modifications can be accomplished more effectively in full-day programs. "Pull-out programs," where students are pulled out of the regular classroom for services, give everyone the impression that the students are only gifted for a few hours on Tuesdays (Betts, 2012). James Gallagher (2000) calls these minimal programs "educational fraud," as they offer a *nontherapeutic educational dosage* of the amount of time needed to make an actual difference (p. 10).

Full-day programs actually cost less than pull-out programs. It can be argued that the most beneficial aspect of special programs for the gifted is connecting with intellectual peers who are also serious about learning. The interplay of gifted minds accelerates the drive to learn (Coleman, 2012). Interaction with true peers allows gifted students to develop lasting friendships. Instructional modifications needed for gifted students include:

- an Advanced Learning Plan (ALP)
- diagnostic assessment
- allowing students to learn at their own rate
- compacting material
- differentiated homework
- higher levels of abstraction
- autonomy
- less time on basics and more time for in-depth explorations
- inquiry and problem-based learning
- access to more sophisticated resources
- mentors (Silverman, 1995b)

An ALP should be designed in collaboration with the parents and the student. A diagnostic/prescriptive approach is recommended, where students are able to demonstrate what they have already mastered before being taught new material. Preassessment enables teachers to determine the appropriate level of instruction at the beginning of an instructional unit. Psychological assessment is fundamental to the preassessment process. Standardized achievement tests paint a global picture of the child's level of mastery and provide an objective basis for accelerated learning.

Students in Kanevsky's (2011) study ranked "learning at my own speed" first out of 110 preferences (p. 288); it was endorsed by over 90% of her sample. Instruction should be streamlined, as gifted students are capable of learning "twice as much in half the time as other students" (VanTassel-Baska, 2012a, p. 497).

> *Pacing* is a critical strategy to use in ensuring that gifted students can move at their own rate of learning.... The strategy of appropriate pacing involves the deliberate use of informal assessment of mastery and readiness to learn more rapidly. It also involves the use of questioning gifted learners about what they understand about a topic and how they might master it more rapidly. Often

informal discussion clarifies the need for a faster pace in learning. (VanTassel-Baska, 2012a, p. 498)

Covering the same amount of material in less than the usual time has various names: telescoping, compacting, and compressing. Gifted children usually retain information permanently the first time a concept is presented; they do not need extra practice. Therefore, *differentiated homework* is as important as differentiated instruction. They should be allowed to skip most drill exercises. Instead, they can be asked to answer only the most difficult questions on each page of exercises. It is actually too hard for some of them to do homework that is too easy. Highly gifted children protest that being required to "practice" basic skills they mastered years ago is "sheer torture."

Imagine if you were required to take Driver's Education after you had been driving for many years. How hard would it be to deconstruct the skills that have become automatized? When a complex set of skills is mastered, such as driving, it is not accessible to the part of the brain that learned the isolated skills in the first place. Information is stored in long-term memory, which decreases the need for attention and maximizes efficiency. Once you've mixed a cake batter, how do you remove an egg? That element has become part of the whole. Similarly, a basic skill that has become automatic, and then melded with higher order thinking and conceptual awareness, cannot be pulled out and practiced in isolation.

A high level of abstraction is manna for these hungry minds. Gifted students can engage in hypothetical reasoning, discuss complex issues, make abstract inferences, and utilize systematic procedures in their quest for knowledge. Their curriculum should involve critical analysis, creative synthesis, and evaluation. Material containing several levels of meaning, such as metaphor, analogy, and paradox, is ideal for their abstract minds. Gifted students need autonomy and enjoy independent study projects (Chan, 2011; Kanevsky, 2011). In order to delve as deeply as they would like, they need large chunks of time to devote to their projects, "many times requiring whole days away from school in order to carry out aspects of learning not possible in a school setting" (VanTassel-Baska, 2012a, pp. 500–501).

There are special opportunities for children who score 145 or above on standardized IQ tests and standardized achievement tests (>3 SD), such as the Davidson Young Scholar program (www.davidsongifted.org). *Challenging Highly Gifted Learners* (Gilman, 2008b) serves as a concise blueprint for teachers to work effectively with this population. In addition to the other provisions discussed earlier, all forms of acceleration need to be seriously considered. Even within a school or full-day program for the gifted, these children learn faster and need more advanced content.

Acceleration is a no-cost option that has been researched for over 80 years—more extensively than any other intervention (Colangelo, Assouline, & Gross, 2004; Gross, 2009; Kuo & Lohman, 2011; VanTassel-Baska, 2012a). It adjusts the curriculum to the appropriate level of challenge, pace of instruction, and complexity of the thought process of the learner (Kuo & Lohman, 2011; Wood, Portman, Cigrand, & Colangelo, 2010). Research consistently indicates that acceleration has a positive impact on academic achievement and a slightly positive impact on social–emotional development (Steenbergen-Hu & Moon, 2011). *A Nation Deceived* (Colangelo, Assouline, & Gross, 2004; Southern & Jones, 2004) outlines 18 forms of acceleration, including:

- early entrance to school,
- subject acceleration,
- grade skipping,
- curriculum compacting,
- continuous progress,
- Advanced Placement courses,
- concurrent enrollment in high school and college,
- mentoring,
- early graduation,
- early entrance to college.

This two-volume definitive report (www.nationdeceived.org) is a must read!

The timing of this intervention is essential. Girls mature faster than boys and appear to be better candidates for early entrance to Kindergarten. They tend to be precocious readers, often 2 years ahead of gifted boys (Kerr, 2012). During elementary school, girls are more likely than boys to skip grades (Wells, Lohman, & Marron, 2009); it is better to accelerate them before they become owned and operated by their third-grade peers. Later grade-skipping allows boys to mature socially and physically—both in stature and fine motor coordination (Colangelo, Assouline, & Lupkowski-Shoplik, 2004). However, children who accelerated during the primary grades had higher math and reading achievement by 12th grade than those who skipped later grades (Kuo & Lohman, 2011).

Acceleration results in early readiness for college and many highly gifted children attend college early (Solow & Rhodes, 2012). In their meta-analysis, Steenbergen-Hu and Moon (2011) found that early entrants "believed that they benefited greatly in academic and social-emotional development" (p. 51). Boazman and Sayler (2011) also reported that "early college entrants expressed greater global satisfaction with their lives than age peers" (p. 76). A list of early college entrance programs is available at www.hoagiesgifted.com.

At the fourth standard deviation (SD) above the mean (160+ IQ), exceptionally gifted children may need to accelerate several times throughout their educational career. Full-time gifted programs, acceleration, homeschooling, and partial homeschooling are all viable options for various gifted children at different points in their development.

Just as children who are 5 SD below the norm (25 IQ) are not served in regular schools, children who are 5 SD above the norm, in the profoundly gifted range (175+ IQ), are often too far advanced for typical public school programs and private schools for the gifted. Most parents homeschool, or do partial homeschooling, combined with distance learning. A wealth of distance learning opportunities is now available. Profoundly gifted children are ready for college work much earlier than colleges are ready for them. Those who attend college extremely early are accompanied by their parents. They thrive when they find each other online or at special conferences and gatherings designed for exceptionally and profoundly gifted children. See www.hoagiesgifted.com for homeschooling curricula and opportunities for profoundly gifted students.

Optimal development of giftedness is feasible and affordable. The only obstacle is a value system that denies gifted children the right to struggle (Kane & Fiedler, 2011); it is only through struggling that true learning occurs. Parents of the gifted have the right to ask for more challenging work for their children. Psychologists can support gifted students in obtaining harder work and can negotiate various forms of accelerated learning. Assessment is often the first step in that process. Parents of gifted children need a safe harbor where they will be treated with decency and respect, instead of derision. Psychologists can also be on the forefront of ending the blatant discrimination, stereotyping, and stigmatizing of this segment of the population.

Where Do We Go From Here?

We need to care for and understand the human Soul and make its uncluttered growth and development a priority over all other goals in education, politics, and all our interactions.

Annemarie Roeper

o here we are, caught between two worldviews. In one camp, we have educators and academics, attempting to overthrow the "old guard"—those of us who define giftedness through the narrow lens of IQ tests. They are hoping to establish a *raison d'etre* for gifted education—a field with a wobbly foundation. In the other camp, we have parents and the psychologists who specialize in working with the gifted, railing against the externalizing of giftedness. They want the inner world of the gifted to be recognized and appreciated. Are IQ tests elitist? Isn't replacing IQ tests by grooming children toward eminence even more elitist? Neither camp seems to be able to dodge the bullet of elitism.

There is no truce in sight. Controversy has dogged the study of giftedness since its inception, and is likely to continue into the foreseeable future. Multiple views will somehow have to learn to coexist.

Is it worthwhile for you to enter such a fractured domain of study? Yes, I think so. As nothing is set in stone yet, there is ample room for new ideas to be explored. The psychology of giftedness is a fledgling. You can make a difference. You can make a difference to the field by adding your energy, your exploration, your insights, your research on interesting questions about the human mind, and the study of outliers. You can make a difference to parents, who feel dismissed and battered. You can make a difference to gifted adults, whose bewildering experiences beg for meaning. You can make a difference to twice exceptional adolescents, helping them gain accommodations on College Board exams, so that they get into good colleges where they will shine. You can make a difference to gifted children, who have had to camouflage who they are in order to survive.

What does giftedness mean to you? If you are feeling some inexplicable attraction to this population, perhaps you are a gifted person in disguise—or denial. Be forewarned that if you ally with this unpopular cause, you, too, will feel the sting of anti-intellectualism aimed at you. You will soon learn firsthand about the prejudice that exists toward the gifted and their advocates. Expect to be derided at cocktail parties when you tell people what you do. An impressive number of people think they know more about the gifted than you do and they are delighted to share their opinions. Should you become a guardian of the gifted, know that there is no glory in it. This is not the route to eminence. When the scythe appears, you will have thrown in your lot with the tall poppies.

But I promise you an exciting ride. You will encounter a kaleidoscope of interesting people. It is often frustrating, but never boring. Studying the gifted has fascinated me for over 50 years. Know, without any doubt, that you are needed. There is so much work to be done.

Annemarie Roeper is gone, but her work needs to be carried on. She was the champion of children and the champion of intuition. When it is my time, will there be others who have the strength of conviction to bring their intuitive judgment to the table in interpreting a child's abilities? Or will the numbers be left on their own to tell the story? It's because we thought numbers could speak for themselves that people stopped trusting them. With no mediators, eventually the numbers will be discarded, and these precious minds will become even more invisible. Obviously, the numbers tell only a small part of the story, but they do convince the pragmatic, empirical, and scientific communities of the existence of a child with special needs. A child who is measurably different. IQ tests are dragon detectors.

Perhaps your calling is to work with those who are learning disabled. Be aware that among these children are twice exceptional learners whose weaknesses have been in the limelight, while their gifts have gone unnoticed. When I entered graduate school at USC in Special Education, I was introduced to one of my soon-to-be professors in the following manner: "This is Linda Silverman; she is interested in studying learning disabilities in the gifted." Bob McIntyre instantly retorted, "What you *should* be studying is giftedness in the learning disabled." You can do both. There is a ferocious need for professionals who understand twice exceptional children and adults. They are complexity quadrupled.

Are you a budding researcher? The files of the 6,000+ children we have assessed are in the process of being scanned and made available to graduate students to enable them to answer their burning questions about giftedness. This is the largest data bank on this population in existence.

Even if this is not a path you wish to pursue, you can make a difference. You can have the courage to take a stand against prejudice. When you hear someone being cut down for being "too smart," step in and say something. When you witness parent bashing, do not remain silent. All who stand on the sidelines of bigotry, and do nothing, silently condone it. The child you protect may be your own.

You can also ask your instructors for more information about the gifted and about the twice exceptional. Information follows the law of supply and demand. If enough people ask for this kind of training in the field of psychology or education, teachers will start assigning the chapter on giftedness that they glossed over for lack of time. Or they'll start writing chapters if there aren't any in the textbooks. Eventually, this could lead to a course on the needs of the gifted. You can write your papers about the gifted and inform your instructors. I did. When I was an undergraduate, I tied my passion for the gifted to every paper I wrote—even in geography. I compared the education of the gifted in Great Britain and the United States. My instructor wrote on my paper, "This is an A paper. It has nothing to do with geography." He gave me an A anyway.

If the gifted and twice exceptional should become your passion as well, you will be paid in appreciation. Your work will be a wellspring of creativity. You'll be outside the box anyway, eyed suspiciously by the system, so you might as well enjoy the freedom to access your creativity. Create a lair for stealth dragons to congregate. Become the choir master for a chorus of singing poppies. Ask frequently, "What do you need?" Let these delicious minds and hearts lead you in directions you never would have dreamed.

I believe that there are more and more gifted and creative children being born. No, I can't prove that. We are finding an increasing number of shockingly gifted children. For the first 10 years, GDC found no children with IQ scores above 200. Since then, we have found 97 children with IQ scores exceeding 200. Few know they exist. I don't think people want to know they exist. An IQ score of 130 is scary enough. What do they need? What can we learn from them? If I'm right, the need for professionals who "get" this population will continue to increase.

Where do we go from here? The future is up to you. I hope that this book has helped you "get it" and that you can help others to "get it," too. I pray that the psychology of the gifted is your calling. And I hope that you will listen.

Appendix

What We Have Learned About Gifted Children

30th Anniversary (1979 to 2009)

Linda Silverman

GIFTED DEVELOPMENT CENTER

The Gifted Development Center has been in operation since June, 1979, and we have assessed over 5,600 children in the last 30 years. By concentrating totally on the gifted population, we have acquired a considerable amount of knowledge about the development of giftedness. In 1994 to 1995, three noted researchers spent postdoctoral internships assisting us in coding our clinical data to enable statistical analysis: Drs. Frank

Falk and Nancy Miller of the University of Akron, and Dr. Karen Rogers of the University of St. Thomas. Here are some of the highlights of what we have learned so far:

1. Parents are excellent identifiers of giftedness in their children: 84% of 1,000 children whose parents felt that they exhibited three fourths of the traits in our *Characteristics of Giftedness Scale* tested in the superior or gifted range. Over 95% demonstrated giftedness in at least one area, but were asynchronous in their development, and their weaknesses depressed their composite IQ scores.

2. Giftedness can be observed in the first 3 years by rapid progression through the developmental milestones. These milestones should be documented and taken seriously as evidence of giftedness. Early identification of advanced development is as essential as early identification of any other exceptionality. Early intervention promotes optimal development in all children.

3. When parents fail to recognize a child's gifts, teachers may overlook them as well. Rita Dickinson (1970) found that half of the children she tested with IQs of 132 or above were referred for behavior problems and not seen as gifted by their teachers or parents. Parent advocacy is critical for gifted children's emotional and academic growth. GDC's Associate Director, Gilman's (2008a) award-winning book, *Academic Advocacy for Gifted Children: A Parent's Complete Guide*, can guide parents in effectively advocating for their children. *Challenging Highly Gifted Learners* (Gilman, 2008b) is an excellent book for teachers and parents.

4. Children and adults can be assessed at any age. However, the ideal age for testing is between 5 and 8½ years. By the age of 9, highly gifted children may hit the ceiling of the tests, and gifted girls may be socialized to hide their abilities. Unless they are absolutely certain they are right, gifted girls are often unwilling to guess, which lowers their IQ scores.

5. Brothers and sisters are usually within 5 or 10 points in measured ability. Parents' IQ scores are often within 10 points of their children's; even grandparents' IQ scores may be within 10 points of their grandchildren's. We studied 148 sets of siblings and found that over one third were within 5 points of each other, over three fifths were within 10 points, and nearly three fourths were within 13 points. When one child in the family is identified as gifted, the chances are great that all members of the family are gifted.

6. Second children are recognized as gifted much less frequently than firstborns or only children. They often go in the opposite direction of their older siblings and are less likely to be achievement oriented. Even the firstborn identical twin has a greater chance of being accepted in a gifted program than the secondborn!

7. IQ testing in childhood clearly demonstrates the equality of intelligence between males and females. Until the IQ test was developed, most of society believed in the "natural superiority of males." Even now, the fact that most of the eminent are men leads some to believe that males are innately more intelligent than females. On the contrary, we have found more than 100 girls with IQ scores above 180. The highest IQ score on record at our Center was attained by a girl, and four of the five highest scores were earned by girls. However, parents are more likely to bring their sons for assessment and overlook their daughters, and this inequity appears to be getting worse. From 1979 to 1989, 57% of the children brought for testing were male, and 43% were female; whereas 51% above 160 IQ were male and 49% female (see Table A1). In 2008, 68% of the children brought for testing were male and only 32% female, while the distribution in the highest IQ ranges is 60% male and 40% female.

8. Gifted girls and gifted boys have different coping mechanisms and are likely to face different problems. Gifted girls hide their abilities and learn to blend in with other children. In elementary school, they direct their mental energies into

TABLE A1   **GENDER DISTRIBUTION ABOVE 160 IQ**

	Males Above 160 IQ	Females Above 160 IQ	Total
1979–1989	94	89	183
1990–2009	507	298	805
1979–2009	601	387	988

developing social relationships; in junior high school, they are valued for their appearance and sociability rather than for their intelligence. Gifted boys are easier to spot, but they are often considered "immature" and may be held back in school if they cannot socialize with children their own age with whom they have no common interests.

9. Gifted children are asynchronous. Their development tends to be uneven, and they often feel out-of-sync with age peers and with age-based school expectations. They are emotionally intense and have greater awareness of the perils of the world. They may not have the emotional resources to match their cognitive awareness. They are at risk for abuse in environments that do not respect their differences.

10. This asynchrony is often seen in large discrepancies between index scores on the fourth edition of the *Wechsler Intelligence Scale for Children* (WISC-IV). In these cases, the Full Scale IQ score should *not* be used to select gifted students for programs. Instead, the General Ability Index (GAI), which omits Working Memory and Processing Speed, provides a better estimate of the child's reasoning ability. The GAI has been endorsed by the National Association for Gifted Children: http://www.nagc.org/index.aspx?id=375. Extended norms are now available for the WISC-IV: http://pearsonassess.com/NR/rdonlyres/C1C19227-BC79-46D9-B43C-8E4A114F7E1F/0/WISCIV_TechReport_7.pdf

11. The fifth edition of the *Stanford-Binet Intelligence Scale* (SB5) measures mathematical and visual-spatial abilities better than abstract verbal reasoning abilities. When the SB5 is used for selection of gifted students for programs, the cut-off score for admission should be lowered to 120 IQ. Different scoring options are available for gifted children, including Rasch-ratio scores. The publisher permits the administration of the older version of the *Stanford-Binet (Form L-M)* to assess abstract verbal abilities, especially in exceptionally gifted children, and recommends that it be administered in conjunction with the SB5 so that various scores can be compared (Carson & Roid, 2004).

12. Creative children, culturally diverse children, mathematically talented children, children with attention deficits, highly gifted children, learning disabled children, and underachievers often are visual-spatial learners who require different teaching methods. Visual-spatial learners usually think in pictures or rely on "sensing" or feeling, whereas auditory-sequential learners usually think in words. Typical educational strategies are a better match for auditory-sequential learners than for visual-spatial learners. We have developed methods of identifying this learning pattern and effective strategies for teaching visual-spatial learners (Silverman, 2002). Our *Visual-Spatial Identifier* can be used with entire school districts or classes, as well as individually. Please visit www.VisualSpatial.org for free information about strategies for teaching visual-spatial learners.

13. Gifted children have better social adjustment in classes with children like themselves. The brighter the child, the lower his or her social self-concept is likely to be in the regular classroom. Social self-concept improves when children are placed with true peers in special classes.

14. Perfectionism, sensitivity, and intensity are three personality traits associated with giftedness. They are derived from the complexity of the child's cognitive and emotional

development. According to Dabrowski's theory, these traits—related to overexcitabilities—are indicative of potential for high moral values in adult life. The brighter the child, the earlier and more profound may be his or her concern with moral issues. But this potential usually does not develop in a vacuum. It requires nurturing in a supportive environment.

15. About 60% of gifted children are introverted. Approximately 75% of highly gifted children are introverted. Introversion correlates with introspection, reflection, the ability to inhibit aggression, deep sensitivity, moral development, high academic achievement, scholarly contributions, leadership in academic and aesthetic fields in adult life, and smoother passage through midlife; however, it is very likely to be misunderstood and "corrected" in children by well-meaning adults.

16. Mildly, moderately, highly, exceptionally, and profoundly advanced children are as different from each other as mildly, moderately, severely, and profoundly delayed children are from each other, but the differences among levels of giftedness are rarely recognized.

17. There are far more exceptionally gifted children in the population than anyone realizes. Approximately 18% of the 5,600+ children we have assessed in the last 30 years are exceptionally gifted, with IQ scores above 160 IQ. As of January 1, 2009, we found at least 988 children above 160 IQ, including 281 above 180 IQ and 87 above 200 IQ. We have entered massive data on 241 of these children—the largest sample in this IQ range ever to be studied (K. Rogers & Silverman, 1997). Only two comprehensive studies have been published to date on children in these ranges. Leta Hollingworth (1942) found 12 children above 180 IQ between 1916 and 1939 and Miraca Gross (1993/2004) studied 60 Australian children with IQ scores above 160.

18. Many cases of underachievement are linked to chronic early ear infections (nine or more in the first 3 years), with residual effects of auditory-sequential processing deficits and attentional problems. Spelling, arithmetic, handwriting, rote memorization, attention, and motivation to do written work are all typically affected.

19. Gifted children may have hidden learning disabilities. Approximately one-sixth of the gifted children who come to the Center for testing have some type of learning disability—often undetected before the assessment—such as central auditory processing disorder (CAPD), difficulties with visual processing, sensory processing disorder, spatial disorientation, dyslexia, attention deficits, and Asperger syndrome. Giftedness masks disabilities and disabilities depress IQ scores. Higher abstract reasoning enables children to compensate to some extent for these weaknesses, making them harder to detect. However, compensation requires more energy, affects motivation, and breaks down under stress or when the child is fatigued.

20. Twice exceptional children and visual-spatial learners usually have at least one parent with the same learning pattern. Visual-spatial learners and children with dual exceptionalities tend to get smarter as they get older and often become successful adults.

21. Difficult birth histories, such as long labor, heads too large for the birth canal, four or more hours of Pitocin to induce labor, emergency C-sections, cords wrapped around any part of the infant's body, and oxygen at birth, can lead to sensory processing disorder (SPD). Parents, teachers, and pediatricians should be alerted that the critical period for ameliorating sensory–motor deficits is from birth to age 7. When gross or fine motor weaknesses are seen, pediatric occupational therapy should be sought immediately, rather than waiting for the child to "outgrow" the problem.

22. Giftedness is not elitist. It cuts across all socioeconomic, ethnic, and national groups (Dickinson, 1970). In every

culture, there are developmentally advanced children who have greater abstract reasoning and develop at a faster rate than their age peers. Though the percentage of gifted students among the upper classes may be higher, a much greater number of gifted children come from the lower classes, because the poor far outnumber the rich (Zigler & Farber, 1985). Therefore, when provisions are denied to the gifted on the basis that they are "elitist," it is the poor who suffer the most. The rich have other options.

23. The more egalitarian gifted programs attempt to be, the less defensible they are. Children in the top and bottom 3% of the population have atypical developmental patterns and require differentiated instruction. Children in the top and bottom 10% of the population are not statistically or developmentally different from children in the top and bottom 15%, and it is not justifiable to single them out for special treatment. More and more school districts are realizing this in this new millennium, and are providing in-depth services for those who need them the most. Self-contained, multiage programs for the gifted and radical acceleration are gaining in popularity.

References

Albert, R. S. (1978). Observations and suggestions regarding gifted-ness, familial influence, and the achievement of eminence. *Gifted Child Quarterly, 22*, 201–211.

Albert, R. S. (1980). Exceptionally gifted boys and their parents. *Gifted Child Quarterly, 24*, 174–179.

Alexander, E. (1992). Learning to fly: A homeschooling retrospective. *Understanding Our Gifted, 5*(1), 1, 11–14.

Ali, R. (2012, January 19). *Dear colleague letter.* Office of Assistant Secretary, Office of Civil Rights. Retrieved February 4, 2012, from www2.ed.gov/about/offices/list/ocr/letters/colleague-201109.html

Alomar, B. O. (2003). Parental involvement in the schooling of children. *Gifted and Talented International, 18*, 95–100.

Alsop, G. (1997). Coping or counseling: Families of intellectually gifted students. *Roeper Review, 20*, 28–34.

Alsop, G. (2003). Asynchrony: Intuitively valid and theoretically reliable. *Roeper Review, 25*, 118–127.

Amend, E. R., & Beljan, P. (2009). The antecedents of misdiagnosis: When normal behaviors of gifted children are misinterpreted as pathological. *Gifted Education International, 25*, 131–143.

Amend, E. R., & Peters, D. B. (2012). Misdiagnosis and missed diagnosis of gifted children: The importance of accurate assessment. In T. L. Cross & J. R. Cross (Eds.), *Handbook for counselors serving students with gifts & talents: Development, relationships, school issues, and counseling needs/interventions* (pp. 585–596). Waco, TX: Prufrock Press.

American Association for Gifted Children. (1978). *On being gifted.* New York, NY: Walker.

American Heritage Dictionary of the English Language (4th ed.). (2000). Boston, MA: Houghton Mifflin. Retrieved February 9, 2012, from http://ahdictionary.com/word/search.html?q=gifted

American Psychiatric Association. (1994). *Diagnostic and statistical manual of mental disorders* (4th ed.). Washington, DC: Author.

American Psychiatric Association. (2013). *Diagnostic and statistical manual of mental disorders* (5th ed.). Washington, DC: Author. Retrieved February 21, 2012, from www.dsm5.org/proposedrevision/pages/proposedrevision.aspx?rid=384

Andreasen, N. C. (1987). Creativity and mental illness: Prevalence rates in writers and their first-degree relatives. *American Journal of Psychiatry, 144,* 1288–1292.

Aristotle. (1962). *On the generation of animals, IV:6* (A. Platt, Trans.). New York, NY: Great Books, Encyclopedia Britannica.

Assouline, S. G., Foley Nicpon, M., & Huber, D. H. (2006). The impact of vulnerabilities and strengths on the academic experiences of twice-exceptional students: A message to counselors. *Professional School Counseling, 10*(1), 14–24.

Assouline, S. G., Foley Nicpon, M., & Whiteman, C. (2010). Cognitive and psychosocial characteristics of gifted students with written language disability. *Gifted Child Quarterly, 54,* 102–115.

Asynchrony. (2011). *Encyclopaedia Brittanica.* Retrieved January 8, 2011, from www.britannica.com/EBchecked/topic/134273/asynchrony

Babcock, W. L. (1895). On the morbid heredity and predisposition to insanity of the man of genius. *Journal of Nervous and Mental Disease, 20,* 749–769.

Bailey, C. L. (2011). An examination of the relationships between ego development, Dabrowski's theory of positive disintegration, and the behavioral characteristics of gifted adolescents. *Gifted Child Quarterly, 55,* 208–222.

Barber, C., & Mueller, C. T. (2011). Social and self-perceptions of adolescents identified as gifted, learning disabled, and twice-exceptional. *Roeper Review, 33,* 109–120.

Baska, A. (2009). The eminent remains: The life, studies, and archives of Sir Francis Galton. In B. MacFarlane & T. Stambaugh (Eds.), *Leading change in gifted education: The festschrift of Dr. Joyce VanTassel-Baska* (pp. 469–479). Waco, TX: Prufrock Press.

Baum, S. M. (2009). Learning disabilities. In B. Kerr (Ed.), *Encyclopedia of giftedness, creativity and talent* (Vol. 2, pp. 527–529). Thousand Oaks, CA: Sage.

Baum, S. M., & Owen, S. V. (2004). *To be gifted and learning disabled: Strategies for helping bright students with LD, ADHD, and more.* Mansfield Center, CT: Creative Learning Press.

Beljan, P. (2005). Behavioral management of gifted children: A neuropsychological approach. *2e Twice-Exceptional Newsletter, 9*, 1, 16–18.

Benbow, C. P. (1990). Leta Stetter Hollingworth: A pilgrim in research in her time and ours. *Roeper Review, 12*(3), 210–215.

Beneventi, A. (2012, March). The Annemarie Roeper Method of Qualitative Assessment. *Gifted Development Center Newsletter.* Available from www.gifteddevelopment.com

Berche Cruz, X. (1987, August). *Developmental differences in gifted and average children.* Paper presented at the Seventh World Conference on Gifted and Talented Children, Salt Lake City, UT.

Besjes-de Bock, K. M., & de Ruyter, D. J. (2011). Five values of giftedness. *Roeper Review, 33*, 198–207.

Betts, G. (2012, January). *Celebrations and new directions.* Presented at the Colorado Academy for Educators of Gifted, Talented and Creative, Golden, CO.

Bianco, M., Harris, B., Garrison-Wade, D., & Leech, N. (2011). Gifted girls: Gender bias in gifted referrals. *Roeper Review, 33*, 170–181.

Binet, A. (1909/1975). *Les idees modernes sur les enfants.* Paris: Ernest Flammarion. (Translated and reprinted from *Modern ideas about children*, by S. Heisler, Trans., 1975, Menlo Park, CA: Suzanne Heisler.)

Binet, A. (1911). Avant-propos: Le bilan de psychologie en 1910. *L'Année Psychologique, 17*, 5–11.

Binet, A., & Henri, V. (1896). La psychologie individuelle. *L'Annee Psychologique, 2*, 411–465.

Binet, A., & Simon, T. (1905). Application des methods nouvelle au diagnostic du niveau intellectual chez des enfants normaux et anormaux d'hospice et d'ecole primaire. *L'Annee Psychologique, 11*, 191–244.

Binet, A., & Simon, T. (1908). Le developpement de l'intelligence chez les enfants. *L'Annee Psychologique, 14*, 1–94.

Bland, L. C. (2012). Achievement-based conceptions of giftedness. In T. L. Cross & J. R. Cross (Eds.), *Handbook for counselors serving students with gifts & talents: Development, relationships, school issues, and counseling needs/interventions* (pp. 21–38). Waco, TX: Prufrock Press.

Bloom, B. S. (Ed.). (1985). *Developing talent in young people.* New York, NY: Ballantine Books.

Boazman, J., & Sayler, M. (2011). Early college entrance and life satisfaction. *Roeper Review, 33,* 76–85.

Bonner, F. A., II, Lewis, C. W., Bowman-Perrott, L., Hill-Jackson, V., & James, M. (2009). Definition, identification, identity, and culture: A unique alchemy impacting the success of gifted African American millennial males in school. *Journal for the Education of the Gifted, 33,* 176–202.

Boring, E. G. (1950). *A history of experimental psychology.* Englewood Cliffs, NJ: Prentice-Hall.

Borland, J. H. (1990). Leta Hollingworth's contributions to the psychology and education of the gifted. *Roeper Review, 12,* 162–166.

Borsting, E., Mitchell, G. L., Kulp, M. T., Scheiman, M., Amster, D. M., Cotter, S., . . . CITT Study Group. (2012). Improvement in academic behaviors after successful treatment of convergence insufficiency. *Optometric & Vision Science, 89*(1), 12–18.

Bouchard, T. J., Jr., & Lykken, D. T. (1999). Achievement in a sample of twins reared apart: Estimating the role of genetic and environmental influences. In N. Colangelo & S. G. Assouline (Eds.), *Talent development III: Proceedings from the 1995 Henry B. and Jocelyn Wallace national research symposium on talent development* (pp. 81–97). Scottsdale, AZ: Gifted Potential Press.

Burns, D. D. (1980, November). The perfectionist's script for self-defeat. *Psychology Today,* pp. 34–52.

Cain, S. (2012). *Quiet.* New York, NY: Crown.

Campbell, J. R., & Verna, M. A. (2007). Effective parental influence: Academic home climate linked to children's achievement. *Educational Research & Evaluation, 13,* 501–519.

Carroll, J. B. (1993). *Human cognitive abilities: A survey of factor analytic studies.* New York, NY: Cambridge University Press.

Carson, D., & Roid, G. (2004). *Acceptable use of the Stanford-Binet Form L-M: Guidelines for the professional use of the Stanford-Binet Intelligence Scale, Third Edition (Form L-M).* Itasca, IL: Riverside.

Cayton, T. (2008, November). *Wechsler's "ability to an extraordinary degree": Extended norms on the WISC-IV.* Paper presented at the meeting of the National Association for Gifted Children, Tampa, FL.

Chan, D. W. (2005). Family environment and talent development of Chinese gifted students in Hong Kong. *Gifted Child Quarterly, 49*, 211–221.

Chan, D. W. (2007). Positive and negative perfectionism among Chinese gifted students in Hong Kong: Their relationships to general self-efficacy and subjective well-being. *Journal for the Education of the Gifted, 31*, 77–102.

Chan, D. W. (2009). Dimensionality and typology of perfectionism: The use of the Frost Multidimensional Perfectionism Scale with Chinese gifted students in Hong Kong. *Gifted Child Quarterly, 53*, 174–187.

Chan, D. W. (2010). Healthy and unhealthy perfectionists among academically gifted Chinese students in Hong Kong: Do different classification schemes make a difference? *Roeper Review, 32*, 88–97.

Chan, D. W. (2011). Characteristics and competencies of teachers of gifted learners: The Hong Kong student perspective. *Roeper Review, 33*, 160–169.

Chan, D. W. (2012). Life satisfaction, happiness, and the growth mindset of healthy and unhealthy perfectionists among Hong Kong Chinese gifted students. *Roeper Review, 34*, 224–233.

Charyton, C., Elliott, J. O., Aahman, M. A., Woodard, J. L., & DeDios, S. (2011). Gender and science: Women Nobel Laureates. *Journal of Creative Behavior, 45*(3), 203–214.

Cho, S., & Campbell, J. R. (2011). Differential influences of family processes for scientifically talented individuals' academic achievement along developmental stages. *Roeper Review, 33*, 33–45.

CITT (Convergence Insufficiency Treatment Trial) Study Group. (2008). Randomized clinical trial of treatments for symptomatic convergence insufficiency in children. *Archives of Ophthalmology, 126*, 1336–1349.

Clance, P. (1985). *The imposter phenomenon*. Atlanta, GA: Peachtree.

Clark, B. (1983). *Growing up gifted: Developing the potential of children at home and at school* (2nd ed.). Columbus, OH: Charles E. Merrill.

Colangelo, N. (2002, May). *Anti-intellectualism in universities, schools, and gifted education*. Keynote address presented at the Sixth Biennial Wallace National Research Symposium on Talent Development, University of Iowa, Iowa City, IA.

Colangelo, N., Assouline, S. G., & Gross, M. U. M. (2004). *A nation deceived: How schools hold back America's brightest students* (Vols. 1–2).

Iowa City, IA: The Connie Belin & Jacqueline N. Blank International Center for Gifted Education and Talent Development.

Colangelo, N., Assouline, S. G., & Lupkowski-Shoplik, A. E. (2004). Whole-grade acceleration. In N. Colangelo, S. G. Assouline, & M. U. M. Gross (Eds.), *A nation deceived: How schools hold back America's students* (Vol. 2, pp. 77–86). Iowa City, IA: The Connie Belin & Jacqueline N. Blank International Center for Gifted Education and Talent Development, University of Iowa.

Cole, L. C., & DellaVecchia, R. M. (1993). "Pushy and domineering": A stigma placed on parents of gifted children. *Understanding Our Gifted, 6*(1), 1, 8–10.

Coleman, L. J. (2012). Lived experience, mixed messages, and stigma. In T. L. Cross & J. R. Cross (Eds.), *Handbook for counselors serving students with gifts & talents: Development, relationships, school issues, and counseling needs/interventions* (pp. 371–392). Waco, TX: Prufrock Press.

Columbus Group. (1991, July). *Unpublished transcript of the meeting of the Columbus Group.* Columbus, OH.

Columbus Group. (2013). *Off the charts. Asynchrony and the gifted child.* Unionville, NY: Royal Fireworks Press.

Cornell, D. G. (1984). *Families of gifted children.* Ann Arbor, MI: UMI Research Press.

Cox, C. M. (1926). *Genetic studies of genius: Vol. 2. The early mental traits of three hundred eminent geniuses.* Stanford, CA: Stanford University Press.

Cross, J. R. (2012). Peer relationships. In T. L. Cross & J. R. Cross (Eds.), *Handbook for counselors serving students with gifts & talents: Development, relationships, school issues, and counseling needs/interventions* (pp. 409–425). Waco, TX: Prufrock Press.

Csikszentmihalyi, M. (1990). *Flow: The psychology of optimal experience.* New York, NY: Harper & Row.

Dabrowski, K. (1964). *Positive disintegration.* London: Little, Brown.

Dabrowski, K. (1967). *Personality-shaping through positive disintegration.* Boston, MA: Little, Brown.

Dabrowski, K. (1972). *Psychoneurosis is not an illness.* London: Gryf.

Dai, D. Y. (2009). Essential tensions surrounding the concept of giftedness. In L. V. Shavinina (Ed.), *International handbook on giftedness* (Part 1, pp. 39–80). Amsterdam: Springer Science.

Daniels, S., & Piechowski, M. M. (Eds.). (2009). *Living with intensity: Understanding the sensitivity, excitability, and emotional development of gifted children, adolescents, and adults.* Scottsdale, AZ: Great Potential Press.

Darwin, C. R. (1859). *On the origin of the species by means of natural selection, or the preservation of favoured races in the struggle for life.* London: John Murray.

Darwin, C. R. (1897). *The descent of man and selection in relation to sex* (Rev. ed.). New York, NY: D. Appleton.

Dauber, S. L., & Benbow, C. P. (1990). Aspects of personality and peer relations of extremely talented adolescents. *Gifted Child Quarterly, 34,* 10–15.

Davis, R. D. (with Braun, E. M.). (2010). *The gift of dyslexia: Why some of the smartest people can't read . . . and how they can learn (revised).* New York, NY: Perigee.

Delbridge-Parker, L., & Robinson, D. C. (1989). Type and academically gifted adolescents. *Journal of Psychological Type, 17,* 66–72.

Dembinski, R. J., & Mauser, A. J. (1978). Parents of the gifted: Perceptions of psychologists and teachers. *Journal for the Education of the Gifted, 1,* 5–14.

DeVries, A., & Webb, J. (2007). *Gifted parent groups: The SENG model* (2nd ed.). Scottsdale, AZ: Great Potential Press.

Dickinson, R. M. (1956). *A technique for locating and for assessing the unmet needs of gifted children in the public schools* (Unpublished doctoral dissertation). University of Denver, Denver, CO.

Dickinson, R. M. (1970). *Caring for the gifted.* North Quincy, MA: Christopher.

Dixon, S. G., Eusebio, E. C., Turton, W. J., Wright, P. W. D., & Hale, J. B. (2011). Forest Grove School District v. T.A. Supreme Court case: Implications for school psychology practice. *Journal of Psychoeducational Assessment, 29*(2), 103–113. doi: 10.1177/0734282910388598

Drews, E. (1972). *Learning together: How to foster creativity, self-fulfillment, social awareness in today's students and teachers.* Englewood Cliffs, NJ: Prentice-Hall.

DuBois, P. H. (1970). *A history of psychological testing.* Boston, MA: Allyn & Bacon.

Dweck, C. S. (1986). Motivational processes affecting learning. *American Psychologist, 41,* 1040–1048.

Dweck, C. S. (2006). *Mindset: The new psychology of success.* New York, NY: Random House.

Dweck, C. S. (2011). Giftedness: A motivational perspective. *Images: Michigan Alliance for Gifted Education Newsletter, 21*(1), 1, 3, 12–13.

Eddles-Hirsch, K., Vialle, W., McCormick, J., & Rogers, K. (2012). Insiders or outsiders: The role of social context in the peer relations of gifted students. *Roeper Review, 34*, 53–62.

Educational Policies Commission. (1950). *Education of the gifted.* Washington, DC: National Education Association.

Ehrlich, V. Z. (1986). Recognizing superior cognitive abilities in disadvantaged, minority, and other diverse populations. In J. R. Whitmore (Ed.), *Intellectual giftedness in young children: Recognition and development* (pp. 55–70). New York, NY: The Haworth Press.

Eide, B. L., & Eide, F. F. (2006). *The mislabeled child.* New York, NY: Hyperion.

Eide, B. L., & Eide, F. F. (2011). *The dyslexic advantage: Unlocking the hidden potential of the dyslexic brain.* New York, NY: Hudson Street Press.

Elementary and Secondary Educational Amendments of 1969, Provisions Related to Gifted and Talented Children, Pub. L. No. 91–230, 84 Stat. 191 (1970).

Emerick, L. J. (1992). Academic underachievement among the gifted: Students' perceptions of factors that reverse the pattern. *Gifted Child Quarterly, 36*, 140–146.

Ericsson, K. A. (2006). The influence of experience and deliberate practice on the development of superior expert performance. In K. A. Ericsson, N. Charness, P. Feltovich, & R. R. Hoffman (Eds.), *Cambridge handbook of expertise and expert performance* (pp. 685–706). Cambridge, UK: Cambridge University Press.

Ericsson, K. A., Nandagopal, K., & Roring, R. W. (2009). An expert performance approach to the study of giftedness. In L. V. Shavinina (Ed.), *International handbook on giftedness* (Part 1, pp. 129–153). Amsterdam: Springer Science.

Esquierdo, J. J., & Arreguín-Anderson, M. (2012). The "invisible" gifted and talented bilingual students: A current report on enrollment in GT programs. *Journal for the Education of the Gifted, 35*, 35–47.

Fagan, T. K. (1990). Contributions of Leta Hollingworth to school psychology. *Roeper Review, 12*(3), 157–161.

Falk, R. F. (2012). *Two factors of emotional overexcitability: Emotional sensitivity and empathy.* Unpublished data. (Available from the Institute for the Study of Advanced Development, 8120 Sheridan Boulevard, Suite C-111, Westminster, CO 80003).

Falk, R. F., & Miller, N. B. (2009). Building firm foundations: Research and assessments. In S. Daniels & M. M. Piechowski (Eds.), *Living with intensity: Understanding the sensitivity, excitability and emotional development in gifted children, adolescents and adults* (pp. 239–259). Scottsdale, AZ: Great Potential Press.

Falk, R. F., Miller, N. B., & Silverman, L. K. (2009, November). *Parents' perceptions of their gifted child's overexcitability.* Paper presented at the 56th annual convention of the National Association for Gifted Children, St. Louis, MO.

Falk, R. F., Piechowski, M. M., & Lind, S. (1994). *Criteria for rating the intensity of overexcitabilities* (Unpublished manuscript). Department of Sociology, University of Akron, Akron, OH. (Available from the Institute for the Study of Advanced Development, 8120 Sheridan Boulevard, Suite C-111, Westminster, CO 80003).

Feagans, L. (1986). Otitis media: A model for long term effects with implications for intervention. In J. Kavanaugh (Ed.), *Otitis media and child development* (pp. 192–208). Parkton, MD: York Press.

Feiring, C., Louis, B., Ukeje, I., & Lewis, M. (1997). Early identification of gifted minority kindergarten students in Newark, NJ. *Gifted Child Quarterly, 41,* 76–82.

Feldhusen, J. (1992). *Talent identification and development in education (TIDE).* Sarasota, FL: Center for Creative Learning.

Feldhusen, J. F. (1998). Identification and assessment of talented learners. In J. VanTassel-Baska (Ed.), *Excellence in educating gifted and talented learners* (3rd ed., pp. 193–210). Denver, CO: Love.

Feldhusen, J. F., & Kroll, M. D. (1985). Parent perceptions of gifted children's educational needs. *Roeper Review, 7*(4), 249–252.

Feldman, D. H. (1984). A follow-up of subjects scoring above 180 IQ in Terman's "Genetic Studies of Genius." *Exceptional Children, 50,* 518–523.

Feldman, D. H. (with Goldsmith, L. T.). (1986). *Nature's gambit: Child prodigies and the development of human potential.* New York, NY: Basic Books.

Feldman, D. H. (1992). Has there been a paradigm shift in gifted education? In N. Colangelo, S. G. Assouline, & D. L. Ambroson (Eds.), *Talent development: Proceedings from the 1991 Henry B. and Jocelyn Wallace National Research Symposium on Talent Development* (pp. 89–94). Unionville, NY: Trillium.

Fiedler, E. (2012). You don't outgrow it! Giftedness across the lifespan. *Advanced Development, 13,* 23–41.

Fisher, K. (1990, April). Interaction with infants is linked to later abilities. *The APA Monitor*, p. 10.

Flanagan, D. P., & Kaufman, A. S. (2004). *Essentials of WISC-IV assessment*. Hoboken, NJ: John Wiley.

Foley Nicpon, M., Allman, A., Siek, B., & Stinson, R. D. (2011). Empirical investigation of twice-exceptionality: Where have we been and where are we going? *Gifted Child Quarterly, 55*, 3–17.

Ford, D., Moore, J. L., & Scott, M. T. (2011). Key theories and frameworks for improving the recruitment and retention of African American students in gifted education. *Journal of Negro Education, 80*, 239–253.

Frank, J. (2006). *Portrait of an inspirational teacher of the gifted* (Unpublished doctoral dissertation). University of Calgary, Calgary, AL.

French, L. R., Walker, C. L., & Shore, B. (2011). Do gifted students really prefer to work alone? *Roeper Review, 33*, 145–159.

Friedrichs, T. P. (2012). Counseling gifted GLBT students along paths to freedom. In T. L. Cross & J. R. Cross (Eds.), *Handbook for counselors serving students with gifts & talents: Development, relationships, school issues, and counseling needs/interventions* (pp. 153–177). Waco, TX: Prufrock Press.

Gagné, F. (1985). Giftedness and talent: Reexamining a reexamination of the definitions. *Gifted Child Quarterly, 29*, 103–112.

Gagné, F. (2012). Differentiated model of giftedness and talent. In T. L. Cross & J. R. Cross (Eds.), *Handbook for counselors serving students with gifts & talents: Development, relationships, school issues, and counseling needs/interventions* (pp. 3–19). Waco, TX: Prufrock Press.

Gallagher, J. J. (1979). Issues in education of the gifted. In A. H. Passow (Ed.), *The gifted and the talented: Their education and development* (pp. 28–44). The 78th Yearbook of the National Society for the Study of Education, Part I. Chicago, IL: University of Chicago Press.

Gallagher, J. J. (2000). Unthinkable thoughts: Education of gifted students. *Gifted Child Quarterly, 44*, 5–12.

Gallagher, J. J. (2004). No child left behind and gifted education. *Roeper Review, 26*, 121–123.

Gallagher, J., & Moss, J. (1963). New concepts of intelligence and their effect on exceptional children. *Exceptional Children, 30*(1), 1–5.

Gallagher, S. A. (1990). Personality patterns of the gifted. *Understanding Our Gifted, 3*(1), 1, 11–13.

Galton, F. (1869). *Hereditary genius: An inquiry into its causes and consequences.* London: Macmillan.

Galton, F. (1883). *Inquiries into human faculty and its development.* New York, NY: Macmillan.

Gardner, H. G. (1983). *Frames of mind: A theory of multiple intelligences.* New York, NY: Basic Books.

Gardner, J. W. (1961). *Excellence: Can we be equal and excellent, too?* New York, NY: Harper & Row.

Garn, A. C., Matthews, M. S., & Jolly, J. L. (2010). Parental influences on the academic motivation of gifted students: A self-determination theory perspective. *Gifted Child Quarterly, 54,* 263–272.

Garrett, T., Antrop-Gonzalez, R., & Velez, W. (2010). Examining the success factors of high-achieving Puerto Rican male high-school students. *Roeper Review, 32,* 106–115.

Garrison, C. G., Burke, A., & Hollingworth, L. S. (1917). The psychology of a prodigious child. *Journal of Applied Psychology, 1,* 101–110.

Gaunt, R. I. (1989). *A comparison of the perceptions of parents of highly and moderately gifted children* (Unpublished doctoral dissertation). Kent State University, Kent, OH.

Geake, J. G., & Gross, M. U. M. (2008). Teachers' negative affect toward academically gifted students: An evolutionary psychological study. *Gifted Child Quarterly, 52,* 217–231.

Gentry, M., Steenbergen-Hu, S., & Choi, B. -Y. (2011). Student-identified exemplary teachers: Insights from talented teachers. *Gifted Child Quarterly, 55,* 111–125.

George, P. (1988). Tracking and ability grouping. *Middle School Journal, 20*(1), 21–28.

George, P. (1992). *How to untrack your school.* Alexandria, VA: Association for Supervision and Curriculum Development.

Gifted and Talented Children's Education Act. Pub. L. No. 95–561, 20 U.S.C. 3312 § 902 (1978).

Gilger, J. W., & Hynd, G. W. (2008). Neurodevelopmental variation as a framework for thinking about the twice exceptional. *Roeper Review, 30,* 214–228.

Gilman, B. J. (2008a). *Academic advocacy for gifted children: A parent's complete guide.* Scottsdale, AZ: Great Potential Press.

Gilman, B. J. (2008b). *Challenging highly gifted learners.* Waco, TX: Prufrock Press.

Gilman, B. J., Robinson, N., Kearney, K., Wasserman, J. D., & Silverman, L. K. (2010, November). *Exploring ideal elements of tests of ability for gifted students*. Paper presented as a signature session at the 57th annual convention of the National Association for Gifted Children, Atlanta, GA. (Available from www.gifteddevelopment.com/ PDF_files/NAGC%25202010%2520Handout%2520Exploring %2520Ideal%2520Elements%2520of%2520Tests%2520of%252 0Ability.pdf).

Gladwell, M. (2008). *Outliers: The story of success*. New York, NY: Little, Brown.

Goertzel, T. G., & Hansen, A. (2004). *Cradles of eminence: Childhoods of more than 700 famous men and women* (2nd ed.). Scottsdale, AZ: Great Potential Press.

Gogel, E. M., McCumsey, J., & Hewett, G. (1985). What parents are saying. *G/C/T, Issue 41*, 7–9.

Goleman, D. (1995). *Emotional intelligence: Why it can matter more than IQ*. New York, NY: Bantam Books.

Goodwin, C. B., & Gustavson, M. (2010, September). The bow tie: A conceptual model for understanding the educational needs of the twice-exceptional (2e) child. *Parenting for High Potential*, 21–24. Retrieved from http://issuu.com/jmlawler13/docs/php_ sept10_1

Goodwin, C. B., & Gustavson, M. (2011). *Making the choice: When typical school doesn't fit your atypical child*. Ashland, OR: GHF Press.

Goodwin, C. B., & Gustavson, M. (2012). Education outside of the box: Homeschooling your gifted or twice-exceptional child. *Understanding Our Gifted, 24*(4), 8–11. Retrieved from www.our-gifted.com/

Goss, D. A., Downing, D. B., Lowther, A. H., Horner, D. G., Blemker, M., Donaldson, L., Malsom, T., Gray, K. H. (2007). The effect of HTS [home therapy system] vision therapy conducted in a school setting on reading skills in third and fourth grade students. *Optometry & Vision Development, 38*(1), 27–32.

Gottfredson, L. S. (2003). The science and politics of intelligence in gifted education. In N. Colangelo & G. A. Davis (Eds.), *Handbook of gifted education* (3rd ed., pp. 24–40). Boston: Allyn & Bacon.

Gottfredson, L. S. (2005). Implications of cognitive differences for schooling within diverse societies. In C. L. Frisby & C. R. Reynolds

(Eds.), *Comprehensive handbook of multicultural school psychology* (pp. 517–554). New York, NY: Wiley.

Gottfredson, L. S. (2011). Intelligence and social inequality: Why the biological link? In T. Chamorro-Premuzic, A. Furnham, & S. von Stumm (Eds.), *Handbook of individual differences* (pp. 538–575). Wiley-Blackwell.

Gottfried, A. W., Gottfried, A. E., Bathurst, K., & Guerin, D. W. (1994). *Gifted IQ. Early developmental aspects: The Fullerton longitudinal study*. New York, NY: Plenum Press.

Gottfried, A. W., Gottfried, A. E., & Guerin, D. W. (2006). The Fullerton Longitudinal Study: A long-term investigation of intellectual and motivational giftedness. *Journal for the Education of the Gifted, 29*, 430–450.

Gowan, J. C. (1977). Background and history of the gifted-child movement. In J. C. Stanley, W. C. George, & C. H. Solano (Eds.), *The gifted and the creative: A fifty-year perspective* (pp. 5–27). Baltimore, MD: The Johns Hopkins University Press.

Gowan, J. C. (1980). Issues on the guidance of gifted and creative children. In J. C. Gowan, G. D. Demos, & C. J. Kokaska (Eds.), *The guidance of exceptional children* (2nd ed., pp. 66–70). New York, NY: Longman.

Grant, B., & Piechowski, M. M. (1999). Theories and the good: Toward a child-centered gifted education. *Gifted Child Quarterly, 43*, 4–12.

Grantham, T. C. (2011). New directions for gifted Black males suffering from bystander effects: A call for upstanders. *Roeper Review, 33*, 263–272.

Gray, T. (1751/1949). Elegy written in a country churchyard. In W. H. Davenport, L. C. Wimberly, & H. Shaw (Eds.), *Dominant types in British and American literature, Volume 1. Poetry and drama* (pp. 250–252). New York, NY: Harper.

Greenspon, T. S. (2012). Perfectionism: A counselor's role in a recovery process. In T. L. Cross & J. R. Cross (Eds.), *Handbook for counselors serving students with gifts & talents: Development, relationships, school issues, and counseling needs/interventions* (pp. 597–613). Waco, TX: Prufrock Press.

Grobman, J. (2009). A psychodynamic psychotherapy approach to the emotional problems of exceptionally and profoundly gifted adolescents and adults. *Journal for the Education of the Gifted, 33*, 106–125.

Gross, M. U. M. (1998). The "me" behind the mask: Intellectually gifted students and the search for identity. *Roeper Review, 20,* 167–174.

Gross, M. U. M. (2004). *Exceptionally gifted children* (2nd ed.). London: Routledge Falmer.

Gross, M. U. M. (2006). Exceptionally gifted children: Long-term outcomes of academic acceleration and non-acceleration. *Journal for the Education of the Gifted, 29,* 404–429.

Gross, M. U. M. (2009). Highly gifted young people: Development from childhood to adulthood. In L. V. Shavinina (Ed.), *International handbook on giftedness* (Part 1, pp. 337–351). Amsterdam: Springer Science.

Haas, S. (2011, December). *The Visual-Spatial Identifier. Gifted Development Center Newsletter.* Available from www.gifteddevelopment.com

Hafenstein, N. L., & Honeck, E. (Eds.). (2011). *Greatest potential, greatest need: Soaring beyond expectations. Conference proceedings and selected articles focusing on the highly gifted.* Denver, CO: The Institute for the Development of Gifted Education, University of Denver.

Hamachek, D. E. (1978). Psychodynamics of normal and neurotic perfectionism. *Psychology, 15,* 27–33.

Harris, B., Plucker, J. A., Rapp, K. E., & Martinez, R. S. (2009). Identifying gifted and talented English language learners: A case study. *Journal for the Education of the Gifted, 32,* 368–393.

Harrison, C. (2004). Giftedness in early childhood: The search for complexity and connection. *Roeper Review, 26,* 78–84.

Harvey, S., & Seeley, K. (1984). An investigation of the relationships among intellectual and creative abilities, extracurricular activities, achievement, and giftedness in a delinquent population. *Gifted Child Quarterly, 28,* 73–79.

Hebert, T. P. (2011). *Understanding the social and emotional lives of gifted students.* Waco, TX: Prufrock Press.

Hebert, T. P., Pagnani, A. R., & Hammond, D. R. (2009). Paternal influence on high-achieving gifted males. *Journal for the Education of the Gifted, 33,* 241–274.

Henderson, L. M., & Ebner, F. F. (1997). The biological basis for early intervention with gifted children. *Peabody Journal of Education, 72*(3 & 4), 59–80.

Hermann, K. M., & Lawrence, C. (2012). Family relationships. In T. L. Cross & J. R. Cross (Eds.), *Handbook for counselors serving students with gifts & talents: Development, relationships, school issues, and counseling needs/interventions* (pp. 393–407). Waco, TX: Prufrock Press.

Hewitt, P. L., & Flett, G. L. (1991). Dimensions of perfectionism in unipolar depression. *Journal of Abnormal Psychology, 100*, 98–101.

Hildreth, G. H. (1966). *Introduction to the gifted.* New York, NY: McGraw-Hill.

Hirsch, N. D. M. (1931). *Genius and creative intelligence.* Cambridge, MA: Sci-Art.

Hoagies' Gifted Education Page. *Psychologists familiar with testing the gifted and exceptionally gifted.* Retrieved October 14, 2012, from www.hoagiesgifted.org/psychologists.htm

Hoehn, L., & Bireley, M. K. (1988). Mental processing preferences of gifted children. *Illinois Council for the Gifted Journal, 7*, 28–31.

Hollingworth, L. S. (1913). The frequency of amentia as related to sex. *Medical Record, 84*, 753–756.

Hollingworth, L. S. (1923). *Special talents and defects.* New York, NY: Macmillan.

Hollingworth, L. S. (1926). *Gifted children: Their nature and nurture.* New York, NY: Macmillan.

Hollingworth, L. S. (1930). Personality development of special class children. *University of Pennsylvania Bulletin: Seventeenth Annual Schoolmen's Week Proceedings, 30*, 442–446.

Hollingworth, L. S. (1931). The child of very superior intelligence as a special problem of social adjustment. *Mental Hygiene, 15*(1), 3–16.

Hollingworth, L. S. (1932). Who is the gifted pupil? *University of Pennsylvania Bulletin, Nineteenth Annual Schoolmen's Week Proceedings, 30*, 239–246.

Hollingworth, L. S. (1939). What we know about the early selection and training of leaders. *Teachers College Record, 40*, 575–592.

Hollingworth, L. S. (1942). *Children above 180 IQ Stanford-Binet: Origin and development.* Yonkers-on-Hudson, NY: World Book.

Howley, A., & Howley, C. (2012). Counseling the rural gifted. In T. L. Cross & J. R. Cross (Eds.), *Handbook for counselors serving students with gifts & talents: Development, relationships, school issues, and counseling needs/interventions* (pp. 121–136). Waco, TX: Prufrock Press.

Hubbard, E. T., & Whitley, C. T. (Eds.). (2012). *Trans-Kin: A guide for family and friends of transgender people.* Boulder, CO: Bolder Press.

Individuals with Disabilities Education Improvement Act of 2004, Pub. L. No. 108–446, 20 U.S.C. § 1401, 118 Stat. 2657 (2004).

Jackson, P. S., & Moyle, V. F. (2009). Inner awakening, outward journey: The intense gifted child in adolescence. In S. Daniels & M. M. Piechowski (Eds.), *Living with intensity: Understanding the sensitivity, excitability, and emotional development of gifted children, adolescents, and adults* (pp. 57–71). Scottsdale, AZ: Great Potential Press.

Jackson, P. S., Moyle, V. F., & Piechowski, M. M. (2009). Emotional life and psychotherapy of the gifted in light of Dabrowski's theory. In L. V. Shavinina (Ed.), *International handbook on giftedness* (Part 1, pp. 437–465). Amsterdam: Springer Science.

Jackson, P. S., & Peterson, J. (2003). Depressive disorder in highly gifted adolescents. *Journal of Secondary Gifted Education, 14*, 175–189.

Jensen, A. R. (1980). *Bias in mental testing.* New York, NY: The Free Press.

Johnson, W., Nijenhuis, J. T., & Bouchard, T. J., Jr. (2008). Still just 1 g: Consistent results from five test batteries. *Intelligence, 36*, 81–95.

Jones, E. D., & Southern, W. T. (1991). Objections to early entrance and grade skipping. In W. T. Southern & E. D. Jones (Eds.), *The academic acceleration of gifted children* (pp. 51–73). New York, NY: Teachers College Press.

Jung, C. G. (1923/1938). *Psychological types or the psychology of individuation* (H. G. Baynes, Trans.). London: Kegan Paul, Trench, Trubner.

Jung, J. Y., McCormick, J., & Gross, M. U. M. (2012). The forced choice dilemma: A model incorporating idiocentric/allocentric cultural orientation. *Gifted Child Quarterly, 56*, 15–24.

Kagan, J. (1998). *Galen's prophecy.* New York, NY: Basic Books.

Kagan, J., & Snidman, N. (2004). *The long shadow of temperament.* Cambridge, MA: Harvard University Press.

Kalbfleisch, M. L. (2009). The neural plasticity of giftedness. In L. V. Shavinina (Ed.), *International handbook on giftedness* (Part 1, pp. 275–293). Amsterdam: Springer Science.

Kane, M., & Fiedler, E. (2011). Into the stratosphere: Providing curriculum for highly, exceptionally, and profoundly gifted students. In N. L. Hafenstein & E. Honeck (Eds.), *Greatest potential, greatest need: Soaring beyond expectations. Conference proceedings and selected articles focusing on the highly gifted* (pp. 71–114). Denver, CO: The Institute for the Development of Gifted Education, University of Denver.

Kanevsky, L. K. (1994). A comparative study of children's learning in the zone of proximal development. *European Journal of High Ability, 5*(2), 163–175.

Kanevsky, L. (2011). Deferential differentiation: What types of differentiation do students want? *Gifted Child Quarterly, 55,* 279–299.

Kaufman, A. S. (1992). Evaluation of the WISC-III and WPPSI-R for gifted children. *Roeper Review, 14,* 154–158.

Kaufman, A. S. (1994a). *Intelligent testing with the WISC-III.* New York, NY: John Wiley.

Kaufman, A. S. (1994b). A reply to Macmann and Barnett: Lessons from the blind men and the elephant. *School Psychology Quarterly, 9,* 199–207.

Kaufman, A. S. (2009). *IQ testing 101.* New York, NY: Springer.

Kaufman, J. C. (2009). *Creativity 101.* New York, NY: Springer.

Kaufmann, F. A., & Sexton, D. (1983). Some implications for home-school linkages. *Roeper Review, 6,* 49–51.

Kay, K., Robson, D., & Brenneman, J. F. (Eds.). (2007). *High IQ kids: Collected insights, information and personal stories from the experts.* Minneapolis, MN: Free Spirit.

Kearney, K. (1992). Life in the asynchronous family. *Understanding Our Gifted, 4*(6), 1, 8–12.

Kearney, K. (2009, November). *Move over, Galton! Hidden, surprising 19th century sources regarding conceptions of giftedness.* Presented at the National Association for Gifted Children 56th Annual Convention, St. Louis, MO. [Available from author.]

Kearney, K. (2011, March). *Homeschooling gifted children.* Presented at the Homeschoolers of Maine 21st Annual Convention, Rockland, ME.

Kearney, K., & LeBlanc, J. (1993). Forgotten pioneers in the study of gifted African-Americans. *Roeper Review, 15,* 192–199.

Kennedy, D. M., & Banks, R. S. (with Grandin, T.) (2011). *Bright not broken: Gifted kids, ADHD, and autism.* San Francisco, CA: Jossey-Bass.

Kerr, B. A. (1990). Leta Hollingworth's legacy to counseling and guidance. *Roeper Review, 12*(3), 178–181.

Kerr, B. A. (1991). *A handbook for counseling the gifted and talented.* Alexandria, VA: American Association for Counseling and Development.

Kerr, B. A. (1994). *Smart girls two.* Dayton, OH: Ohio Psychology Press.

Kerr, B. A. (Ed.). (2010). *The encyclopedia of giftedness, creativity and talent.* Thousand Oaks, CA: Sage.

Kerr, B. A. (2012). Developmental issues for gifted and creative girls: Milestones and danger zones. In T. L. Cross & J. R. Cross (Eds.), *Handbook for counselors serving students with gifts & talents: Development, relationships, school issues, and counseling needs/interventions* (pp. 315–331). Waco, TX: Prufrock Press.

Kipfer, B. A. (2010). *Roget's international thersaurus* (7th ed., Rev., Updated). New York, NY: Harper Collins.

Kitano, M. (2012). Social-emotional needs of gifted students of color. In T. L. Cross & J. R. Cross (Eds.), *Handbook for counselors serving students with gifts & talents: Development, relationships, school issues, and counseling needs/interventions* (pp. 209–225). Waco, TX: Prufrock Press.

Kuipers, W. (2010). *Enjoying the gift of being uncommon: Extra intelligent, intense, and effective.* Zoetermeer, the Netherlands: Free Musketeers.

Kulieke, M. J., & Olszewski-Kubilius, P. (1989). The influence of family values and climate on the development of talent. In J. VanTassel-Baska & P. Olszewski-Kubilius (Eds.), *Patterns of influence on gifted learners: The home, the self, and the school* (pp. 40–59). New York, NY: Teachers College Press.

Kuo, Y. -L., & Lohman, D. F. (2011). The timing of grade skipping. *Journal for the Education of the Gifted, 34,* 731–741.

Latz, A. O., & Adams, C. M. (2011). Critical differentiation and the twice oppressed: Social class and giftedness. *Journal for the Education of the Gifted, 34,* 773–789.

Lawrence, B. K. (2009). Rural gifted education: A comprehensive literature review. *Journal for the Education of the Gifted, 32,* 461–494.

Lee, S. -Y., Matthews, M. S., & Olszewski-Kubilius, P. (2008). A national picture of talent search and talent search educational programs. *Gifted Child Quarterly, 52,* 55–69.

Lee, S. -Y., Olszewski-Kubilius, P., & Peternel, G. (2010). Achievement after participation in a preparatory program for verbally talented students. *Roeper Review, 32,* 150–163.

Lefrancois, G. R. (1981). *Adolescence* (2nd ed.). Belmont, CA: Wadsworth.

LeGuin, U. K. (1976). *Very far away from anywhere else.* New York, NY: Bantam.

Lehrer, J. (2012). *Imagine: How creativity works.* Boston, MA: Houghton Mifflin Harcourt.

Leman, K. (1984). *The birth order book: Why you are the way you are.* Old Tappan, NJ: Fleming H. Revell.

Leviton, L. P. (1995). Blossoms in Satir's garden: Lynne Azpeitia's work with gifted adults. In L. K. Silverman (Ed.), *Advanced development: A collection of works on giftedness in adults* (pp. 127–146). Denver, CO: Institute for the Study of Advanced Development.

Leviton, L. P. (2011, May). Gotta dance. *Gifted Development Center Newsletter.* Retrieved from www.gifteddevelopment.com

Leviton, L. P. (in press). *Peace within, peace between: Powerfully transforming relationships using Satir practices.* Palo Alto, CA: Science and Behavior Books.

Lewis, B. A. (1998). *The kids' guide to social action: How to solve the social problems you choose—and turn creative thinking into positive action* (2nd ed.). Minneapolis, MN: Free Spirit.

Lewis, M., & Louis, B. (1991). Young gifted children. In N. Colangelo & G. A. Davis (Eds.), *Handbook of gifted education* (pp. 365–381). Boston, MA: Allyn & Bacon.

Lips, H. M. (2005). *Sex and gender: An introduction* (5th ed.). Boston, MA: McGraw-Hill.

Livingston, A., & Nachazal, T. (Eds.) (with Planty, M., Hussar, W., Snyder, T., Kena, G., Kewal Romani, A., Kemp, J., ... Ferguson, K.). (2009, June). *The condition of education, 2009.* Report number NCES 2009–081. Washington, DC: US Department of Education, National Center for Education Statistics, Institute of Education Sciences.

Lombroso, C. (1888/1905). *L'uomo di genio in rapporto alla psichiatria, alla storia, ed al estetica* [The man of genius (2nd ed.). New York, NY: Robert Scott]. Torino: Fratelli Bocca.

Louis, B. (1993). How parents identify giftedness in young children. *Understanding Our Gifted, 5*(5), 1, 7–10.

Louis, B., & Lewis, M. (1992). Parental beliefs about giftedness in young children and their relation to actual ability level. *Gifted Child Quarterly, 36,* 27–31.

Lovecky, D. V. (1986). Can you hear the flowers singing? *Journal of Counseling and Development, 64,* 572–575.

Lovecky, D. V. (1990/1995). Warts and rainbows: Issues in the psychotherapy of the gifted. In L. K. Silverman (Ed.), *Advanced development: A collection of works on giftedness in adults* (pp. 107–125). Denver, CO: Institute for the Study of Advanced Development. (Reprinted from *Advanced Development,* 1990, *2,* 65–83.)

Lovecky, D. V. (1991). The divergently thinking child. *Understanding Our Gifted, 4*(4), 3–4.

Lovecky, D. V. (1994). Exceptionally gifted children: Different minds. *Roeper Review, 17,* 116–120.

Lovecky, D. V. (2004). *Different minds: Gifted children with AD/HD, Asperger syndrome, and other learning deficits.* London: Jessica Kinglsey.

Lovecky, D. V. (2009). Moral sensitivity in young gifted children. In D. Ambrose & T. Cross (Eds.), *Morality, ethics and gifted minds* (pp. 161–176). New York, NY: Springer Science.

Lovecky, D. V. (2011). Friendship and the gifted. In N. Hafenstein & E. Honeck (Eds.), *Greatest potential, greatest need: Soaring beyond expectations. Conference proceedings and selected articles focusing on the highly gifted* (pp. 142–176). Denver, CO: The Institute for the Development of Gifted Education, University of Denver.

Lovecky, D. V., Kearney, K., Falk, R. F., & Gilman, B. J. (2005, August). *A comparison of the Stanford-Binet 5 and the Stanford-Binet Form L-M in the assessment of gifted children.* Paper presented at the 16th biennial conference of the World Council for Gifted and Talented Children, New Orleans, LA.

Lovett, B. J., & Lewandowski, L. J. (2006). Gifted students with learning disabilities? Who are they? *Journal of Learning Disabilities, 39,* 515–585.

Lubin, B., Wallis, R. R., & Paine, C. (1971). Patterns of psychological test usage in the United States: 1935 – 1969. *Professional Psychology, 2,* 70–74.

Luther, M. (1533/1967). *Table talk: To Conrad Cordatus, Feb./Mar., 1533* (T. G. Tappert, Trans.). In J. Pelikan & H. T. Lehmann (Eds.), *Luther's works, Vol. 54.* Philadelphia, PA: Fortress Press.

MacKinnon, D. W. (1962). The nature and nurture of creative talent. *American Psychologist, 17,* 484–495.

Mahoney, A. S. (1998). In search of the gifted identity: From abstract concept to workable counseling constructs. *Roeper Review, 20,* 222–226.

Maker, C. J. (1986). Qualitatively different: Is it a key concept in defining giftedness? In C. J. Maker (Ed.), *Critical issues in gifted education: Defensible programs for the gifted* (pp. 1–4). Austin, TX: Pro-Ed.

Marland, S. P., Jr. (1971/1972). *Education of the gifted and talented: Report to the Congress of the United States by the U.S. Commissioner of Education, Volume 1.* Pursuant to Public Law 91–230, Section 806. Washington, DC: U.S. Government Printing Office.

Martin, L. T., Burns, R. M., & Schonlau, M. (2010). Mental disorders among gifted and nongifted youth: A selected review of epidemiologic literature. *Gifted Child Quarterly, 54,* 31–41.

Martinson, R. A. (1974). *The identification of the gifted and talented.* Ventura, CA: Office of the Ventura County Superintendent of Schools.

Maslow, A. H. (1962). *Toward a psychology of being.* Princeton, NJ: D. Van Nostrand.

Maslow, A. H. (1971). *The farther reaches of human nature.* New York, NY: Viking Press.

Matthews, M. A. (2009). Gifted learners who drop out: Prevalence and prevention. In L. V. Shavinina (Ed.), *International handbook on giftedness* (Part 1, pp. 527–536). Amsterdam: Springer Science.

Matthews, M. S., & Kirsch, L. (2011). Evaluating gifted identification practice: Aptitude testing and linguistically diverse children. *Journal of Applied School Psychology, 27,* 155–180.

Maxwell, E. (1995). The changing developmental needs of the gifted: Birth to maturity. In J. L. Genshaft, M. Bireley, & C. L. Hollinger (Eds.), *Serving gifted and talented students: A resource for school personnel* (pp. 17–30). Austin, TX: Pro-Ed.

May, K. M. (2000). Gifted children and their families. *The Family Journal, 8,* 58–60.

McBee, M. (2010). Examining the probability of identification for gifted programs in Georgia elementary schools: A multilevel path analysis study. *Gifted Child Quarterly, 54,* 283–297.

McCoach, D. B., & Siegle, D. (2007). What predicts teachers' attitudes toward the gifted? *Gifted Child Quarterly, 51,* 246–255.

McDermott, P. A., Fantuzzo, J. W., & Glutting, J. J. (1990). Just say no to subtest analysis: A critique on Wechsler theory and practice. *Journal of Psychoeducational Assessment, 8,* 290–302.

McGuffog, C., Feiring, C., & Lewis, M. (1987). The diverse profile of the extremely gifted child. *Roeper Review, 10*(2), 82–88.

McKenzie, R. G. (2010). The insufficiency of response to intervention in identifying gifted students with learning disabilities. *Learning Disabilities Research & Practice, 25*(3), 161–168.

Meckstroth, E. (1989). On testing. *Understanding Our Gifted, 1*(5), 4.

Meckstroth, E. (1991). Guiding the parents of gifted children: The role of counselors and teachers. In R. M. Milgram (Ed.), *Counseling gifted and talented children: A guide for teachers, counselors, and parents* (pp. 95–120). Norwood, NJ: Ablex.

Meeker, M. N., Meeker, R. J., & Roid, G. H. (1985). *Structure of Intellect Learning Abilities Test (SOI-LA) manual.* Los Angeles, CA: Western Psychological Services.

Mendaglio, S. (2008). *Dabrowski's theory of positive disintegration.* Scottsdale, AZ: Great Potential Press.

Merrill, J. (2012). *If this is a gift, can I send it back? Surviving in the land of the gifted and twice exceptional.* Ashland, OR: GHF Press.

Mika, E. (2006). Giftedness, ADHD, and overexcitabilities: The possibilities of misinformation. *Roeper Review, 28,* 238–242.

Miller, A. L., & Speirs Neumeister, K. L. (2012). Multiple variables for predicting creativity in high ability adults. *Advanced Development, 13,* 84–102.

Montague, H., & Hollingworth, L. S. (1914). The comparative variability of the sexes at birth. *The American Journal of Sociology, 20,* 335–370.

Moon, S. M. (2003). Counseling families. In N. Colangelo & G. A. Davis (Eds.), *Handbook of gifted education* (3rd ed., pp. 388–402). Boston, MA: Allyn & Bacon.

Mooney, J. (2007). *The short bus: A journey beyond normal.* New York, NY: Henry Holt.

Morawska, A., & Sanders, M. R. (2009). Parenting gifted and talented children: Conceptual and empirical foundations. *Gifted Child Quarterly, 55,* 163–173.

Morrison, W. F., & Rizza, M. G. (2007). Creating a toolkit for identifying twice-exceptional students. *Journal for the Education of the Gifted, 31,* 57–76.

Morrissey, A. -M., & Brown, P. M. (2009). Mother and toddler activity in the zone of proximal development for pretend play as a predictor of higher child IQ. *Gifted Child Quarterly, 53,* 106–120.

Mrazik, M., & Dombrowski, S. C. (2010). The neurobiological foundations of giftedness. *Roeper Review, 32,* 224–234.

Mudrak, J. (2011). 'He was born that way': Parental constructions of giftedness. *High Ability Studies, 22,* 199–217.

Munger, A. (1990). The parent's role in counseling the gifted: The balance between home and school. In J. VanTassel-Baska (Ed.),

A practical guide to counseling the gifted in a school setting (2nd ed., pp. 57–65). Reston, VA: The Council for Exceptional Children.

Myers, I. B., & McCaulley, M. H. (1985). *Manual: A guide to the development and use of the Myers-Briggs Type Indicator.* Palo Alto, CA: Consulting Psychologists Press.

National Aeronautics and Space Administration [NASA]. (2012, May 22). *Coaching.* Retrieved August 19, 2012, from http://ohcm.ndc. nasa.gov/career/csa5.htm

National Association for Gifted Children. (2008, January). *Use of the WISC-IV for gifted identification.* Retrieved January 23, 2008, from www.nagc.org/index.aspx?id=375

National Association for Gifted Children. (2011a). *Redefining giftedness for a new century: Shifting the paradigm.* Retrieved January 25, 2012, from www.nagc.org/index.aspx?id=6404

National Association for Gifted Children. (2011b). *What is giftedness? Other definitions from the field.* Retrieved January 2, 2011, from www.nagc.org/index.aspx?id=574

National Association for Gifted Children Britain. (2007). *Giftedness and high ability: Definitions of giftedness.* Retrieved January 17, 2007, from www.nagcbritain.org.uk/giftedness/definitions.html

National Research Council. (2002). *Minority students in special and gifted education* (Committee on minority representation in special education, M. S. Donovan & C. T. Cross, Eds.). Washington, DC: National Academy Press.

Neihart, M. (2007). The socioaffective impact of acceleration and ability grouping: Recommendations for best practice. *Gifted Child Quarterly, 51,* 330–341.

Neihart, M., Reis, S. M., Robinson, N. M., & Moon, S. M. (Eds.). (2002). *The social and emotional development of gifted children. What do we know?* Waco, TX: Prufrock Press.

Neumann, L. C. (2009). Twice exceptional. In B. Kerr (Ed.), *Encyclopedia of giftedness, creativity, and talent* (Vol. 2, pp. 906–910). Thousand Oaks, CA: Sage.

Newland, T. E. (1976). *The gifted in socio-educational perspective.* Englewood Cliffs, NJ: Prentice-Hall.

Nisbet, J. F. (1893). *The insanity of genius and the general inequality of human faculty physiologically considered.* London: Ward & Downey.

No Child Left Behind Act of 2001, 20 U.S.C. 70 §6301 et seq. (2002).

Office of Educational Research and Improvement [OERI]. (1993). *National excellence: A case for developing America's talent.* Washington, DC: U. S. Government Printing Office.

Olsen Laney, M. (2002). *The introvert advantage: How to thrive in an extrovert world.* New York, NY: Workman.

Panter, B. (2009). *Creativity & madness—Psychological studies of art and artists* (Vol. 2). Los Angeles, CA: AIMED Press.

Paolini, C. (2003). *Eragon: Inheritance Book One.* New York, NY: Alfred A. Knopf.

Parker, W. D. (1997). An empirical typology of perfectionism in academically talented children. *American Educational Research Journal, 34*, 545–562.

Parker, W. D. (2000). Healthy perfectionism in the gifted. *The Journal of Secondary Gifted Education, 11*, 173–182.

Parker, W. D., & Stumpf, H. (1995). An examination of the Multidimensional Perfectionism Scale with a sample of academically talented children. *Journal of Psychoeducational Assessment, 13*, 372–383.

Parkinson, M. L. (1990). Finding and serving gifted preschoolers. *Understanding Our Gifted, 2*(5), 1, 10–13.

Pearson, K. (1914). *The life, letters and labours of Francis Galton* (Vol. 1). Cambridge: University Press.

Perrone-McGovern, K. M., Boo, J. N., & Vannatter, A. (2012). Marital and life satisfaction among gifted adults. *Roeper Review, 34*, 46–52.

Persson, R. S. (2009). The unwanted gifted and talented: A sociobiological perspective of the societal functions of giftedness. In L. V. Shavinina (Ed.), *The international handbook of giftedness* (Part 2, pp. 913–924). Amsterdam: Springer Science.

Peter, R., & Stern, W. (1922). *Die auslese befahigter Volksschuler in Hamburg.* Leipzig: Barth.

Peterson, J., & Ray, K. (2006). Bullying among the gifted: The subjective experience. *Gifted Child Quarterly, 50*, 252–269.

Pfeiffer, S. (2003). Challenges and opportunities for students who are gifted: What the experts say. *Gifted Child Quarterly, 47*, 161–169.

Piechowski, M. M. (1991a). Emotional development and emotional giftedness. In N. Colangelo & G. A. Davis (Eds.), *Handbook of gifted education* (pp. 285–306). Boston, MA: Allyn & Bacon.

Piechowski, M. M. (1991b). Giftedness for all seasons: Inner peace in a time of war. In N. Colangelo, S. G. Assouline, & D. L. Ambroson

(Eds.), *Talent development* (pp. 180–203). Proceedings of the Henry B. and Jocelyn Wallace National Research Symposium on Talent Development. Unionville, NY: Trillium Press.

Piechowski, M. M. (2006). *"Mellow out," they say. If I only could. Intensities and sensitivities of the young and bright.* Madison, WI: Yunasa Books.

Piirto, J. (2009). Eminent women. In B. Kerr (Ed.), *Encyclopedia of giftedness, creativity, and talent* (Vol. 1, pp. 314–318). Thousand Oaks, CA: Sage.

Piirto, J., & Fraas, J. (2012). A mixed-methods comparison of vocational and identified-gifted high school students on the Overexcitability Questionnaire. *Journal for the Education of the Gifted, 35,* 3–34.

Plato. (n.d./1944). *The republic* (B. Jowett, Trans.). New York, NY: The Heritage Press.

Plomin, R., & Asbury, K. (2005). Nature and nurture: Genetic and environmental influences on behavior. *Annals of the American Academy of Political and Social Science, 600,* 86–94.

Plomin, R., & Price, T. S. (2003). The relationship between genetics and intelligence. In N. Colangelo & G. A. Davis (Eds.), *Handbook of gifted education* (3rd ed., pp. 113–123). Boston, MA: Allyn & Bacon.

Plucker, J. A. (2000). Flip sides of the same coin or marching to the beat of different drummers? A response to Pyryt. *Gifted Child Quarterly, 44,* 193–195.

Plucker, J. A., Callahan, C. M., & Tomchin, E. M. (1996). Wherefore art thou, multiple intelligences? Alternative assessments for identifying talent in ethnically diverse and low income students. *Gifted Child Quarterly, 40,* 81–92.

Postma, M., Peters, D., Gilman, B., & Kearney, K. (2011, June). RTI and the gifted child: What every parent should know. *Parenting for High Potential,* 16–23 (Available at www.gifteddevelopment.com).

Pramathevan, G. S., & Garces-Bascal, R. M. (2012). Factors influencing altruism in the context of overseas learning experiences among gifted adolescent girls in Singapore. *Roeper Review, 34,* 145–157.

Pritchard, M. C. (1951). The contributions of Leta S. Hollingworth to the study of gifted children. In P. A. Witty (Ed.), *The gifted child* (pp. 47–85). American Association for Gifted Children. Boston, MA: D. C. Heath.

Probst, B., & Piechowski, M. M. (2012). Overexcitabilities and temperament. In T. L. Cross & J. R. Cross (Eds.), *Handbook for counselors serving* students with gifts & talents: Development, relationships, school issues, and counseling needs/interventions (pp. 53–73). Waco, TX: Prufrock Press.

Pyryt, M. C. (2000). Finding "g": Easy viewing through higher order factor analysis. *Gifted Child Quarterly, 44,* 190–192.

Reams, R., Chamrad, D., & Robinson, N. (1990). The race is not necessarily to the swift: Validity of WISC-R bonus points for speed. *Gifted Child Quarterly, 34,* 108–110.

Reichenberg, A., & Landau, E. (2009). Families of gifted children. In L. V. Shavinina (Ed.), *International handbook of giftedness* (Part 2, pp. 873–883). Amsterdam: Springer Science.

Renzulli, J. S. (1977). *The enrichment triad model: A guide for developing defensible programs for the gifted.* Mansfield, CT: Creative Learning.

Renzulli, J. S. (1978). What makes giftedness? Reexamining a definition. *Phi Delta Kappan, 60,* 180–184.

Renzulli, J. S., & Park, S. (2000). Gifted dropouts: The who and the why. *Gifted Child Quarterly, 44,* 261–271.

Renzulli, J. S., & Reis, S. M. (2003). The schoolwide enrichment model: Developing creative and productive giftedness. In N. Colangelo & G. A. Davis (Eds.), *Handbook of gifted education* (3rd ed., pp. 184–203). Boston, MA: Allyn & Bacon.

Renzulli, J. S., Reis, S. M., & Smith, L. H. (1981). The revolving door model: A new way of identifying the gifted. *Phi Delta Kappan, 62,* 648–649.

Reynolds, C. R., & Kamphaus, R. W. (2007). *Reynolds Intellectual Assessment Scale—Interpretive report system* (RIAS-IR). Lutz, FL: Psychological Assessment Resources.

Reynolds, C. R., & Shaywitz, S. E. (2009). Response to intervention: Ready or not? Or, from wait-to-fail to watch-them-fail. *School Psychology Quarterly, 24,* 130–145.

Rimm, S. (2008). Underachievement syndrome: A psychological defense pattern. In S. I. Pfeiffer (Ed.), *Handbook of giftedness in children* (pp. 139–160). New York, NY: Springer Science.

Rimm, S. (2009). Underachievement. In B. Kerr (Ed.), *Encyclopedia of giftedness, creativity and talent* (Vol. 2, pp. 911–914). Thousand Oaks, CA: Sage.

Rimm, S., Gilman, B. J., & Silverman, L. K. (2008). Non-traditional applications of traditional testing. In J. VanTassel-Baska (Ed.), *Alternative assessments with gifted and talented students* (pp. 175–202). Waco, TX: Prufrock Press.

Rivero, L. (2002). *Creative home schooling: A resource guide for smart families.* Scottsdale, AZ: Great Potential Press.

Robertson, S. G., Pfeiffer, S. I., & Taylor, N. (2011). Serving the gifted: A national survey of school psychologists. *Psychology in the Schools, 48*(8), 786–799.

Robinson, H. B. (1981). The uncommonly bright child. In M. Lewis & L. A. Rosenblum (Eds.), *The uncommon child* (pp. 57–81). New York, NY: Plenum Press.

Robinson, N. M. (1993). Identifying and nurturing gifted, very young children. In K. A. Heller, F. J. Monks, & A. H. Passow (Eds.), *International handbook of research and development of giftedness and talent* (pp. 507–524). Oxford: Pergamon Press.

Robinson, N. M. (1996). Counseling agendas for gifted young people: A commentary. *Journal for the Education of the Gifted, 20,* 128–137.

Robinson, N. M. (2004). Effects of academic acceleration on the social-emotional status of gifted students. In N. Colangelo, S. G. Assouline, & M. U. M. Gross (Eds.), *A nation deceived: How schools hold back America's brightest students* (Vol. 2, pp. 59–67). Iowa City, IA: The Connie Belin & Jacqueline N. Blank International Center for Gifted Education and Talent Development.

Robinson, N. M. (2005). In defense of a psychometric approach to the definition of academic giftedness: A conservative view from a die-hard liberal. In R. J. Sternberg & J. E. Davidson (Eds.), *Conceptions of giftedness* (2nd ed., pp. 280–294). New York, NY: Cambridge University Press.

Robinson, N. M. (2008a). The social world of gifted children and youth. In S. I. Pfeiffer (Ed.), *Handbook of giftedness in children: Psycho-educational theory, research, and best practices* (pp. 33–51). New York, NY: Springer Science.

Robinson, N. M. (2008b). The value of traditional assessments as approaches to identifying academically gifted students. In J. VanTassel-Baska (Ed.), *Alternative assessments with gifted and talented students* (pp. 157–174). Waco, TX: Prufrock Press.

Robinson, N. M., & Noble, K. D. (1991). Social-emotional development and adjustment of gifted children. In M. C. Wang, M. C. Reynolds, & H. J. Walberg (Eds.), *Handbook of special education: Research and practice, Volume 4: Emerging programs* (pp. 57–76). New York, NY: Pergamon Press.

Robinson, N. M., & Olszewski-Kubilius, P. M. (1996, December). Gifted and talented children: Issues for pediatricians. *Pediatrics in Review, 17*(12), 427–434.

Robinson, N. M., & Robinson, H. (1992). The use of standardized tests with young gifted children. In P. S. Klein & A. J. Tannenbaum (Eds.), *To be young and gifted* (pp. 141–170). Norwood, NJ: Ablex.

Robinson, N. M., Zigler, E., & Gallagher, J. (2000). Two tails of the normal curve: Similarities and differences in the study of mental retardation and giftedness. *American Psychologist, 55,* 1413–1424.

Roedell, W. C. (1988). "I just want my child to be happy": Social development and young gifted children. *Understanding Our Gifted, 1*(1), 1, 7, 9–11.

Roedell, W. C. (1989). Early development of gifted children. In J. VanTassel-Baska & P. Olszewski-Kubilius (Eds.), *Patterns of influence on gifted learners: The home, the self, and the school* (pp. 13–28). New York, NY: Teachers College Press.

Roeper, A. (1982). How the gifted cope with their emotions. *Roeper Review, 5*(2), 21–24.

Roeper, A. (1991/1995). Gifted adults: Their characteristics and emotions. In L. K. Silverman (Ed.), *Advanced development: A collection of works on giftedness in adults* (pp. 21–34). Denver, CO: Institute for the Study of Advanced Development. (Reprinted from *Advanced Development,* 1991, 3, 85–98.)

Roeper, A. (2011a). *Beyond old age: Essays on living and dying.* Berkeley, CA: Azalea Art Press.

Roeper, A. (2011b, June). For the symposium on gifted adults. *Gifted Development Center Newsletter.* Retrieved February 21, 2012, from www.gifteddevelopment.com/Speakers_Bureau/SymposiumSpeech.html

Roeper, A. (2012). *The AMR method of qualitative assessment.* Retrieved March 7, 2012, from http://roeperconsultationservice.blogspot.com/p/annemarie-roeper-method-sm-of.html

Roeper, A., & Silverman, L. K. (2009). Giftedness and moral promise. In D. Ambrose & T. L. Cross (Eds.), *Morality, ethics, and gifted minds* (pp. 251–264). New York, NY: Springer Science.

Rogers, C. R. (1961). *On becoming a person: A therapist's view of psychotherapy.* Boston, MA: Houghton Mifflin.

Rogers, C. R. (1969). *Freedom to learn.* Columbus, OH: Charles E. Merrill.

Rogers, K. B. (2004, July). *Keeping gifted learners in school: Can education plans make a difference?* Presented at the 25th anniversary conference of the Gifted Development Center, Denver, CO.

Rogers, K. B., & Silverman, L. K. (1997, November 7). *Personal, social, medical and psychological factors in 160+ IQ children.* National Association for Gifted Children 44th Annual Convention, Little Rock, AK.

Rogers, K. B., & Silverman, L. K. (2001). The physical, social, emotional and environmental differences of profoundly gifted children: A comparative study. In N. Colangelo & S. G. Assouline (Eds.), *Talent development IV: Proceedings from the 1998 Henry B. and Jocelyn Wallace National Research Symposium on Talent Development* (pp. 419–423). Scottsdale, AZ: Great Potential Press.

Rogers, M. T. (1986). *A comparative study of developmental traits of gifted and average youngsters* (Unpublished doctoral dissertation). University of Denver, Denver, CO.

Rogers, M. T., & Silverman, L. K. (1988). Recognizing giftedness in young children. *Understanding Our Gifted, 1*(2), 5, 16–17, 20.

Roid, G. H. (2003). *Stanford-Binet Intelligence Scales interpretive manual: Expanded guide to the interpretation of SB5 test results.* Itasca, IL: Riverside.

Ronvik, R. W. (1993). Re-examining the foundations of giftedness. *Understanding Our Gifted, 5*(6), 1, 8–10, 14.

Rothenberg, A. (1990). *Creativity and madness: New findings and old stereotypes.* Baltimore, MD: The Johns Hopkins Press.

Rudasill, K. M., Capper, M. R., Foust, R. G., Callahan, C. M., & Albaugh, S. B. (2009). Grade and gender differences in gifted students' self-concepts. *Roeper Review, 32,* 340–367.

Ruf, D. L. (2003). *Use of the SB5 in assessment of high abilities.* Assessment Service Bulletin No. 3. Itasca, IL: Riverside.

Saint-Exupery, A. de. (1943). *The little prince.* New York, NY: Harcourt, Brace & World.

Sankar-DeLeeuw, N. (2002). Gifted preschoolers: Parent and teacher views on identification, early admission, and programming. *Roeper Review, 24,* 172–177.

Sankar-DeLeeuw, N. (2004). Case studies of gifted kindergarten children: Profiles of promise. *Roeper Review, 26,* 192–207.

Schechtman, Z., & Silektor, A. (2012). Social competencies and difficulties of gifted children compared to nongifted children. *Roeper Review, 34,* 63–72.

Schlesinger, J. (2009). Creative mythconceptions: A closer look at the evidence for the "mad genius" hypothesis. *Psychology of Aesthetics, Creativity, and the Arts, 3*(2), 62–72.

Schopenhauer, A. (1851/1914). *Parerga and paralipomena, II* (T. B. Saunders, Trans.). In K. Francke (Ed.), *The German classics of the nineteenth and twentieth century: Vol. 15.* New York, NY: The German Publication Society.

Schuler, P. A. (2000). Perfectionism and the gifted adolescent. *The Journal of Secondary Gifted Education, 11,* 183–196.

Schultz, D. (1981). *A history of modern psychology* (3rd ed.). New York, NY: Academic Press.

Schultz, S. M. (2012). Twice-exceptional students enrolled in Advanced Placement classes. *Gifted Child Quarterly, 56,* 119–133.

Seagoe, M. V. (1975). *Terman and the gifted.* Los Altos, CA: William Kaufmann.

Seeley, K. (1998). Facilitators for talented students. In J. VanTassel-Baska (Ed.), *Excellence in educating gifted and talented learners* (3rd ed., pp. 473–488). Denver, CO: Love.

Seeley, K. (2003). High risk gifted learners. In N. Colangelo & G. A. Davis (Eds.), *Handbook of gifted education* (3rd ed., pp. 444–451). Boston, MA: Allyn & Bacon.

Shah, N. (2012, January 31). Feds say more students may qualify for disability services: OCR urges schools to reconsider who gets special services. *Education Week.* Retrieved February 4, 2012, from www.edweek.org/ew/articles/2012/02/01/19speced.h31.html?tkn=XPXFX6bli

Shah, P., & Miyake, A. (Eds.). (2005). *The Cambridge handbook of visuospatial thinking.* New York, NY: Cambridge University Press.

Shaywitz, S. E., Holahan, J. M., Freudenheim, D. A., Fletcher, J. M., Makuch, R. W., & Shaywitz, B. A. (2001). Heterogeneity within the gifted: Higher IQ boys exhibit behaviors resembling boys with learning disabilities. *Gifted Child Quarterly, 45,* 16–34.

Sheely, A. R. (2007). Birds and bees: Sex and the high-IQ adolescent. In K. Kay, D. Robson, & J. F. Brenneman (Eds.), *High IQ kids: Collected insights, information and personal stories from the experts* (pp. 300–310). Minneapolis, MN: Free Spirit.

Shin, H. S., Park, S. C., & Maples, W. C. (2011). Effectiveness of vision therapy for convergence dysfunctions and long-term stability after vision therapy. *Opthalmic & Physiological Optics, 31,* 180–189.

Silverman, L. K. (1978). Characteristics of giftedness. *Colorado Association for the Gifted and Talented Newsletter, 5*(2), 8. Updated version available at www.gifteddevelopment.com

Silverman, L. K. (1986a). The IQ controversy—Conceptions and misconceptions. *Roeper Review, 8,* 136–140.

Silverman, L. K. (1986b). Parenting young gifted children. *Journal of Children in Contemporary Society, 18,* 73–87.

Silverman, L. K. (1986c). What happens to the gifted girl? In C. J. Maker (Ed.), *Critical issues in gifted education, Vol. 1: Defensible programs for the gifted* (pp. 43–89). Austin, TX: Pro-Ed.

Silverman, L. K. (1988, October). The second child syndrome. *Mensa Bulletin, 320,* 18–20.

Silverman, L. K. (1989). Invisible gifts, invisible handicaps. *Roeper Review, 12*(1), 37–42.

Silverman, L. K. (1992). Scapegoating the gifted: The new national sport. *CAG Communicator, 22*(3), 16–19.

Silverman, L. K. (Ed.). (1993a). *Counseling the gifted and talented.* Denver, CO: Love.

Silverman, L. K. (1993b). Parent bashing. *Understanding Our Gifted, 6*(1), 15.

Silverman, L. K. (1993c). Social development, leadership, and gender issues. In L. K. Silverman (Ed.), *Counseling the gifted and talented* (pp. 291–327). Denver, CO: Love.

Silverman, L. K. (1995a). Highly gifted children. In J. Genshaft, M. Bireley, & C. L. Hollinger (Eds.), *Serving gifted and talented students: A resource for school personnel* (pp. 217–240). Austin, TX: Pro-Ed.

Silverman, L. K. (1995b, August 3). *Instructional strategies* (translated into Chinese). Eleventh World Council conference on gifted and talented children, Hong Kong. Available from www.gifteddevelopment.com

Silverman, L. K. (1998a). Developmental stages of giftedness: Infancy through adulthood. In J. VanTassel-Baska (Ed.), *Excellence in educating gifted and talented learners* (3rd ed., pp. 145–166). Denver, CO: Love.

Silverman, L. K. (1998b). Personality and learning styles of gifted children. In J. VanTassel-Baska (Ed.), *Excellence in educating gifted & talented learners* (3rd ed., pp. 29–65). Denver, CO: Love.

Silverman, L. K. (2001). Diagnosing and treating visual perceptual issues in gifted children. *Journal of Optometric Vision Development, 32*, 153–176.

Silverman, L. K. (2002). *Upside-down brilliance: The visual-spatial learner.* Denver, CO: DeLeon.

Silverman, L. K. (2003). *Characteristics of Giftedness Scale: Research and review of the literature.* Available from the Gifted Development Center website: www.gifteddevelopment.com

Silverman, L. K. (2007). A new era in identification of the gifted. *Gifted Education Communicator, 8*(1), 26–31.

Silverman, L. K. (2008). The theory of positive disintegration in the field of gifted education. In S. Mendaglio (Ed.), *Dabrowski's theory of positive disintegration* (pp. 157–174). Scottsdale, AZ: Great Potential Press.

Silverman, L. K. (2009a). The measurement of giftedness. In L. Shavinina (Ed.), *The international handbook on giftedness* (Part 2, pp. 947–970). Amsterdam: Springer Science.

Silverman, L. K. (2009b). Searching for asynchrony. A new perspective on twice-exceptional children. In B. MacFarlane & T. Stambaugh (Eds.), *Leading change in gifted education: The Festschrift of Dr. Joyce VanTassel-Baska* (pp. 169–181). Waco, TX: Prufrock Press.

Silverman, L. K. (2009c). The two-edged sword of compensation: How the gifted cope with learning disabilities. *Gifted Education International, 25*(2), 115–130.

Silverman, L. K. (2009d). Visual-spatial learners. In B. Kerr (Ed.), *Encyclopedia of giftedness, creativity and talent* (Vol. 2, pp. 928–931). Thousand Oaks, CA: Sage.

Silverman, L. K. (2009e, March). *What we have learned about gifted children, 30th anniversary: 1979–2009.* Second national symposium on assessing gifted learners, Van Nuys, CA. (See Appendix.)

Silverman, L. K. (2011). Effective practices for secondary school students. In N. L. Hafenstein & E. Honeck (Eds.), *Greatest potential, greatest need: Soaring beyond expectations. Conference proceedings and selected articles focusing on the highly gifted* (pp. 139–141). Denver, CO: The Institute for the Development of Gifted Education, University of Denver.

Silverman, L. K. (2012a). Asynchronous development: A key to counseling the gifted. In T. L. Cross & J. R. Cross (Eds.), *Handbook for counselors serving students with gifts & talents: Development, relationships, school issues, and counseling needs/interventions* (pp. 261–279). Waco, TX: Prufrock Press.

Silverman, L. K. (2012b). [The percentage of female Nobel Laureates]. Unpublished raw data compiled from The Nobel Foundation website, http://nobelprize.org/ and Female Nobel Prize Laureates listed on The Nobel Prize Internet Archive, http://almaz.com/nobel.html. Retrieved February 4, 2012.

Silverman, L. K. (2012c). [Reasons parents seek assessment for their gifted children]. Unpublished raw data.

Silverman, L. K., Cayton, T., & Raiford, S. (2008, November). *Taking the top off the WISC-IV: Extending norms for exceptionally gifted students.* Presented at the National Association for Gifted Children 55th annual convention, Tampa, FL.

Silverman, L. K., Chitwood, D. G., & Waters, J. L. (1986). Young gifted children: Can parents identify giftedness? *Topics in Early Childhood Special Education, 6*(1), 23–38.

Silverman, L. K., & Conarton, S. A. (2005). Gifted development: It's not easy being green. In D. Comstock (Ed.), *Diversity and development: Critical contexts that shape our lives and relationships* (pp. 233–251). Pacific Grove, CA: Wadsworth/BrooksCole.

Silverman, L. K., Gilman, B. J., & Falk, R. F. (2004, November). *Who are the gifted using the new WISC-IV?* Paper presented at the National Association for Gifted Children 51st annual convention, Salt Lake City, UT.

Silverman, L. K., & Kearney, K. (1989). Parents of the extraordinarily gifted. *Advanced Development, 1*, 41–56.

Silverman, L. K., & Miller, N. B. (2009). A feminine perspective of giftedness. In L. Shavinina (Ed.), *The international handbook on giftedness* (Part 1, pp. 99–128). Amsterdam: Springer Science.

Simonton, D. (2003). When does giftedness become genius? And when not? In N. Colangelo & G. A. Davis (Eds.), *Handbook of gifted education* (3rd ed., pp. 359–387). Boston, MA: Allyn & Bacon.

Simonton, D. K. (2009). *Genius 101.* New York, NY: Springer.

Singal, D. J. (1991). The other crisis in American education. *The Atlantic Monthly, 268*(5), 59–74.

Snyderman, M., & Rothman, S. (1990). *The IQ controversy, the media and public policy.* New Brunswick, NJ: Transaction.

Solow, R., & Rhodes, C. (2012). *College at 13: Young, gifted, and purposeful*. Scottsdale, AZ: Great Potential Press.

Southern, W. T., & Jones, E. D. (Eds.). (1991). *The academic acceleration of gifted children*. New York, NY: Teachers College Press.

Speirs Neumeister, K. L. (2004a). Factors influencing the development of perfectionism in gifted college students. *Gifted Child Quarterly, 48*, 259–274.

Speirs Neumeister, K. L. (2004b). Understanding the relationship between perfectionism and achievement motivation in gifted college students. *Gifted Child Quarterly, 48*, 219–231.

Stalnacke, J., & Smedler, A. -C. (2011). Psychosocial experiences and adjustment among adult Swedes with superior general mental ability. *Journal for the Education of the Gifted, 34*, 900–916.

Stambaugh, T. (2009). Promising students of poverty: Pathways and perils to success. In B. MacFarlane & T. Stambaugh (Eds.), *Leading change in gifted education: The festschrift of Dr. Joyce VanTassel-Baska* (pp. 135–147). Waco, TX: Prufrock Press.

Stanley, J. C. (1990). Leta Hollingworth's contributions to above-level testing of the gifted. *Roeper Review, 12*(3), 166–171.

Steenbergen-Hu, S., & Moon, S. M. (2011). The effects of acceleration on high ability learners: A meta-analysis. *Gifted Child Quarterly, 55*, 39–53.

Sternberg, R. J. (1985). *Beyond IQ: A triarchic theory of human intelligence*. Cambridge: Cambridge University Press.

Storfer, M. (1990). *Intelligence and giftedness*. San Francisco, CA: Jossey-Bass.

Subotnik, R. F., Olszewski-Kubilius, P., & Worrell, F. C. (2011). Rethinking giftedness and gifted education: A proposed direction forward based on psychological science. *Psychological Science in the Public Interest, 12*(1), 3–54.

Sulloway, F. J. (1996). *Born to rebel*. New York, NY: Vintage.

Sumption, M. R., & Luecking, E. (1960). *Education of the gifted*. New York, NY: The Ronald Press.

Tannenbaum, A. J. (1983). *Gifted children: Psychological and educational perspectives*. New York, NY: Macmillan.

Tannenbaum, A. J. (1992). Early signs of giftedness: Research and commentary. *Journal for the Education of the Gifted, 15*, 104–133.

Taylor, J. B. (2006). *My stroke of insight: A brain scientist's personal journey*. New York, NY: Viking.

Terman, L. M. (1906). Genius and stupidity: A study of some of the intellectual processes of seven "bright" and seven "stupid" boys. *Pedagogical Seminary, 13*, 307–373.

Terman, L. M. (1916a). *The measurement of intelligence.* Boston, MA: Houghton Mifflin.

Terman, L. M. (1916b). *The Stanford revision of the Binet-Simon tests.* Boston, MA: Houghton Mifflin.

Terman, L. M. (1917). The intelligence quotient of Francis Galton in childhood. *American Journal of Psychology, 28*, 209–215.

Terman, L. M. (1925). *Genetic studies of genius, Vol. 1: Mental and physical traits of a thousand gifted children.* Stanford, CA: Stanford University Press.

Terman, L. M. (1931). The gifted child. In C. Murchison (Ed.), *A handbook of child psychology* (pp. 568–584). Worcester, MA: Clark University Press.

Terman, L. M. (1944). Review of Leta Stetter Hollingworth: A biography. *Journal of Applied Psychology, 28*, 357–359.

Terman, L. M., & Merrill, M. A. (1973). *The Stanford-Binet Intelligence Scale: 1973 norms edition.* Boston, MA: Houghton Mifflin.

Terman, L. M., & Oden, M. H. (1947). *Genetic studies of genius, Vol. 4: The gifted child grows up.* Stanford, CA: Stanford University Press.

Terman, L. M., & Oden, M. H. (1959). *Genetic studies of genius, Vol. 5: The gifted group at mid-life.* Stanford, CA: Stanford University Press.

Terman, L. M., et al. (1925–1959). *Genetic studies of genius, Vols. 1–5.* Stanford, CA: Stanford University Press.

Terrassier, J.-C. (1985). Dyssynchrony–uneven development. In J. Freeman (Ed.), *The psychology of gifted children* (pp. 265–274). New York, NY: John Wiley.

The Roeper Institute. (2012). *Annemarie Roeper method of qualitative assessment videotapes.* Retrieved March 8, 2012, from www.roeper. org/RoeperInstitute/index.aspx

Thorndike, E. L. (1910). *Educational psychology* (2nd ed.). New York, NY: Teachers College, Columbia University.

Thorndike, R. L. (1975). Mr. Binet's test 70 years later. *Educational Researcher, 4*, 3–4.

Thorndike, R. L., Hagen, E. P., & Sattler, J. M. (1986). *The Stanford-Binet Intelligence Scale: Fourth edition. Technical manual.* Itasca, IL: Riverside.

Tolan, S. S. (1992). Only a parent: Three true stories. *Understanding Our Gifted*, 4(3), l, 8–10.

Tolan, S. (1994/1995). Discovering the ex-gifted child. In L. K. Silverman (Ed.), *Advanced development: A collection of works on giftedness in adults* (pp. 13–20). Denver, CO: Institute for the Study of Advanced Development. (Reprinted and updated from *Roeper Review*, 1994, 17, 134–138.)

Tolan, S. (1996). *Is it a cheetah?* Retrieved August 4, 2012, from www.stephanietolan.com/is_it_a_cheetah.htm

Tolan, S. (1999). Self-knowledge, self-esteem and the gifted adult. *Advanced Development*, 8, 147–150.

Torrance, E. P. (1974). *Torrance tests of creative thinking.* Bensenville, IL: Scholastic Testing Service.

Treffinger, D. J., & Feldhusen, J. F. (1996). Talent recognition and development: Successor to gifted education. *Journal for the Education of the Gifted*, 19, 181–193.

Tucker, C. C. (2012, February). Twenty plus years and not counting. *Gifted Development Center Newsletter.* Available from www.gifted-development.com

VanTassel-Baska, J. (1989). The role of the family in the success of disadvantaged gifted learners. *Journal for the Education of the Gifted*, 13, 22–36.

VanTassel-Baska, J. (2012a). The importance of teaching strategies in the education of the gifted. In T. L. Cross & J. R. Cross (Eds.), *Handbook for counselors serving students with gifts & talents: Development, relationships, school issues, and counseling needs/interventions* (pp. 495–510). Waco, TX: Prufrock Press.

VanTassel-Baska, J. (2012b, March/April). The role of parents in helping gifted children with learning problems. *2e Twice-Exceptional Newsletter*, 51, 3–4.

VanTassel-Baska, J., & Brown, E. F. (2007). Toward best practice: An analysis of the efficacy of curriculum models in gifted education. *Gifted Child Quarterly*, 51, 342–358.

VanTassel-Baska, J., & Little, C. (Eds.). (2011). *Content-based curriculum for high ability learners* (2nd ed.). Waco, TX: Prufrock Press.

Vernon, P. E. (1987). The demise of the Stanford-Binet Scale. *Canadian Psychology/Psychologie Canadienne*, 28(3), 251–258.

Vygotsky, L. S. (1962). *Thought and language.* Cambridge, MA: M.I.T. Press.

Vygotsky, L. S. (1978). *Mind in society: The development of higher psychological processes*. Cambridge, MA: Harvard University Press.

Wallach, M. (1995). The courage to network. In L. K. Silverman (Ed.), *Advanced development: A collection of works on giftedness in adults* (pp. 35–41). Denver, CO: Institute for the Study of Advanced Development.

Wasserman, J. (2003). Assessment of intellectual functioning. In J. R. Graham & J. A. Naglieri (Eds.), *Handbook of psychology, Volume 10: Assessment psychology* (pp. 417–442). Hoboken, NJ: Wiley.

Wasserman, J. (2007). Intellectual assessment of exceptionally and profoundly gifted children. In K. Kay, D. Robson, & J. F. Brenneman (Eds.), *High IQ kids: Collected insights, information, and personal stories from the experts* (pp. 48–65). Minneapolis, MN: Free Spirit.

Watkins, M. W. (2000). Cognitive profile analysis: A shared myth. *School Psychology Quarterly, 15*, 465–479.

Webb, J. T., Gore, J. L., Amend, E. R., & DeVries, A. R. (2007). *A parent's guide to gifted children*. Scottsdale, AZ: Great Potential Press.

Webb, J. T., Gore, J. L., Karnes, F. A., & McDaniel, A. S. (2004). *Grandparents' guide to gifted children*. Scottsdale, AZ: Great Potential Press.

Wechsler, D. (2003). *The WISC-IV technical and interpretive manual*. San Antonio, TX: Pearson Assessments.

Wells, R., Lohman, D., & Marron, M. (2009). What factors are associated with grade acceleration? *Journal of Advanced Academics, 20*, 248–270.

West, T. G. (2009). *In the mind's eye: Creative visual thinkers, gifted dyslexics, and the rise of visual technologies* (2nd ed.). Buffalo, NY: Prometheus Press.

Whipple, G. M. (1924). Historical and introductory. In G. M. Whipple (Ed.), *Report of the society's committee on the education of gifted children,* (Part I, pp. 1–24). National Society for the Study of Education 23rd Yearbook. Bloomington, IL: Public School.

White, B. (1985). Competence and giftedness. In J. Freeman (Ed.), *The psychology of gifted children: Perspectives on development and education* (pp. 59–73). New York, NY: Wiley.

Whitmore, J. R. (1980). *Giftedness, conflict, and underachievement*. Boston, MA: Allyn & Bacon.

Winner, E. (2000). The origins and ends of giftedness. *American Psychologist, 55*, 159–169.

Witty, P. A. (1930). A study of one hundred gifted children. *University of Kansas Bulletin of Education, 2*(7), 3–44.

Witty, P. A. (1940). Contributions to the IQ controversy from the study of superior deviates. *School & Society, 51,* 503–508.

Witty, P. A. (1958). Who are the gifted? In N. B. Henry (Ed.), *Education for the gifted* (Part II, pp. 41–63). The 57th Yearbook of the National Society for the Study of Education, Part II. Chicago, IL: The University of Chicago Press.

Wood, S. (2010). Best practices in counseling the gifted in schools: What is really happening? *Gifted Child Quarterly, 54,* 42–58.

Wood, S., Portman, T. A. A., Cigrand, D. L., & Colangelo, N. (2010). School counselors' perceptions and experience with acceleration as a program option for gifted and talented students. *Gifted Child Quarterly, 54,* 168–178.

Wu, E. H. (2008). Parental influence on children's talent development: A case study with three Chinese American families. *Journal for the Education of the Gifted, 32,* 100–127.

Yoshinaga-Itano, C., Sedey, A. L., Coulter, D. K., & Mehl, A. L. (1998). Language of early- and later-identified children with hearing loss. *Pediatrics, 102,* 1161–1171.

Yssel, N. (2012). Twice-exceptional students. In T. L. Cross & J. R. Cross (Eds.), *Handbook for counselors serving students with gifts & talents: Development, relationships, school issues, and counseling needs/interventions* (pp. 245–257). Waco, TX: Prufrock Press.

Zhu, J., Cayton, T., Weiss, L., & Gabel, A. (2008). *Wechsler Intelligence Scale for children* (4th ed.). *Technical report #7.* Upper Saddle River, NJ: Pearson Education. Retrieved from http://pearsonassess.com/NR/rdonlyres/C1C19227-BC79–46D9-B43C-8E4A114F7E1F/0/WISCIV_TechReport_7.pdf

Zigler, E., & Farber, E. A. (1985). Commonalities between the intellectual extremes: Giftedness and mental retardation. In F. D. Horowitz & M. O'Brien (Eds.), *The gifted and talented: Developmental perspectives* (pp. 387–408). Washington, DC: American Psychological Association.

Index